Paul Chapman
Publishing Ltd

Copyright © 1989 A V Kelly

First published 1989

by Paul Chapman Publishing Ltd.
144 Liverpool Road
London N1 1LA

British Library Cataloguing in Publication Data
Kelly, A. V. (Albert Victor), *1931–*
   The curriculum: theory and practice.–3rd
   ed
   1. Schools. Curriculum
   I. Title
   375

   ISBN 1–85396–018–7

Typeset by Inforum Typesetting, Portsmouth
Printed and bound by St Edmundsbury Press, Bury St Edmunds

'The teacher, like the artist, the philosopher, and the man of letters, can only perform his work adequately if he feels himself to be an individual directed by an inner creative impulse, not dominated and fettered by an outside authority.'

Bertrand Russell, *Unpopular Essays* (1950), p. 159.

CONTENTS

INTRODUCTION

The first edition of *The Curriculum: Theory and Practice* attempted, amongst other things, to draw attention to and to commend the evolutionary nature of curriculum theory and curriculum practice. Indeed, the careful reader will have detected elements of that evolutionary nature within the book itself. For, even as that first edition was in preparation, curriculum evolution was giving way to externally directed change, and the book itself evolved in the writing in an attempt to capture the main features of developments which were already in train. Those developments have gathered massive momentum since that time.

For, in the eleven years since the publication of the first edition, and even in the six years since that of the second, there have been major changes of scene. The background constraints on curriculum planning have moved into the foreground; indeed, constraints have become directives; concern with curriculum evaluation has grown into demands for teacher appraisal and accountability; the role of the teacher in curriculum planning and development, whose centrality both earlier editions were concerned to stress, has been rapidly eroded and dramatically reduced in scope; the evolutionary process of curriculum development has been effectively halted; and, in general, the 'secret garden' of the curriculum has been thrown open to the public – an event which, as in many other stately homes, has led to ossification as well as preservation and to much trampling on the flower-beds.

The current scene, then, is no longer one of continuous curriculum innovation and development; it is one in which there has been dramatic change of an externally imposed kind, change whose culminating effect is likely to be the ending of all curriculum development of an evolutionary nature. This third edition of *The Curriculum: Theory and Practice*, therefore, in attempting the same kind of overview of curriculum theory which was attempted by its forerunners, finds itself surveying a very different scene, one whose major features and whose focuses of interest have been transformed, so that it is not so much a modified and updated edition as a completely new book. Its publication, however, is still predicated on the belief that such an overarching study of the curriculum continues to be necessary, a belief which is indeed strengthened rather than weakened by the awareness that a wide understanding of the theory and practice of curriculum planning and development is now needed not only by teachers but by all the other agencies, not least the politicians and their aides at the Department of Education and Science, who wish to play a part in the control of the school curriculum. This conviction is further reinforced by the sad recognition that it is precisely the depth of understanding which can come only from such a study that is conspicuously missing from the current pronouncements through which is being dictated a new National Curriculum for all our schools.

This third edition sets out not only to offer the overview of curriculum theory of its predecessors or merely to attempt to press further the general theme of the central role of the teacher in the actualities of the school curriculum. It is concerned also to argue that the planning of an educational curriculum is a far more sophisticated activity than most of the present amateur planners seem to recognize, and that it necessitates an intellectual depth of understanding which they manifestly lack. The over-simplification of curricular issues puts education itself at risk and must lead to a lowering of educational standards rather than that raising of standards which current policies purport to be seeking. The education of children, the development of young, unformed minds, is a complex undertaking, and must, therefore, be based on a properly substantial, and indeed substantiated, body of theoretical understandings and considerations. To plan on any other basis, and especially to plan on the assumption that the development of the human mind is a simple matter, is to jeopardize the whole educational enterprise and, further, to offer insult not only to the teaching profession but also to the nation's children themselves – and to their parents.

This edition, then, is centrally concerned to demonstrate the need for such a substantial theoretical basis for curriculum planning, as well as to attempt to make its own contribution to the continuing evolution of such a properly intellectual and professional body of understanding.

1
CURRICULUM PLANNING
AND DEVELOPMENT – AN OVERVIEW

It is stating the obvious to assert that education has changed drastically in the last twenty or thirty years. Both in the United Kingdom and elsewhere many important modifications have been made to all aspects of the education system. Nor is it surprising that the nature and structure of our education system should have been changing so extensively at a time when we have been experiencing social change of an equally dramatic kind, much of it prompted by rapid technological advance. The education system is a social institution which should be expected to change along with other such institutions. It would be more surprising, not to say disturbing, if the education system were to stand still while all else changed. And it is the need to ensure that it continues to develop, and that it responds appropriately not only to other changes in society but also to our increasing understanding of the educational process itself, which is, or should be, the central concern of educational studies and especially of curriculum studies.

For, amidst all this change, nothing has been more significant or as fundamental as the major modifications that have been made to the curriculum. The significance of this lies in the fact that it has manifested itself at all levels of educational activity, from the nursery school through to the university, from the education of the least able pupils to that of the most educationally gifted. Its fundamental nature derives from the fact that the curriculum is the very foundation of any education system, and no amount of tinkering with the structure of the system, the organization of schools or the selection procedures to be used will have more than a peripheral effect unless accompanied by a rethinking of the real substance of education – the curriculum itself.

And so, changes to the structure of the school system, such as the introduction of comprehensive schools and of mixed-ability classes, have been followed by attempts to make corresponding modifications to the curriculum, since it has become clear that, to meet the demands of society, whether they be for more highly skilled and qualified technologists or for the provision of greater educational opportunities for all, close attention must be given to the curriculum itself. Indeed, without curriculum change, modifications to the structure of the system make little sense and have little point, since, as has become apparent from the attempts to promote equality of educational opportunity, in themselves they have but little effect. It is this awareness that has led to the increased attention that has been directed towards the school curriculum since the mid-1970s, both from within and from outside the teaching profession.

One feature that has characterized the curriculum change of recent years, and which must be realized at the outset of this discussion, is the increased incidence of planning and preparation in curriculum development. Most of the curriculum change that we saw in the past was of a kind best described as unplanned 'drift' (Hoyle, 1969a) and a good deal of this still goes on. Recently, however, educationists have begun to see the need for planned innovation, to recognize that if educational change is to keep pace with and match changes in society, if it is at the same time to maintain also those standards and values which may be seen as transcending particular times and particular societies, and if it is to respond to that increased understanding of education and curriculum which has come from recent work in the field of curriculum studies, it must be deliberately managed rather than merely left to happen. To recognize this is not, of course, to be committed to a totally revolutionary approach to curriculum development. The advantages of evolution over revolution are at least as evident in education as elsewhere. It is, however, to acknowledge that the process of evolution can be smoother, quicker and more effective, if it is not left to chance but implemented according to carefully thought-out strategies. It is this that makes the kind of understanding of curriculum development that can come from a deep study of curriculum theory the most essential item in the armoury of the modern teacher.

It is the aim of this chapter to identify what is involved in this, to outline some of the essential ingredients both of the study of curriculum theory and the practice of curriculum planning and development. Almost all of these points will be examined in greater detail in the chapters that follow, but an overall framework, a rationale, a cognitive map offered at the outset may help to establish and maintain the interrelationship of the many factors involved in curriculum planning. For a major problem facing teachers as they recognize their responsibility for curriculum planning is the range of interconnected factors that they must constantly keep in balance. Like jugglers, they must not only keep many balls in the air at the same time, they must also maintain the proper relationships between them if disaster is not to ensue.

WHAT IS 'CURRICULUM STUDIES'?

It is important from the outset to be clear about the kind of study we are involved in when we begin to explore issues related to curriculum planning and development. And there are several points which can be made straight away as a contribution to the attainment of such clarity.

The first is that the area of study which has come to be known as curriculum studies has emerged from the attempts, over the last two decades, of research workers and some of those who have been concerned to teach educational studies to develop an approach to the study of education which would not be limited by being conducted within the confines of other disciplines, such as philosophy, psychology and sociology. The traditional approach to the study of education through these 'contributory disciplines', as they were once and in some places still are called, has led to serious inadequacies not least because of the approach's consequent inability to handle issues in an interdisciplinary way, in spite of the fact that it would be very difficult to identify any single educational issue which does not require a contribution from all these disciplines and often several others too. Quite serious and extensive problems have arisen when the solutions to educational questions have been sought, and accepted, from psychologists or philosophers or sociologists, since inevitably such experts have a limited, one-sided and thus distorted view of the educational issues or practices to which they are applying the techniques and the methodologies of their own disciplines. Thus, for example, major problems were created by the establishment of a whole system of secondary schooling on the basis of the psychologists' view of intelligence and intelligence testing without the complementary and modifying contributions of a philosophical analysis of the concept of intelligence or of a sociological comment on the implications of such a system for the nature of society. Many other examples could readily be found in the history of the development of the schooling system in the United Kingdom or, indeed, in any other country. Curriculum studies, then, has emerged from an attempt to study education and to explore educational problems in their own right and not as philosophical problems or as psychological or sociological phenomena. The concern has been to end the practice of viewing the study of education as a sub-branch of any or all of these other disciplines.

Allied to this has been a concern to study education as a practical activity and not merely as a body of theory, to get to grips with the realities of educational practice and to do so 'from the inside', in a manner that the philosopher, the psychologist or the sociologist can never do. Their studies have essentially and inevitably been conducted from the outside; their concern has been with the effects of educational practice rather than with its nature, with the realities of the classroom. If recently they have begun to turn their attention to these realities, they have in doing so become themselves aspects or sub-branches of curriculum studies.

There is a further crucial point which arises from this, which is their studies must by definition be descriptive rather than prescriptive. It is not the part of any of those experts to tell us what we *ought* to be doing in education, any more than it is the part of the scientist or the technologist to tell us what we ought to do with his or her findings or inventions. Yet educational practice must essentially be concerned with questions of what *ought* to be done. Teachers in their practice must make such decisions – by the day and sometimes by the minute; they must be prescriptive. And so, if they, and curriculum planners generally, are to be assisted in this quite crucial aspect of their task, they need the support of studies which can and do take full account of that aspect, which do not remain at the descriptive level and offer information without advice or, worse, advice which they can offer only by abandoning the rigour and the methodology of their disciplines.

Yet this is what has been offered in the past. As a result, there was a lack of intellectual rigour at this most crucial point of educational practice and decision-making since no one was able to supply or offer that rigour. Psychological research cannot in itself tell us what we should be doing in education; where psychologists have attempted to do so, they have over-stepped their brief and the limits of their discipline. Philosophical analysis cannot tell us what we ought to be doing in education; and where philo-sophers have attempted to do this, they too have been going beyond what their work *qua* philosophers permits. Nor is it possible for sociologists to extend their work into the sphere of prescription. This is one reason why the approach to the study of education through these disciplines has proved not only barren but often positively misleading in relation to educational practice. Again, curriculum studies must be seen as an attempt to put right this deficiency.

In general, these difficulties illustrate the problems and the inadequacies of all attempts to adopt a 'scientific' approach to the study or the planning of education and/or curriculum. Curriculum studies cannot be seen as a science, and especially not as an applied science. The history of attempts to theorize about education is littered with examples of this kind of scientist approach, and all of them have been theoretically misleading and practically harmful. Human beings seem to need the security of certainty in all areas of experience, and thus they are prey to all illusory forms of such certainty. This tendency is particularly odd, since it is the case that the more specifically human an activity is, the less susceptible it is to understanding through a search for objective 'truths'. Education is one such human activity, and thus does not lend itself to study of a narrowly scientific kind. It is what Maurice Holt (1981, p. 80) has described as 'a complex and ultimately impenetrable process'.

Unfortunately, attempts to make this process the object of scientific exploration, and, more seriously, the practice of offering educational prescriptions as if they are the indisputable deductions from, or conclusions of, such scientific study, continue to be made. Nor are these confined to those working in the 'contributory disciplines'. This kind of not-to-be-questioned assertion is all too prevalent, as we shall see later, in those many pronouncements we are now offered from official sources. S. J. Curtis (1948, p. 255) quotes a story about Robert Lowe: 'There is a story that when an HMI went to consult him, Lowe said, "I know what you've come about, the science of education. There is none. Good Morning." ' Whether or not Lowe himself was fully aware of the significance of that assertion – or, indeed, meant it in the sense in which we are taking it here – it is a pity that the said HMI did not pass this pearl of wisdom down to his descendants.

For, if there is no science of education, and thus no scientific and indisputable base for educational prescriptions, it must follow that all such prescriptions will reflect nothing more solid than the preferences, the values, the ideology of those who are offering them. And so, there is an obligation on such persons, first, not to behave as though this were not the case or as though their prescriptions enjoyed some kind of scientific objectivity that those of others do not and, second, having recognized that, to see also the necessity of offering some justification of their views. To offer them as views without justification is to risk being totally ignored; to use a position of power to impose them without justification is to stand convicted of indoctrination and the abuse of authority. The concept of ideology, then, is an important one in curriculum studies, as we shall see, as is the concept of ideologies competing for dominance.

A further problem is that the vacuum which is created by the inadequacies of attempts to study education scientifically and the inability of all kinds of study, whether scientific or not, to assist with the prescriptive dimension of educational practice has too often been filled by theories based on little evidence and less research and thus lacking in any kind of intellectual rigour. Too much educational practice has been based on a kind of folklore or on intuition; and too many teachers have been heard proudly to boast that they have no theory, that they are merely good practitioners, without considering sufficiently closely whether it is logically possible to make both of these claims at the same time. To be fair, this has often been the result of their being offered no kind of theory which they could recognize as being appropriate or relevant to their practice. This vacuum too, curriculum studies has endeavoured to fill by offering an intellectually rigorous study of curriculum which will generate understandings that are both academically respectable and defensible, and practically relevant, a marrying of theory and practice which will do honour and justice to both and which will demean neither.

Curriculum studies, then, is the result of attempts which have been made, over the last two decades or so, to generate research and a resultant body of understanding of education which might make possible the development of a properly rigorous and practically relevant theoretical underpinning to educational practice, which might bridge the gap between or fill the vacuum created by the theoretical researches of people working in other disciplines on the one hand and the unchallenged assumptions and largely intuitive practices of some teachers on the other.

One further point must also be made. Most of what we have said so far could be seen as a definition of what in many courses of teacher education is nowadays known as professional studies. The added ingredient of curriculum studies is the value or prescriptive element to which we referred above, and especially the requirement this places on the student of curriculum to be critical and questioning in his or her approach, to face the value issues central to such studies and, in short, to recognize that the concern is not with mere methodology, with the *how* of educational practice, but much more with questions of the justification of such practice, with the *why* as well as the how. It is this critical dimension that is crucial to curriculum studies, at least as it is conceived throughout this book.

We can take this further. At one level, curriculum studies can be seen, and *is* seen by many, as concerned largely with the mechanics of curriculum planning, development and innovation. There is no doubt that this is an important area of study and that there are many curricula which could profit enormously from the application of the understanding of the mechanics of curriculum planning which has been acquired through recent studies. There is much more to curriculum studies than this, however. We have already seen that, if it is to help teachers and other curriculum planners with the most difficult theoretical task they face – that of justifying their curricular practices or proposals – it must go far beyond this rather limited scientific and technological level. As Bill Reid (1978, p. 29) has suggested, curriculum problems 'are practical problems which are moral rather than technical in nature'. To deal with such problems, curriculum studies must embrace and tackle questions of what education is, or at least of what different approaches to schooling one might adopt. It must recognize that for some people, perhaps most topically, for example, those who have framed that National Curriculum which is currently being imposed on all schools, the term 'education' means little more than instruction or the transmission of certain agreed bodies of knowledge, while for others it carries connotations of the value of what is being transmitted and even, most crucially, the impact on the individual educand of exposure to it. The latter would also wish to raise questions about the former's notion of agreed bodies of knowledge to be transmitted and especially about the criteria by which these have been selected; whether such criteria are economic and utilitarian, for example, or whether they are derived from some broader concept of the intrinsic or personal value of educational experiences.

To evaluate any curriculum plan or practice credibly, therefore, we need not only an understanding of the technicalities of curriculum planning and innovation but also the ability to discern the underlying values and assumptions of the curriculum specification. Indeed, it would not be difficult to argue that the latter may be far more important than the former. For to be subjected to some form of indoctrinatory process through lack of the ability to analyse critically and identify the value positions implicit in the forms of curriculum we are offered or exposed to is, in the long term, inimical to educational development in a way that some lack of understanding of the technicalities of curriculum innovation or planning or dissemination can never be. For, while the latter may diminish the quality of the educational experiences offered, the former must have the effect of rendering those experiences positively anti-educational.

The view of curriculum studies which underpins all that follows in this book will include, indeed emphasize, considerations of this deeper kind. For it is a major assumption that the narrower, mechanical version of curriculum studies, while important, does not in itself warrant a book of this scope or kind. In particular, it does not warrant a book whose prime concern is with the need for a critical approach to the study of the curriculum, since the mechanical view is by definition non-critical, value-neutral and raises no questions of whether the particular curriculum we might be planning is of educational value or not; its concern is merely with the mechanics of planning it. Its concern is that of those who developed nuclear weapons with no responsibility – quite rightly – for decisions about when, where or whether they were to be used.

Too much of what is called 'curriculum studies' these days is concerned with nothing more significant or more intellectually demanding than issues of methodology, usually within particular subject areas. Whatever one calls it, there is a need for a study of curricular theories and practices which goes far beyond this; and it is with that kind of study that we shall be concerned here. Perhaps we should call it 'pedagogialogy', or some such, a term which might have the advantage C. S. Peirce once claimed for one of his linguistic creations, namely of being 'ugly enough to be safe from kidnappers'.

Curriculum studies, then, is seen throughout this book as a critical, analytical exploration of the curriculum as a totality, a theoretical/ conceptual and practical/empirical examination of all the many dimensions of the curriculum debate and of curriculum planning, a critical evaluation of curriculum theories and practices, and a form of inquiry which goes far beyond considerations of mere methodology and transcends both particular subject specialisms and particular age ranges.

As such, it might be regarded as essentially a form of applied philosophy. Certainly, its major concern is conceptual analysis, for its prime purpose must be to achieve conceptual clarity in thinking about the curriculum as a basis for ensuring practical coherence in the implementation of that thinking – again a proper matching of theory and practice. Its concern is to conceptualize the practice of education – at both the general and the particular levels. It requires, therefore, as was suggested earlier, the development of an understanding of a wide range of theories, views and empirical insights of the kind generated by the work of psychologists, sociologists and many others but, more than this, it demands the ability to sort through these ideas, theories and insights to identify and, if possible, resolve logical and conceptual mismatch and its resultant practical incoherence and confusion.

Many, perhaps most, of the concepts essential to any properly rigorous discussion of the curriculum or any attempt to implement curriculum proposals are highly problematic in nature, are complex in meaning and cannot, without detriment to the quality of both that discussion and its implementation, be treated as though they were simple, self-evident and non-controversial. This is another aspect of that attempt, which we commented on earlier, to treat educational planning and policy-making as forms of applied science. Concepts such as 'aims', 'objectives', 'processes', 'approaches', 'standards', 'ability', 'progression', 'continuity', 'coherence', 'evaluation', 'appraisal', 'accountability' and even 'subjects' or individually named subjects are far from being non-problematic in their meanings, just as they are equally far, as we saw above, from being value-free. Nor are they matters of empirical 'fact' or scientific 'truth'. One does not, or at least one should not, go out to 'discover' by empirical experiment aims, objectives, standards or any other of those things. This is another major intellectual flaw in current policies.

In any curriculum debate, therefore, a major concern must be with an analysis of what these concepts may mean and, in the context of the particular debate, what they do mean. In any curriculum planning conceptual clarity is a *sine qua non* of effective practice. And worthwhile and productive research into curricular matters must embrace conceptual as well as empirical inquiry.

Engagement in curriculum studies of this kind, therefore, involves the development of skills with which to make this kind of critical analysis and evaluation of curricular schemes, proposals and theories – whether these are one's own or are offered by others – to explore rigorously their underlying conceptual structures and to make similarly critical evaluations of educational practices – again both one's own and those of others – in terms not only of their effectiveness but also of their educational worth and their conceptual coherence. In short, it necessitates a raising of levels of perception and awareness in relation to all aspects of curricular theory and practice.

Finally, it must be acknowledged that this kind of critical questioning of the school curriculum has been largely pre-empted at the practical level by the institution of the National Curriculum in the United Kingdom. Teachers have now been told what they are to teach, so that questions of the purpose or justification of this, or even of its logical or intellectual coherence, have effectively been removed from their sphere of influence. If, however, as a result of this, they cease to face these questions, even if at present they can approach them only in a largely theoretical way, then those questions will be faced by no one, and there are issues encapsulated in those questions which many would see as vital not only to the future of education but to the quality of the society in which future generations will live. The debate must go on, National Curriculum or not, and it must be conducted at a properly rigorous and critical level. It is that kind of debate curriculum studies endeavours to fuel. And it is that kind of debate to which this book attempts to contribute.

All that follows, therefore, should be seen by the reader as an attempt to provide him or her with the understanding and, particularly, the critical apparatus needed to engage in this kind of rigorous study of curricular practices, both as a sound underpinning for his or her own practice and as a firm basis for appropriately professional contributions to what must be a continuing professional debate.

WHAT IS THE CURRICULUM?

The first need is to achieve some clarity over what we are to understand by the term 'curriculum'. It is a term which is used with several meanings and a number of different definitions of it have been offered, so it is important that we establish at the beginning what it should be taken to signify throughout this book.

To begin with, it will be helpful if we distinguish the use of the word to denote the content of a particular subject or area of study from the use of it to refer to the total programme of an educational institution. Many people still equate a curriculum with a syllabus and thus limit their planning to a consideration of the content or the body of knowledge they wish to transmit. It is also because this view of curriculum has been adopted that many teachers in primary schools once regarded issues of curriculum as of no concern to them, since they have not usually regarded their task as being to transmit bodies of knowledge in this manner. The inadequacies of this view of curriculum as content will be explored more fully in Chapter 2. It will be immediately clear, however, that this kind of definition of curriculum is limiting in more than one way and that it is likely to hamper rather than to assist the planning of curriculum change and development. Indeed, some of the inadequacies of previous attempts at curriculum planning can be attributed to the fact that it has tended to proceed in a rather piecemeal way within subjects rather than according to some overall rationale, so that the curriculum can be seen as 'the amorphous product of generations of tinkering' (Taba, 1962, p. 8).

Both of these dimensions of curriculum development are, of course, important, but it is the rationale of the total curriculum that must have priority. 'Schools should plan their curriculum as a whole. The curriculum offered by a school, and the curriculum received by individual pupils, should not be simply a collection of separate subjects' (DES, 1981, p. 12). At the very least, the total curriculum must be accorded prior consideration, and a major task that currently faces teachers and curriculum planners is to work out a basis on which some total scheme can be built, a task which has now been rendered infinitely more difficult by the imposition of a National Curriculum framed in terms of individual subjects.

Furthermore, as we shall see when we consider this issue at length in Chapter 2, any definition of curriculum, if it is to be practically effective and productive, must offer much more than a statement about the knowledge-content (or, worse, as in the new National Curriculum, merely the subjects) which schooling is to 'teach' or transmit. It must go far beyond this to an explanation, and indeed a justification, of the purposes of such transmission and an exploration of the effects that exposure to such knowledge and such subjects is likely to have, or is intended to have, on its recipients – indeed it is from these deeper concerns, as we shall also see later, that any curriculum planning worthy of the name must start.

These wider concerns will be the focus of our discussions in this book, and we will understand by the term 'curriculum' the overall rationale for the educational programme of an institution, or, indeed, of the individual teacher, and those more subtle features of curriculum change and development, and especially those underlying principles which we have just suggested are the most crucial element in curriculum studies, although much of what is said about curriculum development in this sense will, of course, be of relevance to the problems of developments within individual subject areas.

A further question that needs to be resolved is whether we are to place any limit on the kinds of school activity that we will allow to count as part of the curriculum. Again, the word can be found in use in a number of different contexts and again we need to distinguish these clearly.

For example, some educationists speak of the 'hidden curriculum', by which they mean those things which pupils learn at school because of the way in which the work of the school is planned and organized but which are not in themselves overtly included in the planning or even in the consciousness of those responsible for the school arrangements. Social roles, for example, are learnt in this way, it is claimed, as are sex roles and attitudes to many other aspects of living. Implicit in any set of arrangements are the attitudes and values of those who create them, and these will be communicated to pupils in this accidental and perhaps even sinister way.

Some would argue that the values implicit in the arrangements made by schools for their pupils are quite clearly in the consciousness of teachers and planners and are equally clearly accepted by them as part of what pupils should learn in school, even though they are not overtly recognized by the pupils themselves. In other words, teachers deliberately plan the school's 'expressive culture'. In such instances, therefore, the curriculum is 'hidden' only to or from the pupils. If or where this is so, the values to be learnt clearly form a part of what the teachers plan for their pupils and must, therefore, be accepted as fully a part of the curriculum.

Others, however, take a less definite and perhaps less cynical line on this but wish nevertheless to insist that teachers do have a responsibility here. They accept that some of the values and attitudes learnt via the hidden curriculum are not directly intended by teachers, but believe that, since these things are being learnt as a by-product of what is planned, teachers should be aware of and accept responsibility for what is going on, for what their pupils are learning in this unplanned way (Barnes, 1976). It is this view which is at the heart of those many attempts we currently hear of to eliminate implicit racism and sexism from the experiences children receive at school.

There is no doubting the importance of this notion of the hidden curriculum or the need for curriculum planners and teachers to keep its implications constantly before them. Some, however, would argue that to use the term 'curriculum' to denote such kinds of learning is to render the planning of a total curriculum impossible since the term is being used here expressly to denote experiences that by definition have not been deliberately planned, and which cannot be so, at least without ceasing to be 'hidden' in the sense used. They prefer, therefore, to confine the use of the word 'curriculum' to those activities that are planned or are the result of some intentionality on the part of teachers and planners, and to deal with these other kinds of learning as the hidden results or by-products of the curriculum rather than as part of the curriculum itself.

It is because of the all-pervasive nature of such experiences and hidden forms of learning, however, and also because of the apparent impossibility of eliminating such unplanned, and thus uncontrolled, learning, that some theorists, such as Ivan Illich (1971), have recommended a 'deschooling' of society and have claimed that all forms of organized schooling must involve the imposition of the values implicit in the selection of the content of such schooling on its recipients, and thus constitute an invidious form of social and political control through the distribution of knowledge. This is an important point and one to which we shall return later. What it suggests which is of importance here, however, is that, if we are not to go to the lengths of abolishing schooling altogether, we cannot merely ignore these hidden aspects of the school curriculum, and certainly must not adopt a definition of curriculum which excludes them from all critical consideration. Rather our definition must embrace all the learning that goes on in schools whether it is expressly planned and intended or is a by-product of our planning and/or practice. For it is difficult to exonerate teachers completely from responsibility for these implicit forms of learning. Rather they need to be sensitized to them and helped to recognize and identify the hidden implications of some of the materials and the experiences they offer their pupils.

Much the same point emerges when we consider the distinction which has sometimes been made between the official curriculum and the actual curriculum, or between the planned curriculum and the received curriculum. By the official or planned curriculum is meant what is laid down in syllabuses, prospectuses and so on; the actual or received curriculum is the reality of the pupils' experience. The difference between them may be conscious or unconscious the cause of any mismatch being either a deliberate attempt by the teachers or others to deceive, to make what they offer appear more attractive than it really is, or merely the fact that, since teachers and pupils are human, the realities of any course will never fully match up to the hopes and intentions of those who have planned it. This latter distinction, as we shall see, begins to loom much larger now that we have a statutory requirement in the United Kingdom for the teaching of a National Curriculum. For all the evidence suggests that there is bound to be such a mismatch here between the intentions of those who framed that National Curriculum and the realities of the practices of teachers and the experiences of pupils.

Both of these distinctions are important and we would be foolish to go very far in our examination of the curriculum without acknowledging both the gaps that must inevitably exist between theory and practice and the predilection of some teachers for elaborate 'packaging' of their wares.

Furthermore, we must not lose sight of the fact that curriculum studies must ultimately be concerned with the relationship between these two views of the curriculum, between intention and reality, if it is to succeed in linking the theory and the practice of the curriculum (Stenhouse, 1975).

It becomes even more important, then, that we should not adopt a definition of curriculum which confines or restricts us to considerations only of that which is planned. What is actually received by pupils must be an equally important, or even more important concern, so that the actual or received curriculum must be seen as the teacher's or planner's responsibility every bit as much as the 'hidden' curriculum.

Lastly, we must also recognize the distinction that is often drawn between the 'formal' curriculum and the 'informal' curriculum, between the formal activities for which the timetable of the school allocates specific periods of teaching time or which, as in the case of the primary school, are included in the programme of work to be covered in normal school hours, and those many informal activities that go on, usually on a voluntary basis, at lunchtimes, after school hours, at weekends or during holidays. These latter activities – sports, clubs, societies, school journeys and the like – are often called 'extracurricular' activities and this suggests that they should be seen as separate from, as over and above the curriculum itself.

The reasons for this, however, are difficult to discern unless they are those that derive from the time of the day or week when they take place or the nature of the voluntary participation that usually characterizes them. For activities of this kind are usually seen to have as much educational validity and point as any of the formal arrangements of the school. Indeed, some would even argue that in certain cases they have more point than many such arrangements. It was for this reason that the Newsom Report (CACE, 1963) recommended that they 'ought to be recognized as an integral part of the total educational programme' (§ 135) and that to this end they be included in the formal timetable of an extended day. It is also for this reason that educationists such as Charity James have suggested that they be regarded and planned as one element of the curriculum (James, 1968). The inclusion of this kind of activity in the formal provision made by the school has also been a major feature of the philosophy of many of those concerned with the development of community schools (Cooksey, 1972, 1976a, 1976b).

Again, it would seem that, if we are concerned with curriculum planning, it would be foolish to omit by our definition of the curriculum a whole range of activities which teachers plan and execute with deliberate reasons and intentions. In looking at curriculum planning, therefore, there would appear to be nothing to be gained from leaving out of consideration any planned activity. It is for this reason that John Kerr (1968, p. 16) has defined the curriculum as 'all the learning which is planned and guided by the school, whether it is carried on in groups or individually, inside or outside the school'. Such a definition provides us with a basis for planning all the organized activities of a school.

However, there are real difficulties in attempting to operate with a definition of curriculum which excludes from consideration the unplanned effects of teacher activity, as the notions of the 'hidden' and the 'actual' or 'received' curriculum indicate. There are more aspects to curriculum than are dreamed of in the philosophy of most teachers, and certainly of most politicians, and a definition of curriculum which confines its scope to what teachers, or politicians, actually plan will omit many of those important dimensions of curriculum studies we identified earlier. We need a definition which will take us 'beyond curriculum' (Holly, 1973), or at least beyond the official curriculum, or, rather, we need to recognize that, whatever definition we adopt, it must embrace at least four major dimensions of educational planning and practice: the intentions of the planners, the procedures adopted for the implementation of those intentions, the actual experiences of the pupils resulting from the teachers' direct attempts to carry out their or the planners' intentions, and the 'hidden' learning that occurs as a by-product of the organization of the curriculum, and, indeed, of the school.

The problems of definition are thus serious and complex and it may be that they are best avoided by not attempting to define it too closely. The chapters which follow will reveal that in planning for curriculum change and development we need to be aware of all aspects and dimensions of the educational experiences which pupils have during any period of formal education, and with their underlying principles and rationale. And so, with the proviso that the expert is the person who can keep all or most of those dimensions in view rather than concentrating on one or two of them, we might accept that as the kind of loose definition we need. The importance of this kind of loose definition will become immediately apparent when we look at the problems of curriculum planning and at some of the planning models which have been offered.

PLANNING MODELS

It has been suggested (Tyler, 1949) that the curriculum has to be seen as consisting of four elements, and curriculum planning, therefore, as having four dimensions: objectives, content or subject matter, methods or procedures and evaluation. In short, we must distinguish in our curriculum planning what we are hoping to achieve, the ground we are planning to cover in order to achieve it, the kinds of activity and methods that we consider likely to be most effective in helping us towards our goals and the devices we will use to evaluate what we have done. Tyler's own way of putting this point is to suggest that there are 'four fundamental questions which must be answered in developing any curriculum and plan of instruction' (op. cit., p. i). These he lists as:

1. What educational purposes should the school seek to attain?
2. What educational experiences can be provided that are likely to attain these purposes?
3. How can these educational experiences be effectively organized?
4. How can we determine whether these purposes are being attained? (ibid.)

This analysis, then, if taken just as it stands, would give us a very simple model for curriculum planning, a linear model which requires us to specify our objectives, to plan the content and the methods which will lead us towards them and, finally, to endeavour to measure the extent of our success. It is, however, too simple a model for many reasons, most of which will become apparent when we consider the problems of prespecified objectives in Chapter 3.

One reason why it will not suffice, which must be mentioned here, is that it does not make sufficient allowance for the interrelatedness of the separate elements. At the very least we must allow for the fact that the results of our evaluation processes may be used to modify our planning. Thus it has been suggested that we should employ a cyclical rather than a linear model and link up evaluation with the framing of objectives to create a continuous cycle (Wheeler, 1967).

This would seem to be a step in the right direction but many would claim that the influence of evaluation on curriculum planning should be a continuous process rather than being delayed until the exercise is over and, if we accept that, then we must expect such continuous evaluation to result in regular modifications of our planning. In fact, we must go further than this and acknowledge the interrelationship of all four elements, since the practical experience of most teachers suggests that every one of these four elements is constantly being modified by every other and that the whole business of curriculum planning must be seen as one of constant interaction between the elements. A more suitable model might therefore be derived from the idea of a permutated entry on a football pool with every possible kind of combination allowed for, or the physicist's notion of 'dynamic equilibrium' where stable progress is made possible by the balanced interaction of a variety of forces.

What these models of curriculum planning have in common, however, is their acceptance that curriculum planning must begin with a statement of its objectives and, indeed, it has been argued (Hirst, 1969) that this is necessary if it is to qualify as a rational activity, since, it is argued, what characterizes a rational activity is that it is directed at some clear goal or set of purposes. This view, however, is by no means universally accepted and, as we shall see when we come to examine it in detail in Chapter 3, there are some very compelling arguments against adopting this kind of model for educational planning, not least those that draw attention to the model's inability to shed light on those value questions which we saw earlier are crucial to, and must have priority in, the planning of any educational curriculum. The criteria by which one selects one's objectives must logically be a prior consideration and this model offers no help with such decisions.

The alternative models that are available lay stress on other elements of Tyler's fourfold analysis of curriculum. One approach to curriculum planning has placed the emphasis on the content of education. This, as Paul Hirst (1969) suggests, has been the main characteristic of the traditional approach to educational planning, and it might be argued that this form of curriculum continues to predominate in secondary schools (and, indeed, in institutions of further and higher education) and it is now of course the implicit model for the National Curriculum. To plan a curriculum on this model is to state what subjects are to be studied and perhaps what aspects of them are to be studied. It is not a model, however, which ever begins to ask questions about the point and purposes of such studies, about the justification for their inclusion in the curriculum.

A further planning model, and one whose attractions appear to be becoming increasingly acknowledged, is that which emphasizes that element of Tyler's analysis of curriculum which is usually referred to as 'procedures', although not in quite the sense in which most people have understood it. Paul Hirst (1969) associates this approach with 'progressive' education and the form of curriculum which has been seen in some primary schools. The view he takes of this model is that its main concern is with methods of learning, with such things as project work, inquiry methods and discovery learning generally, and he criticizes it for not paying adequate attention either to the purposes of these activities or to the content of what is learnt by them.

However, that is a highly simplistic interpretation of a form of education which needs to be analysed at a rather more sophisticated level. For this approach to curriculum planning is predicated on the view that education is centrally concerned with certain processes of intellectual or cognitive development, that what is crucial to it, therefore, is not the bodies of knowledge that are assimilated nor is it the behavioural objectives that are attained or the behavioural changes that are brought about, but the processes of development that are promoted (Blenkin and Kelly, 1981, 1987, 1988a). In short, it is based on the belief that to have been educated is to have been helped to develop certain intellectual capacities rather than to have acquired factual knowledge or to have had one's behaviour modified in certain ways.

On this view, then, curriculum planning must start with a clear statement of the processes of development it is concerned to promote and thus the procedural principles upon which the teacher's day-to-day decisions and judgements are to be based. Indeed, as we have seen, it might be argued that such principles are a prerequisite of the other models too, since some criteria of this kind are a necessary basis both for the initial selection of objectives or content and for the continuing modification of these in the light of subsequent evaluations, so that to plan our curricula in this way might be seen as an attempt to get to the roots of truly educational decision-making.

From this kind of thinking, then, and as a reaction against those models which emphasize either content or objectives as the central elements in curriculum planning, there has emerged a 'process' model (Stenhouse, 1975), or a 'developmental' model of educational planning (Blenkin and Kelly, 1988a), which seems to many people to reflect more adequately than the other models available what the process of education might be regarded as being essentially concerned with.

Thus Tyler's analysis of the logic of curriculum planning, useful and interesting as it has been, does not offer us the clear-cut definition or model of curriculum planning that some have seen in it, but rather opens up a number of conflicting possibilities and has thus given rise to the appearance of several different models.

Curriculum planning, therefore, is not the simple matter that some seem to think. For there are, as we have just seen, at least three quite different ways in which we can set about it. No one of these will fit all the situations we may find ourselves planning for; all may have their place; although it will be argued in subsequent chapters that if one's concern is with education, with the development of the educand, rather than with instruction or the transmission of knowledge, if we are planning a curriculum designed to foster the development of its recipients rather than to provide them with socially or commercially useful knowledge, the 'process' or 'developmental' model is the only one which is suitable. Nevertheless, the main point to be made here is that our first decision in curriculum planning, at all levels from the planning by every individual teacher to the planning of a national curriculum, must be the selection of the appropriate model and the justification of our choice, and, to do this, we need a good deal more understanding of the implications of such a choice than many current curriculum planners or advisers seem to possess.

Hitherto, we have spoken rather vaguely of teachers, curriculum planners and curriculum advisers without clearly specifying whom we have in mind. It might be worthwhile at this point, therefore, to attempt briefly to identify the levels at which curriculum planning occurs and the strategies which have been and continue to be adopted for bringing about curriculum change.

LEVELS AND STRATEGIES OF CURRICULUM PLANNING

It must first be stressed that all that is said about curriculum planning and development in this book applies as much to the individual teacher in the preparation of his or her individual 'lessons' or other programmes of work with children as it does to those who find themselves charged with curriculum development at school, local authority or even national level. The issues raised here are as important for the work of the individual in his or her classroom as for those responsible for major national curriculum projects.

The most important point which arises from this (apart, of course, from the obvious implications it has for the level of every teacher's understanding of curriculum theory) is what it means for those national curriculum projects and other attempts to introduce curriculum innovation on a nationwide scale.

There have been many such attempts over the last two or three decades, most notably those sponsored by the Schools Council during its lifetime, some of the recent work of the Assessment of Performance Unit and, most recently, the decision to change the curricula of all schools to fit the demands of the new National Curriculum. All these strategies for external manipulation of the curriculum we shall explore in greater detail in later chapters, and especially in Chapter 5.

The most important point to be noted here, however, is what we have learned from the experience of these projects and activities about the role of the individual teacher in curriculum change and development. We must especially note the failure of all attempts by the Schools Council to produce 'teacher-proof' packages – schemes of work, versions of curriculum, supporting materials and so on of a kind which teachers would accept, use and apply in the precise form that the central planners had in mind. In every case, teachers have adapted and used what they have been offered in their own ways and for their own purposes. Some project directors were inclined to throw up their hands in despair at this phenomenon; others went along with it eventually and built into their schemes proper forms of allowance for this kind of personal and local adaptation by teachers. The Schools Council itself, just before its demise, adopted a policy of supporting school-based curriculum developments, assisting teachers and groups of teachers with the process of developing their own curricula rather than attempting to 'sell' them prepackaged programmes which might not be geared appropriately to the specific needs of the individual school. And some of the recent work of the Assessment of Performance Unit, as we shall see in Chapter 5, has been concerned much more with offering its findings to teachers, while leaving it to them to decide whether and how they might use these in their own contexts, than with attempts at imposing the same solutions to teaching problems on all. In short, there has come a growing awareness that each school is unique and that its curricular needs are thus largely idiosyncratic.

The implications of this kind of experience for the implementation of the new National Curriculum are interesting and will be explored more fully later. We have here another example of the failure or the refusal of the architects of the National Curriculum to take any account or cognizance of the substantial experience and findings of earlier research.

What we must note here, however, is that the teachers have a 'make or break' role in any curriculum innovation. Teachers have been known to sabotage attempts at change; certainly it is clear that such attempts can succeed only when the teachers concerned are committed to them and, especially, when they understand, as well as accept, their underlying principles. We have already noted, and will no doubt do so on many more occasions, that the practice of education cannot be a mechanical, largely mindless activity; it requires constant decisions and judgements by the teacher, and these he or she cannot make properly without fully appreciating and accepting the underlying rationale of any activity. The quality of any educational experience, then, will depend to a very large extent on the individual teacher responsible for it; and any attempt at controlling the curriculum from the outside which does not recognize that must be doomed to failure. An alternative strategy for ensuring compliance to external requirements might of course be to introduce stringent measures for controlling the activities of teachers, through schemes of accountability and appraisal, and this aspect of current policies we must also consider later. Such a strategy, however, cannot ensure commitment or understanding; and obedience to authority on the part of teachers may not be the best basis for the practice of education as we are viewing it here.

Finally, in noting the central role of the teacher in education, we must not lose sight of the fact that he or she is operating in a context hedged about with constraints and pressures of many kinds, social and political as well as physical and organizational. No curriculum planning of any kind can go on in a vacuum; it must take place in an environment which is prey to pressures and constraints of many kinds, most notably at the present time, as we shall see later, the constraints imposed by the statutory requirements of the 1988 Education Act. Again, we shall consider these in much greater detail in later chapters, but it will do no harm here to note in our overview some of the more significant of them.

CONSTRAINTS AND PRESSURES ON CURRICULUM PLANNING

No teacher can be unaware of the constraints and pressures which form the context within which he or she works. It is this that makes a nonsense of the views of those people who seem to think that teacher autonomy implies complete licence for the teacher to do as he or she pleases. For, as we shall see later, education is essentially a political activity and no one who practises it can long remain unaware of the political dimensions of his or her work.

There are several ways in which one might categorize these constraints and pressures. One might identify those which arise from organizational factors and, with them, those created by the physical environment of the school; and one might contrast those with pressures arising from more overtly personal agencies – parents, employers and pressure groups of many kinds. One might also note the more direct influences stemming from political sources – governing bodies, local authorities and central government.

In the context of education in the United Kingdom in the late 1980s and the 1990s, however, it may be more helpful to see these constraints and pressures under two main headings – those indirect influences which are generated by the organizational contexts within which we work and by all the many groups in society which seek to steer the work of schools into certain directions in which they have some vested interest, and the more direct or, since the 1988 Education Act, the very direct impact of political initiatives taken by central government.

Perhaps the most important aspect of the former, indirect influences on curriculum planning to be noted at this stage is the fact that they often conflict and compete with one another. They arise from many different sources: the recommendations of official government reports and other publications; the work of educational theorists from Plato to writers of the present day; the church, or rather from various churches; teachers' subject and age-group associations; other pressure groups, some, for example the Campaign for the Advancement of State Education (CASE), concerned with the general quality of state provision, others, for example the Confederation of British Industry (CBI), wishing to point the attention of schools into certain directions of their own.

These different sources of influence, therefore, represent many different kinds of pressure, so that the school curriculum has been described as a battleground of competing ideologies. At the risk of over-simplification, we might see these as broadly falling into two main camps: one concerned with the vocational, the utilitarian, the economic function of schooling, what the Crowther Report (CACE, 1959) described as education as a national investment; the other stressing the notion of education as a form of personal development and as what the Crowther Report called 'the right of every boy and girl to be educated' (op cit., p. 54), a right which it claimed 'exists regardless of whether, in each individual case, there will be any return' (ibid.). At the risk of further over-simplification, it might also at this stage be claimed that most teachers lean to the second of these ideologies in their own views of education, so that the greater the control teachers themselves wield in curricular decisions, the more likely it is that, in spite of contrary constraints and pressures, the curricula offered by most schools will tend to favour this latter view of education and its purposes.

There can be little doubt that this is the prime reason why the last two decades have seen a rapidly accelerating move to limit, in fact to remove completely, the teachers' own influence over the school curriculum and to create machinery which will ensure that curricular decisions are made, or at least approved, by central government. We will trace this development in some detail in Chapter 6. It is important to note here, however, that its main purpose has clearly been to make the education system more economically productive or, to use the current euphemism, more responsive to the needs of society. This has been clearly stated by all the major political figures associated with the movement, from James Callaghan to Kenneth Baker. Nor can it be doubted that the corollary of this, although for obvious reasons this is never as clearly stated, has been to minimize that other aspect of schooling – education as the right of every child, or education as concerned with individual development.

In this way, the more direct influences of central government on the school curriculum have been slowly converted from influence to intervention and from intervention to direct control. The most important effect of this, as we have noted before, is that teachers now have little or no say in the official curriculum of the nation's schools. On the one hand, therefore, this means that they will be less of a prey to those indirect influences we mentioned earlier, so that these will now need to turn their attention to the bureaucrats and politicians who have taken on the responsibility for curriculum planning at the national level. On the other hand, teachers will now be expected to operate a curriculum which has been imposed upon them from without and to implement curricular policies over whose framing they have had little or no influence.

This latter point raises some interesting issues in the light of what we said earlier about the need for teachers to be committed to the curricular provision they are making if they are to make it properly and effectively. One of the strengths of the previous system was that most teachers did believe in what they were doing, or at least enjoyed a good deal of scope to make of it something they could believe in. No doubt there will be many who will believe in what they are now required to do. But for those who do not there are clearly important problems to be faced and, at a more theoretical level, these are problems which will highlight the distinction we referred to earlier in this chapter between the official and the actual curriculum, between the intention and the reality, between theory and practice. They also resurrect those difficulties we have also noted which arise from earlier attempts to manipulate teachers by remote control or to create teacher-proof curricula.

It is largely for this reason that a major aspect of these recent developments has been a concern to establish not only appropriate means for evaluating curricula and the work of schools but, more crucially, for rendering schools and teachers more accountable and for ensuring that their work can be regularly appraised. This constitutes another major area or set of issues which any attempt to study the curriculum must include – issues to which we turn finally in this brief overview of curriculum theory.

EVALUATION, ACCOUNTABILITY AND APPRAISAL

We shall see in Chapter 7 that a major feature of that increased knowledge and understanding of curriculum which we have acquired through research and study over the last twenty years or so has been what we have learned about the complexities as well as the techniques of curriculum evaluation. What must be stressed here is that one can see at least two purposes in such evaluation. In the early projects, the concern was with evaluating the effectiveness of particular innovations, in terms either of their methodological advantages or of their worth as educational experiences. Thus early discussions of evaluation tend to focus on it as a device for curriculum development and improvement, much as we saw it was viewed in Ralph Tyler's (1949) analysis to which we referred earlier.

However, that move towards more direct political control of the curriculum, which we have just noted, has been accompanied by a shift in the concept of evaluation, or at least in the official view of its purposes. The concern now is much more with evaluation for the accountability of schools and teachers, an examination of particular pieces or kinds of work less to assess their own worth or value as to appraise the work of the teachers responsible for implementing them. Again we can see that this must be the emphasis within a centrally imposed national curriculum, for little development of the curriculum is envisaged, the main purpose of a national curriculum being to inhibit experimentation and any resultant innovation or change. And so, the main purpose of evaluation must now be to appraise the work of individual schools and teachers against the requirements of the National Curriculum, to make them more accountable to outside agencies for its implementation and, indeed, as has been clearly stated more than once by politicians in recent times, to close down schools which seem to be inadequate when measured against these criteria and to fire teachers who seem to reveal similar inadequacies. Thus, as we shall see, evaluation has become appraisal, its concern not with curriculum development so much as with teacher accountability and, in short, it has become another mechanism of central political control.

This does not of course mean that there is no longer a need for teachers to familiarize themselves with the issues and the techniques of curriculum evaluation. Teachers will continue to wish to evaluate their own work and they will still need quite sophisticated techniques and understandings in order to do so. And one hopes that, even with little direct power to bring about change themselves, they will wish to continue to evaluate the National Curriculum, if only to maintain that curriculum debate we suggested earlier is becoming more rather than less important in the new era.

For this reason, Chapter 7 will attempt to explore and outline what we have learned about curriculum evaluation in recent times. It will also, however, trace the development of curriculum evaluation into teacher appraisal and accountability.

SUMMARY AND CONCLUSIONS

This chapter has set out to provide some indication of the underlying rationale of this book and an overview of the survey of the major aspects of curriculum theory which subsequent chapters will offer.

It began by attempting to define curriculum studies or at least to indicate the view of this field of exploration which is adopted here. It stressed that it represents an attempt to study the realities of the classroom in a holistic way, transcending the narrower, more specialist perspectives of what have been called the 'contributory disciplines' of education theory; that it seeks to reconcile theory and practice, to look at the actualities of education from the inside, to get at what is sometimes these days called 'praxis'; that it attempts both of these things in order to generate a body of theory which will have a direct relevance for educational practice; and, finally, but most importantly, that it endeavours to do this in a properly rigorous, critical and analytical manner, seeking to ensure conceptual coherence and raising questions of the ultimate point and purposes of curricular activities and provision and not merely those concerning the mechanics of implementation.

We then went on to consider some definitions of the term 'curriculum' or, rather, some of the many aspects of this notion which have been identified; and we concluded that the most useful definition we could adopt, both for the purposes of this book and for our effective practice as teachers, was one which is loose enough and broad enough to embrace all the learning that actually goes on in schools and all dimensions of the educational process. For, although we could recognize the attractions of limiting the term to those activities which are deliberately planned, we also acknowledged the importance of recognizing the differences which often exist between what is planned and what is achieved, and, in particular, the need for teachers to accept responsibility for all the incidental learning which goes on, for the 'hidden' curriculum.

These first two sections were designed to make clear the broad perspectives from which all the issues later chapters explore will be viewed. It is as important here as in any aspect of curriculum planning to be clear from the outset about one's definitions and conceptions, about one's assumptions and, indeed, about one's value positions.

We then turned to a brief outline of those major issues which will form the substance of subsequent chapters. We looked at the different models of curriculum planning which have emerged from recent studies and stressed their differences and the need to consider carefully the choice of the appropriate model for any innovation. We also suggested that it is the 'process' or 'developmental' model which best enables us to face up to the value questions all educational planning requires us to face and which is thus the most appropriate model for planning any curriculum which is to be justified on educational or developmental rather than on instrumental or utilitarian grounds. We considered some of the strategies which have been adopted for curriculum planning and innovation and the levels at which these can be seen to occur, from that of the individual teacher in the classroom to that of the new National Curriculum, and, in doing so, we stressed the 'make or break' role of the teacher whatever the source of any planned innovation. We looked at some of the constraints and pressures which form the context in which all curriculum planning must go on, and, in particular, that build-up of political pressure which has turned influence into intervention and has resulted in the present centralization of the control of the school curriculum. Finally, we noted the importance of evaluation as a device for keeping questions of the effectiveness and the value of our work constantly under review, although at the same time we recognized the current trend towards seeing this process primarily in terms of teacher appraisal and accountability.

All these issues will be explored in much greater detail in subsequent chapters. This chapter has provided the kind of overview which will enable the reader to see more clearly how these different dimensions of curriculum studies fit together into a body of understanding, both theoretical and practical, whose focus is firmly fixed on classroom practice, and which might offer us a total view of what is involved in curriculum planning and development and thus lead to more coherent educational practice. Above all, however, its main intention has been to stress the need for rigorous and critical examination of all our curricular theories and practices, and an attempt will be made to maintain and to demonstrate that kind of rigour and critical stance in all that follows.

2
CURRICULUM AS CONTENT
AND EDUCATION AS TRANSMISSION

We saw in Chapter 1 that there is a strong case for claiming that in curriculum planning and, indeed, in any debate about the curriculum, we must look beyond considerations of content alone and recognize that questions of the purposes or reasons for our decisions are logically prior to those about their substance. If we accept that curriculum planning must begin with statements about the purposes we hope to attain or the principles upon which our practice is to be based, all decisions about the content of our curriculum must be subsidiary to those prior choices. For, as Ralph Tyler said (1949, p. 1), such decisions will be answers to the question, 'What educational experiences can be provided that are likely to attain these purposes?'

However, we also noted that many people have not fully appreciated the force or the implications of that claim. For many, a curriculum is still a syllabus, and even among those who have discussed and even advocated a more sophisticated approach to planning there are those who continue, at least in the practical recommendations they make, to regard decisions of content as the starting point. Many of these people do operate with a concept of education framed in terms of the developing understanding of the child, the growth of critical awareness (Peters, 1965, 1966) and other such elements which seem more closely related to the idea of education as development than to that of education as the mere transmission of knowledge. They still appear to assume, however, or sometimes endeavour to argue, that only certain kinds of knowledge will promote these forms of development or that exposure to certain kinds of knowledge will do so for all pupils, so that, along with this kind of concept of education, they offer us the further, and incompatible, notion that education is 'initiation into intrinsically worthwhile activities' (Peters, op. cit.). In short, they are adopting a view of knowledge which requires us to see the knowledge-content of the curriculum as in itself the prime source of justification for our curricular decisions, to see it as the chief, and perhaps the sole, determinant, and to plan the curriculum by reference to the knowledge it is designed to transmit rather than the children it is concerned to educate. Thus, for example, Denis Lawton's (1973) model for curriculum planning requires us to select our objectives by reference to the nature of the child, the nature of the society in which he or she lives and the nature of knowledge itself, and thus effectively, if inadvertently, makes decisions of content prior to those concerning purposes. Others too, such as Paul Hirst (1969), while recommending an approach to curriculum planning by way of prestated objectives, have continued to regard analyses of the nature of knowledge as fundamental to the educational debate. Indeed, there is a long tradition of viewing certain subjects or kinds of activity as having some kind of inalienable right to be included in the curriculum without reference to, and even to the deliberate exclusion of, any claims that they might contribute towards the attainment of certain goals. This is one reason why, as we shall see in Chapter 3, some statements of objectives are couched in terms of content, in terms making it apparent that decisions about the value of certain subjects have been reached prior to the choice of the objectives themselves. Talk about the importance of purposes and/or procedures in curriculum planning has by no means banished the traditional emphasis on content in the minds of either practitioners or theorists.

This may well suggest that we are taking too simple a view in attempting, like Ralph Tyler (1949), to place in rank order the questions the curriculum planner must ask. Perhaps we should acknowledge that questions of purposes and principles are inextricably bound up with questions of content and that all must be considered together.

However, even if we do agree that other questions must be asked and answered by the curriculum planner, it remains the case that, in order to deal with questions of content when we reach them, we will need to understand the issues which are involved and to appreciate the different viewpoints, the different epistemological and educational stances, which can be taken up. Thus, if we regard a major purpose of education as being to initiate pupils into the cultural heritage of society or into what is best within it (Lawton, 1973, 1975) or into activities which are intrinsically worthwhile (Peters, 1965, 1966; White, 1973; Thompson and White, 1975) or into the several forms of understanding or rationality (Hirst, 1965), we need to ask many questions about what might be meant by 'our cultural heritage', the basis on which we might select that which is best within it, the grounds for attributing intrinsic value to certain activities, what is meant by a 'form of understanding or rationality' and many other related questions. Similarly, if we take what might be seen as a contrary stance and assert that education should be concerned to develop the knowledge pupils bring into the school with them (Keddie, 1971), or their needs or their interests (Wilson, 1971), or to promote within them the development and the growth of certain abilities, capacities and competences (Blenkin, 1988; Blenkin and Kelly, 1981, 1987, 1988a), we must also explore the epistemological assumptions underlying these claims and the issues which they raise.

We must consider too the implications of viewing education, and especially of planning our curricular provision, as though it were a matter merely of the transmission of knowledge-content. For to see it in this way is not only to take a particular view of the nature of knowledge, it is also to adopt a particular concept of education. What is more it is to adopt a very limited concept of education, one which sees it merely as instruction in certain subjects or bodies of knowledge. The justification of such a view of education as instruction must either be based on the usefulness, the instrumental, utilitarian or even vocational value of certain kinds of knowledge, a view which offers no scope for *educational* debate, since utility not education is the sole concern, or it must be derived from some view, such as those we have just referred to, about the intrinsic value of certain kinds of knowledge. Even if one attempts to mount the latter kind of argument, however, it seems very odd to claim that education consists of transmitting to children certain knowledge-content, whose value somehow resides in itself, regardless of the impact which it has on the children who are to be the recipients of it.

Furthermore, once we accept that some selection must be made of the content to be included in our curriculum, we must acknowledge that we will need some criteria of selection, some set of values by which we will make our choices and undertake our planning, and that these will need not only to be stated clearly but also justified. We must recognize, therefore, that questions of value, and of values, are central to educational planning (even though they may not be an essential part of planning courses of simple instruction), so that the issue of the status of assertions of value must also be examined if we are to achieve a basis for any kind of educational decision, whether its focus be on content, purposes or principles.

Whatever view one takes of education, then, that view will be predicated on certain assumptions about the nature of knowledge and a particular set of values. All these elements need to be examined closely and, in particular, we need to ensure that, whatever our views are, they display a coherence and a consistency, that all these elements are compatible with and in harmony with one another.

Issues of content, then, must remain central to the curriculum debate even if they must not be permitted to continue to dominate it. It is to the issue of what knowledge, if any, must be included in the curriculum and the related issue of the bases upon which we are to make all those value choices which curriculum planning presents us with that we now turn.

KNOWLEDGE AND THE CURRICULUM

The history of education in the western world, from at least as far back as ancient Greece, reveals a concern to distinguish those areas of learning promoted by teachers in order to attain certain social goals from those aspects of learning that have seemed to have some independent and intrinsic right to inclusion in the curriculum and which, therefore, not only do not seek but positively eschew justification in instrumental terms. This was the point of attraction felt and expressed in the ancient world for the idea of a liberal education, of the later concern with the education of the cultured gentleman and the resultant contrasting of liberal and vocational forms of education, a conflict which can still be discerned in the practice of the present day and which has led to some very clear and overt hierarchical distinctions between certain kinds of school subject. The same kind of thinking also expresses itself in modern theory through the differences that are now stressed between education as such, a term which it is suggested should and can be appropriately applied only to those activities that can be viewed and justified as intrinsically worthwhile, and other processes that also involve teaching and that schools also concern themselves with, such as socialization, training, instruction and the like (Peters, 1965, 1966; Hirst and Peters, 1970).

On the whole, such dispute as there has been over the inclusion of vocational or utilitarian learning in the curriculum has centred on the issue of whether this is an appropriate concern of schools, or whether it should be their concern only in relation to the needs of those pupils who cannot cope with the intellectual demands of those subjects that have been felt to be intrinsically valuable (Bantock, 1968, 1971). No one has felt it necessary to challenge their justification beyond that point, since if one accepts the ends to which they are instrumental it must follow that, other things being equal, one accepts the means to those ends.

There has been much disagreement, however, over the question of what is to be included in the curriculum for its own sake. Indeed, this question has been the focal point of educational debate since such debate began. It continues to be a highly controversial issue, since it is by no means a straightforward matter to identify those areas of knowledge that have value in their own right or that are to be seen as intrinsically worthwhile or, indeed, even to demonstrate that there are any areas of knowledge of which this is true.

This question has been a major concern of philosophers since the time of Plato. Indeed, it could be argued that this is the focal point of philosophy itself since all branches of philosophy – ethics, aesthetics, politics and so on – can be seen as centrally engaged in a search for what will constitute knowledge in each particular field. Inevitably a number of different theories about the nature and structure of knowledge have been offered, all or most of which are still in vogue, and for many reasons it would be desirable that we should consider these in great detail; first, because particular theories about the nature of knowledge are implicit in or assumed by all theories that are proposed as bases for curriculum development and planning and, secondly and more importantly, because the assumptions about the nature of knowledge that such theories make are often left unquestioned and accepted uncritically (Kelly, 1986). In other words, the epistemological bases of the curriculum are too little understood by curriculum theorists and most theories about the curriculum need to be looked at very critically and rigorously from this point of view.

However, we must content ourselves here with a brief survey of the main issues, a procedure that may be more acceptable since it begins to appear to me that the most important point for teachers and curriculum planners to understand is perhaps not the details of particular epistemological theories, although clearly they should grasp them if they intend to base their own theories, and especially their practice and their policies, on them, but rather the variety of theories that have been offered and the fact that each of them is inevitably tentative and hypothetical and fails to offer an account of knowledge that is universally acceptable.

Two main kinds of theory have emerged during the development of Western European philosophy: those rationalist views that take as their starting point the supremacy of the intellect over other human faculties and stress that true knowledge is that which is achieved by the mind in some way independently of the information provided by the senses; and those empiricist views which have taken a contrary stance and maintained that knowledge of the world about us can be derived only from the evidence that the world offers us through the use of our senses.

This dispute reflects a distinction that has characterized Western European philosophy from the beginning between the idea of the fallibility of the senses as sources of information and views that some have held of the infallibility of the intellect. Thus such philosophers as Plato, Descartes and Kant have offered various versions of a rationalist epistemology which have shared the basic conviction that the evidence of our senses is misleading but that the rational mind can attain true knowledge independently of the senses by apprehending what lies beyond those sense impressions or in some way introducing a rational structure to our understanding of them.

Such theories, seeing knowledge as essentially independent of the observations of our senses, inevitably lead to a view of knowledge as reified, as in some sense God-given, 'out-there' and independent of the knower, having a status that is untouched by and owes nothing to the human condition of the beings who possess the knowledge they are concerned with. Thus for Plato, and especially for Aristotle, the act of contemplation of the supreme forms of human knowledge is a godlike act, through which humans transcend their human condition and achieve, albeit momentarily, the supreme bliss of the life of pure intellect perpetually enjoyed by God. For St Thomas Aquinas, and indeed for those Thomists who continue to adhere to his doctrine, true knowledge is in a quite literal sense God-given, being 'revealed' by God to humanity. And for Kant too, at a more mundane level, the task of establishing a critique of knowledge is essentially one of discovering those elements of knowledge which owe nothing to our nature as human beings, those which are derived from pure reason and have nothing to do with human feelings or passions.

Such theories give rise to a view of certain kinds of knowledge as timeless, objective, owing nothing to the particular circumstances of individual eras, societies, cultures or human beings. True knowledge, on this view, is independent of all such ephemeral considerations. Furthermore, what is even more important for this debate, as we shall see later, is that these theories seek to embrace not only knowledge of a 'scientific' kind, that concerned with the 'factual' or empirical aspects of existence, but also, and more significantly, human values – aesthetic, moral and even social/political.

Their attractions for some theorists of education can thus be readily understood, and this kind of epistemological belief underlies the claims of some present-day philosophers of education for the inalienable right of certain subjects, those whose intellectual content is high, to be included in the curriculum. For example, Richard Peters's 'transcendental' argument (1966) for the intrinsic value of certain kinds of human activity is in all major respects a reassertion of the rationalist arguments of Immanuel Kant.

It is only relatively recently that doubts have been expressed about the validity of the claim that certain kinds of knowledge are inherently more valuable or more important than others. For Plato there was no doubt that there was a very clear hierarchy of knowledge with philosophy at its peak and this, along with so many of the fundamental assumptions of Platonism, went unquestioned up to the time when the empiricists offered the challenge of a completely new approach to the question of knowledge. The fundamental principle of that hierarchy was that the greater the level of abstraction the more status a particular kind of knowledge had. Thus, in addition to the claims we examined earlier for the superiority of intellectual knowledge over sense-experience of the phenomena of the physical world, Plato also asserts that gradations must be recognized within the realms of intellectual knowledge according to degrees of abstraction, with philosophy, or dialectic as he calls it at this point in his argument, as a form of knowledge that he sees as totally abstract and not hypothetical in any way, at the pinnacle or as the coping stone.

The influence of that kind of thinking on curriculum development, or non-development, over the years should not need to be spelled out to anyone who has spent any time teaching in our schools or colleges or universities.

A major consequence of taking this view of knowledge and its prime role in curriculum planning is that it leads to an inevitable stratification of society. Thus, in Plato's ideal society, all those citizens who have not revealed the talent necessary to be educated as philosophers will be brought up to accept the superior knowledge and judgement of the 'philosopher-kings' and to obey them without question. In other words, this is a view which leads to the generation of two or three levels of culture, two or three kinds of curriculum and two or three classes of people within society.

It is thus a view which makes the attainment of educational equality impossible (Kelly, 1980a, 1986). For, once one accepts a definition of education in terms of certain 'high status' subjects or bodies of knowledge, once one adopts the belief that, for example, to be educated is to have studied Latin and/or Greek or, indeed, whatever subjects one selects to put at the top of one's hierarchy, then it must follow, as the night the day, and as Plato fully appreciated, that anyone who cannot cope with the bodies of knowledge so designated cannot by definition be educated, but must be content with involvement in lower-status activities and with what is literally a second-class form of upbringing.

The best way to recognize what others have found unsatisfactory in this kind of view is to look at the basic tenets of the other main kind of epistemological theory, empiricism. For empiricism is best seen as a reaction to the mysticism of these rationalist views. Its fundamental tenet is well expressed in the claim of John Locke, the founder of the empiricist movement, that no knowledge comes into the mind except through the gates of the senses. The mind of the newborn child is seen as a *tabula rasa*, a clean sheet, 'void of all characters, without any ideas'. Such knowledge as it acquires, it acquires through experience. For the empiricist, there is no other source of knowledge, since he or she denies the validity of all a priori knowledge, that is, all knowledge which does not derive ultimately from experience.

A basic position such as this leads inevitably to a less confident view of knowledge and to a greater awareness of the tentative nature of human knowledge, since it is agreed by everyone that the rationalists are right in claiming that the evidence of our senses is unreliable. Indeed, one of the earliest and most ardent exponents of the empiricist view of knowledge, David Hume, came to the conclusion that no knowledge was possible at all or, at least, that we could have little certainty in our knowledge of the world about us. 'If we believe that fire warms or water refreshes, 'tis only because it costs us too much pains to think otherwise.' It is not perhaps necessary to go as far to the other extreme as this, but it is necessary, if one takes such a view, to recognize at the very least the hypothetical nature of knowledge, as present-day empiricist theories do (Ayer, 1936, 1946).

Thus a number of recent theories of knowledge and theories of education have begun from the conviction that human knowledge has to be treated in a far more tentative way than many who take a rationalist view would concede and that, in relation to curriculum planning, we are in no position to be dogmatic about its content. The whole pragmatist movement, as promoted by John Dewey, which has been highly influential in the recent development of educational practice, has been founded on a view of knowledge as hypothetical and therefore subject to constant change, modification and evolution. Such a view requires us to be hesitant about asserting the value of any body of knowledge or its right to inclusion in the curriculum and encourages us to accept that knowledge is to be equated rather with experience, so that what it means for children to acquire knowledge is that they should have experiences which they can themselves use as the basis for the framing of hypotheses to explain and gain control over the environment in which they live. In other words, we cannot impose what is knowledge for us upon them; we must assist them to develop their own knowledge, their own hypotheses, which will be different from ours if the process of evolution is to go on.

This certainly results in a view of education as a much more personal activity than any rationalist could acknowledge. It may also suggest that knowledge itself is personal and subjective. Thus some have stressed the phenomenological or existentialist claim that all knowledge is personal and subjective, that every individual's knowledge is the result of his or her own completely unique perceptions of his or her own world.

This, however, is not a view that Dewey himself subscribed to. He believed that the proper model for all knowledge is that of scientific knowledge, where hypotheses are framed and modified according to publicly agreed criteria, so that while such knowledge has no permanent status it is objective in so far as it at least enjoys current acceptance by everyone. Mary Warnock (1977) is making the same point (although she develops quite different conclusions from it) when she speaks of 'received bodies of knowledge'.

Others have disputed this, however, and have suggested that knowledge cannot be seen as having even a current universal acceptance. This is the main thrust of the recent developments in sociology towards the generation of a sociology of knowledge, or a recognition of the 'politics of knowledge'. For it has been argued here not only that knowledge is a human product but that it is the product of particular social groups, 'a product of the informal understandings negotiated among members of an organized intellectual collectivity' (Blum, 1971, p. 117). On this view, then, knowledge is socially constructed and, since socially constructed knowledge is ideology, any attempt to make decisions about the content of the curriculum that are based on some views of what kinds of knowledge are valuable has to be seen as an attempt to impose one particular ideology on children and thus to achieve some kind of social control over them either deliberately or merely as a by-product of one's practice. Debate about the content of the curriculum is thus seen as dispute between conflicting ideologies. As a result of arguments of this kind, we have had demands from people like Illich (1971), Freire (1972) and others that society should be deschooled and the process of education made less formal. It is also for this reason, amongst others, that it has been suggested that we should endeavour to base the content of the curriculum on the 'common sense knowledge' of the pupil rather than the 'educational knowledge' of the teacher (Keddie, 1971). In this way it is suggested we will avoid the alienation which, it is claimed, is experienced by children who see no point or meaning in the content of what is presented to them. In addition, we will repudiate the charge that we are endeavouring to gain control of them by indoctrinating them with the values, the ideology, of one dominant section of the community.

It is this debate which bedevils not only any attempt to establish a firm philosophical or epistemological basis for curriculum planning but also, as we shall see in the next section, any attempt to base our decisions on the nature of society or on some notion of education as cultural transmission.

For this also requires that we discover some criteria within the nature of knowledge itself which will enable us to choose between conflicting cultures or to make a selection from what might seem to be the common culture, and this we have just seen we cannot do. There is no universally accepted theory of knowledge and the theories that appear to have the strongest claims on our acceptance are those that tell us that they cannot establish the kind of objective status for knowledge we require in order to make decisions about the content of the curriculum entirely on the basis of this kind of consideration.

In fact, our brief survey of some of the major features of what philosophers and others have said about knowledge has suggested that epistemological considerations in themselves can provide no positive help to curriculum planners, since one can find no clear, hard-and-fast theory of knowledge upon which any firm choice of curriculum content can be based. Similarly, as we shall see later, they offer no clear-cut basis for the development of an objective framework of values within which such decisions can be made.

This also highlights a fundamental tension, or even a contradiction, in Denis Lawton's model of curriculum planning which we mentioned briefly at the beginning of this chapter (Lawton, 1973, 1975). He is suggesting that in making decisions about the curriculum we look to both philosophical assertions about the nature of knowledge and to sociological considerations about such things as social and technological change and that we balance these against each other. It should now be apparent, however, that if those philosophical assertions are such as to promote a view of knowledge as having a 'God-given' status, they must also require of us that we do not, or even cannot, modify or compromise this God-given status by reference to mundane sociological considerations of the here-and-now of particular societies. If, on the other hand, these philosophical considerations do not lead to this view of knowledge, they must lead to a view of it as socially constructed in some way, so that they are not fundamentally different kinds of consideration from the sociological considerations themselves.

Again, therefore, either epistemological considerations of a purely philosophical kind must dominate curriculum planning, no matter how socially irrelevant the curriculum they lead to, or it must be accepted that they are of no real help in curriculum planning at all, beyond of course what they can contribute to the attainment of intellectual and conceptual clarity.

For, if epistemology is of any value to the curriculum planner, that value derives only from the fact that this kind of inquiry can illuminate and introduce some clarity into our discussions of the curriculum, since such excursions into the theory of knowledge do help to point up some of the difficulties that curriculum planners face in this area and to bring out the assumptions implicit in some theories about the curriculum, especially those which endeavour to press 'hard' views about the superior value of certain kinds of knowledge. They also provide some negative evidence as to where solutions to these problems are not to be found and suggest, therefore, both that we look elsewhere for solutions and that there are real dangers in expecting these solutions ever to be so conclusive that we can be dogmatic about them. For they also reveal that some of the difficulties we meet in curriculum planning are a direct result of the adoption of one particular theory of knowledge on the assumption that it can not only help to solve our problems but that it can in itself provide a final answer to them.

This same difficulty, as has just been suggested, bedevils also the attempt to base curriculum planning on an analysis of the nature of society and it is to an examination of this view that we now turn.

CULTURE AND THE CURRICULUM

First, then, let us consider the case for basing decisions about the content of the curriculum on an analysis of the nature of society.

It must be recognized that schools exist in advanced or sophisticated societies as agencies for the handing on of the culture of the society, so that at least in part their purposes must be seen in terms of socialization or acculturation, attending to that induction of children into the ways of life of society which is achieved in more primitive societies by less formal methods. On this basis it has been argued that a good deal of what is to be taught in schools can be decided by reference to the culture of the society they are created to serve. This has been one of the root justifications of those who take a hard line on the question of curriculum content, since it has been argued that a major task of the school is to hand on to the next generation the 'common cultural heritage' of the society (Lawton, 1973, 1975). Indeed, Denis Lawton has asserted elsewhere (1980, p. vii) that his and his colleagues' approach to the study of the curriculum has been one 'which has as its central concept the definition of curriculum in terms of "a selection from the culture of a society" '.

Even if one accepts the force of this claim in principle, in practice it creates more difficulties than it resolves. To begin with, difficulties arise because the term 'culture' has several different meanings (Kelly, 1986). In particular, confusions are created by the fact that the term is used, by anthropologists for example, to denote in a purely descriptive sense all aspects of the ways of life of a particular society, as when we speak of the cultural patterns of a primitive community. On the other hand, it is also used to denote what is regarded as being best in the art and literature of any particular society. Thus a 'cultured individual', is not one who knows his or her way about the ways of life, the habits and beliefs of his or her society; he or she is an individual who has been brought to appreciate those works of his or her fellows that are regarded as being among the finer achievements of the culture.

When people talk, then, of basing the curriculum on the culture of the society, some of them are suggesting that we socialize the young, while others are encouraging us to frame the curriculum in terms of what is regarded as being best or most valuable among the intellectual and artistic achievements of the society. A leaning towards the latter interpretation, since it reflects that Platonic view of knowledge we considered earlier, is likely to lead to a view of two or more cultures, a high and a low, or an upper-class and a folk culture (Eliot, 1948; Bantock, 1968, 1971), and this has serious implications for curriculum planning and the practice of education generally which we must later examine. In particular, problems of both a theoretical and a practical kind arise when the distinction becomes associated with social class or ethnic differences (Kelly, 1981, 1986).

A second problem arises from the difficulty of establishing what is or should be the relationship between schools and the society in which they function. We have spoken so far as if the function of the schools is to transmit the culture of society, but there are those who would wish to argue that they exist rather to transform that culture, to act as positive agents of change. Do schools change society or do they themselves change in response to prior changes in society? These are nice questions. Even nicer are the issues we raise if we ask whether schools ought to be attempting to change society or merely to adjust to social changes. In reality, and perhaps in ideal terms too, it may be sufficient to recognize that both are interlinked and subject to many of the same influences and constraints so that changes occur in both *pari passu*, and this perhaps is how things should be.

Whatever view one takes of this issue, a further difficulty arises for those who wish to base decisions about the content of the curriculum on considerations of the culture of the society when we attempt to state in specific terms what that culture is. For it is clear that in a modern advanced industrial society no one pattern of life that can be called the culture of that society can be identified. Most modern societies are pluralist in nature; that is, it is possible to discern in them many different, and sometimes incompatible, cultures or subcultures. It does not follow that we must regard such subcultures as hierarchically related to one another but it is necessary to recognize them as being different from one another. It is also important to appreciate that most individual members of a society will participate in more than one of these subcultures at different times or in different aspects of their lives. Thus not only do most modern societies contain different ethnic groups, each with its own traditions, habits, beliefs, customs and so on, but they also contain different religious groups, different social groups, artistic groups, groups held together by many different shared interests, each of which will have its own norms, its own 'culture'.

The question whether schools should endeavour to promote a common culture or help diverse groups to develop their own different cultures is a vexed one, not least in relation to those minority ethnic groups that are to be found in most societies (Jeffcoate, 1984; Kelly, 1986). What concerns us more directly here, however, is the implication that even if we believe that the content of the curriculum should be based on the culture of the society, it will be impossible to assert with any real expectation of general acceptance what that culture is and therefore what the content of the curriculum should be. All that this line of argument will achieve is to remind us of the view of the curriculum as a battleground of competing ideologies and to bring us face to face with age-old issues concerning the appropriate educational provision for different social and ethnic groups, as we shall see when we come to consider the question of a common or national curriculum. In fact, it is a line of argument which in the last analysis leads to a recognition of the need for diversity rather than uniformity of educational provision, and thus to an awareness of the inadequacies of any form of curriculum planning that lays too great a stress on the consideration of curriculum content.

The problem is aggravated by the fact that most societies are far from static entities and this implies that one feature of their culture is that it is changing, evolving, developing. Furthermore, western cultures 'are characterized not only by rapid change but also by deliberate change' (Taba, 1962, p. 54). Technological change must also lead to changes in the norms, the values, the beliefs, the customs of a society; in other words, it must lead to a fluid culture. Moral change too is more difficult in many ways to handle. It is slower to take effect, since people shed or change their values more slowly and more reluctantly than they exchange their cars or their washing machines. Thus there is a time-lag between the technological changes and those that follow in the norms, customs and social institutions of the society (Taba, 1962).

There are several aspects of this that have serious implications for education and the curriculum. First, it emphasizes the impossibility of the task of deciding into which aspects of the culture schools should initiate their pupils. Second, it raises again the question of what the role of the school is or should be in relation to the culture of society, in particular whether it is there to transmit that culture or to transform it. Third, it raises questions about what schools should be attempting to do for their pupils in a society that is subject to rapid change.

A recognition of the rapidity of social change and of the need for people to be equipped to cope with it and even to exercise some degree of control over it suggests that schools should in any case go beyond the notion of initiation of pupils into the culture of the society, beyond socialization and acculturation, to the idea of preparing pupils for the fact of social change itself, to adapt to and to initiate changes in the norms and values of the community. This requires that pupils be offered much more than a selection of the culture of the society as it exists at the time when they happen to be in schools, even if this could be identified and defined clearly enough for adequate educational practice. It also constitutes, as we have seen, a strong argument for planning the curriculum by reference to the capacities we are endeavouring to promote in pupils rather than the bodies of knowledge we are concerned to pass on to them.

Furthermore, if we are right to suggest that this is the only viable role the school can take in a rapidly changing society, if it can equip pupils to take their place in such a society only by developing in them the ability to think for themselves and make their own choices, then the question whether the school is there to transmit or to transform the culture of society has already in part been answered. For the adoption of this kind of role takes the school well beyond the mere transmission of knowledge – a role that in a changing society would seem to be in any case untenable. If the school is not itself to transform the culture, it is certainly there to produce people who can and will transform it.

This is one source of a further problem that arises if we attempt to establish as the content of our curriculum those things which we regard as being the essential valuable elements of the culture. Recent practice has revealed very clearly that this can lead to the imposition on some pupils of a curriculum that is alien to them, which lacks relevance to their lives and to their experience outside the school and can ultimately bring about their alienation from and rejection of the education they are offered. This is probably the root cause of most of the problems that the educational system is facing today and it is certainly a real hazard if not an inevitable result of this kind of approach to curriculum planning.

These last points lead us on to a much more general weakness of this line of argument. For it will be apparent that even if we see it as the task of our schools to initiate pupils into the culture of the society, it will not be possible to offer them the whole of that culture, however it is defined. A selection will have to be made and, since this is so, any notion of the culture of the society, no matter how acceptable in definition or content, will in itself not provide us with appropriate criteria of selection. We will need to look elsewhere for justification of the selection we do make so that the arguments for a curriculum content based on the culture or cultures of society will not in themselves take us very far towards finding a solution to our problem.

This brings us lastly to the realization that attempts to base decisions about the content of the curriculum on a consideration of the nature of society are, if interpreted in this way, essentially utilitarian arguments; they seek a social or sociological justification for curriculum content and therefore imply that that justification is to be sought outside the activity or the knowledge or the content itself, a procedure which we have already suggested is incompatible with the notion of education as such.

This charge can be avoided only if they go further and argue that what is valuable in the culture is valuable not merely because it is part of the culture but because it has some intrinsic merit which justifies its place not only on the curriculum but also in society itself. There are many people who would wish to argue that there are certain elements in the culture of any advanced society which go beyond the particularities of that society and reflect certain values which are timeless and, indeed, transcendental in every sense. It is on grounds such as these that many would want to press the case for the introduction of pupils to literature, music, art and ideas that are felt to be 'great' and to constitute a cultural heritage which is the heritage of humanity in general rather than of one particular nation.

To take this view is, of course, to propound a completely different argument from that which seeks justification in the culture itself and it does bring us back to the whole issue of the nature of knowledge and the question whether any body of knowledge has or can have an intrinsic, objective, absolute value or status. The focus of the matter, therefore, continues to be the nature of knowledge, and any attempt to seek a justification of curriculum content in terms that are not instrumental or utilitarian must start with an examination of what knowledge is. We have already seen, however, the problems which that raises.

Appeals to the nature of society, then, like analyses of the nature of knowledge, fail to provide us with unassailable criteria of choice in curriculum planning. They also reveal the problematic nature of any framework of values we may set up to enable us to make choices, whether among bodies of knowledge or among the cultures and subcultures of society. They thus highlight the problem created for curriculum planners by the lack of any firm basis of values, and we must now consider that problem in a little more detail, noting as we do so that it is a problem that must be faced whether we are making choices of content, purposes or principles in the process of curriculum planning.

VALUES AND THE CURRICULUM

We noted earlier that those who have adopted a rationalist or 'transcendental' view of knowledge as objective, timeless and independent of particular societies, cultures or individuals, have extended this view beyond knowledge of a 'scientific' kind and have seen it as providing a basis for knowledge, in the same full sense, in the realm of values – aesthetic, moral and social/political. Those who have built their theories of education on such an epistemology, therefore, have sought to claim that their educational recipes and prescriptions are similarly objective, timeless and independent of particular societies, cultures and individuals. In short, they have wished to be seen as offering not *a* view of education and curriculum but *the* view, not *their* preferred list of subjects and bodies of knowledge-content but *the* list of those which have an indisputable right to inclusion in an educational curriculum, not their own *ideology* but the *only rational and objective view* which can be adopted by anyone who has properly thought the issues through and discovered the basic 'truths'.

Those who, as we have seen, have questioned this view of knowledge and truth have also, therefore, opposed this view of values to which it inevitably must lead, and have argued that, since major doubts can be raised about the validity of the rationalist position, serious dangers must arise from any acceptance of its value claims as anything other than the expression of a particular – and questionable – ideology. It is for this reason that those, such as John Dewey, who, as we have seen, have viewed knowledge as evolutionary in nature, and especially those who, like many sociologists of education in recent times, have insisted that it is socially constructed (Young, 1971), have suggested that there are serious, even sinister, implications in too ready an acceptance of the right of certain bodies of knowledge to inclusion in the curriculum, not least because this entails the acceptance of the values implicit in those bodies of knowledge.

Thus the conflict between these two views of knowledge must be seen as embracing not only the question whether there are certain kinds of knowledge, or certain cultural achievements, which have intrinsic or 'timeless' value, but also the issue of the validity of the value positions from which different people reach their conclusions on such matters and, especially, from which they derive the criteria by which they select what should be included in the curriculum (Wilson, 1967; Peters, 1967a).

This battle is clearly of crucial importance. It has resulted in a questioning of the content of education of a kind which at one time would have been unthinkable. For as long as the view of values as fixed and unchangeable held sway, the model of education it gave rise to remained virtually unquestioned: the Platonic model of the slow ascent of the individual up the ladder of knowledge towards greater degrees of abstraction or, to use his own simile, the gradual emergence from the dark cave of ignorance into the light of the sun and finally to the contemplation of the sun itself. This is a view that can still be detected today as much in the unquestioned assumptions of some people's thinking about education as in certain explicit statements about it. Even the metaphors are similar, the child being seen as the barbarian at the gates and education as the process of gradual admission to the citadel of civilization (Peters, 1965). The arguments too have a familiar ring to them since the superiority of certain kinds of human activity is still argued, as we have seen, in terms of such things as cognitive content, seriousness and intrinsic value (Peters, 1966). The means/end aspect of the Platonic model has been rightly criticized and rejected but all else remains fundamentally much the same.

There are many difficulties, however, in attempts to establish the claim that any kind of activity has an intrinsic value over and above the value that individual human beings place on it or that value is in some way inherent in certain kinds of activity. Values are not entities having some kind of existence of their own, even in some metaphysical sense. Valuing is an activity; it is something people do. Only confusion can result when we allow such activities to become reified because the vagaries of English grammar allow certain verbal functions to be performed by the use of nouns. This is a fallacy common to a number of philosophical problems. Valuing can only be an activity and, as with all activities, different people do it differently.

Furthermore, such a view of values as objective is based on a view of knowledge as 'out-there' and God-given, a view that we saw earlier is at the very least highly questionable. If knowledge is not seen as having this sort of objective status independent of the knower, it is difficult to know what basis there could be for claiming that some activities have an intrinsic value independent of the value placed on them by individual human beings, and even more difficult to establish what these activities are.

Several further points must be made which derive from this basic feature of values. In the first place, a view of values as deriving their validity from the actual choices made by individuals is an essential feature of a view of humans as active rather than passive beings, creatures whose behaviour is the result of their own choices and purposes and not merely of the causal effects of external events. Such a view of values, therefore, follows naturally from the idea of the autonomy of the individual and must lead to the rejection of any study of education or planning of the curriculum that is based on a behaviourist model of humanity.

It is worth going further too and stressing again that it is this which makes it possible to distinguish education from other activities such as training or conditioning. We have noted already the claim that the development of autonomy is an essential feature of any distinctive concept of education (Peters, 1965, 1966). We are here faced with one of the implications of that claim. Such a concept of education must acknowledge that autonomy for the individual implies his or her right to do his or her own valuing and not merely to be brought to recognize certain values for which, in Platonic style, objective status is claimed.

We must recognize, however, that to be engaged in educating anybody is to be committed *ipso facto* to the belief that some human activities are of more value than others. Education is, indeed, a matter of initiation into intrinsically worthwhile activities, even though there are no grounds for claiming that we can objectively identify or determine what those intrinsically worthwhile activities are. To say that qualitative differences between kinds of knowledge and kinds of human activity cannot be demonstrated is not to say that we will accept them all as being of equal merit. Of course, we will all make distinctions of this kind. We must realize, however, that our basis for making such distinctions is insecure and shifting, and that the values we adhere to will represent our own favoured ideological position rather than our grasp on any eternal truths. This is the important thrust of those recent developments in the sociology of knowledge to which we have already referred (Young, 1971), and it adds strength to those criticisms of attempts to treat the study of education and curriculum as some kind of exact science, which we considered in Chapter 1.

It must follow from this that whoever takes decisions about the curriculum or contributes to the taking of such decisions must be encouraged to appreciate the slender nature of the foundations on which any system of values or set of criteria he or she is using will be based. His or her choices should, therefore, be tentative and of such a kind as to avoid dogmatism. Furthermore, they should be open to continuous evaluation and modification since that is the essence of curriculum development. If knowledge were God-given and if values enjoyed a similar status, curriculum development could have only one meaning as the slow progression towards perfection that Plato had in mind. Such a notion is no longer tenable.

It is considerations such as this which raise doubts about the validity of the view of education as transmission or curriculum as content; and it is to an exploration of some of these doubts that we now turn.

CURRICULUM AS CONTENT

It was suggested earlier that many people, from a variety of standpoints, continue to see curriculum merely as content and the process of education as no more than the transmission of knowledge-content, that they adopt a content model of curriculum planning, assuming that no more is required of any curriculum planner than that he or she list the subjects, 'the overall content, knowledge, skills and processes' (DES, 1987a, p. 10) that the curriculum is concerned to transmit. It was suggested, too, that this is a very limited and unsophisticated view both of curriculum and of the demands of curriculum planning. It will perhaps now be clear why this claim was made.

In spite of that, however, we must recognize that this view, simplistic as it is, is becoming increasingly prevalent in current curricular policies. It is the view of curriculum which clearly underpins most recent official statements emerging from the Department of Education and Science, not only from the civil servants there, who might not be expected to show any depth of understanding of the complexities of educational planning, but also from Her Majesty's Inspectorate, whose ambitions to be regarded as being at the top of the teaching profession would seem to suggest that they should. Thus the recent series of publications under the general title *Curriculum Matters* (DES, 1984a, 1985a, b, c, d, 1986a, b, 1987b, c) has been planned, like most earlier statements emanating from the same source, in terms of separate curriculum subjects, and each has concentrated very largely on outlining what its authors feel should be the essential content of those subjects. When they are not outlining content they are listing objectives and thus demonstrating a different, although related, lack of understanding and sophistication, as we shall see in the next chapter.

It is not surprising, therefore, that this same, simple model has been adopted by the politicians and their aides for the planning of the new National Curriculum, whose core is, as we saw just now, 'the overall content, knowledge, skills and processes' (DES, 1987a, p. 10) of every subject listed as an essential ingredient of the new national programme of instruction and testing. We will examine many aspects of this policy in later chapters, but we must note here that it is not only a good example but also a prominent and pressingly topical example of this view of education as transmission and of curriculum as content. And the major weakness we should note is that at no stage does one find any justification, or even any attempt at justification, for either the subjects or their content, except in vague and unanalysed phrases such as 'which they need to learn' (op. cit., p. 4), 'relevant to today's needs' (op. cit., p. 10), or in overtly utilitarian considerations such as 'practical applications and continuing value to adult and working life' (op. cit., p. 4) and 'the challenge of employment in tomorrow's world' (op. cit., p. 2). We hear of 'bench-marks', of 'attainment targets' and of 'standards', all defined in terms of subject-content and offered as though they are non-problematic, and we get an impression that attempts are being made to 'cash in' on the kinds of philosophical argument we considered earlier, but these arguments are nowhere adduced nor are the utilitarian arguments made explicit, so that to all appearances these definitions are 'plucked from the air'.

Yet, as we have seen, justification is needed for any curriculum plan and, unless that justification is to be offered only in utilitarian terms (and this never seems to be openly acknowledged), some form of educational justification must be provided or at least sought. The lack of this is the major weakness of the content model of curriculum and the transmission model of education. There is nothing in the model itself which demands of us that we justify our curricular prescriptions, so that it becomes all too easy to let tradition plan our curricula for us, to let the curriculum 'drift' as we saw in Chapter 1 it once did at a time when, at least at secondary level, it was seen only in subject-knowledge and transmission terms, or to let instrumentalism have its way.

Even when we do attempt justification, however, we have seen that, if this is not to be instrumental and utilitarian, the only other source of justification is to be found in certain rationalist theories of knowledge which, first, are by no means universally accepted, which in fact have been roundly and cogently challenged in recent years, and which, second, can in any case offer us justification only in terms of views about the nature of knowledge, and not in terms of views of education or of the nature of children.

The idea of education as transmission or of curriculum as content, then, is simplistic and unsophisticated because it leaves out of the reckoning major dimensions of the curriculum debate and, in particular, discourages that critical stance which we suggested in Chapter 1 is central to any properly rigorous study of the curriculum. It does not raise, and cannot answer, questions about the purposes of education, unless it sees these merely in utilitarian terms. And it does not encourage or help us to take any account of the children who are the recipients of this content and the objects of the process of transmission, or of the impact of that content and that process on them. Their task is to learn as effectively as they can what is offered to them. If the effect of the process on them is of any significance, this model offers us no means of exploring or evaluating that effect, beyond assessing the extent of their assimilation of what has been fed to them, any other consequences of such learning being beyond its scope. So far as this model is concerned, these are an irrelevance, for to ask this kind of question is to go well beyond what the model permits or acknowledges. Yet many would wish to argue that it is precisely that effect or these consequences which are at the heart of what we might mean by the term 'education', unless, as we have seen, it is to be synonymous with instruction or even training. And for that reason it is claimed by many that this model is inadequate for proper educational planning; it does not go far enough; it asks one kind of question only and takes into account only one kind of consideration; it thus offers a distorted view of education and of curriculum and a seriously flawed and limited model for educational planning.

For this reason, too, many people have wished to argue that we must go well beyond content and consider questions of the purposes or the objectives of our curriculum (Tyler, 1949; Hirst, 1969), or that we should explore the procedural principles which underlie our planning and our practice (Stenhouse, 1975) and the developmental processes it is our concern to promote (Blenkin and Kelly, 1981, 1987, 1988a; Kelly, 1986; Blenkin, 1988). We are thus offered what would appear to be two alternative approaches to education and two alternatives to the content model of curriculum planning. The next two chapters will be devoted to an exploration of both of these.

SUMMARY AND CONCLUSIONS

This chapter has attempted to explore the major aspects and difficulties of that approach to curriculum planning which stresses content as the first, or even the only, consideration. We began by recognizing that, if this is to be our stance, then unless we are adopting a completely utilitarian, and thus non-educational, view of schooling and the school curriculum and offering justification of our chosen content in terms of social and/or vocational and economic utility, we must adopt and be clear about a theory of knowledge which will support that stance. We thus considered next, albeit briefly and somewhat superficially, the age-old debate about the nature and the status of human knowledge, the validity of knowledge claims and the justification of educational prescriptions based on these. We were forced to the conclusion that the very continuation of the debate reinforces the view that there are no hard-and-fast answers to be found and thus no firm basis for the important curricular decisions which have to be made and which are often made far more dogmatically than is warranted by the shifting and uncertain nature of this ground.

We then considered those theories which would have us select the content of our curriculum on the basis of some kind of analysis of the culture of society. We saw that in many ways these theories created even more difficulties, especially in the context of societies characterized by cultural pluralism, and in any case merely forced us back ultimately to those same epistemological theories we had already explored and found wanting.

The notion of selection in turn raised questions about the criteria of selection and the justification of the value systems which underpin such criteria and such selections. Again we found the task of justifying these in any objective way or to the point of any kind of universal acceptance to be not only difficult but impossible. And it was suggested that this should make us tentative in our claims and especially in our prescriptions, and discourage us from dogmatic assertions. In fact, we had already noted the arguments of those who, taking this view of the uncertainty and the problematic nature of values, see the curriculum as the battleground of competing ideologies and the curriculum at any given time as reflecting the ideology of whichever group is dominant in that battle; and we noted this as a serious danger and one which can be avoided only if we adopt an open stance and acknowledge the need for continuous evaluation, change and development in our curricula.

This led us finally to a discussion of the general issue of curriculum as content and of education as transmission. We noted that this is the simplistic model which has been adopted in current official policies for curriculum planning, and especially as the basis for the implementation of the new National Curriculum in the United Kingdom (although at no stage did we wish to appear to be suggesting that this adoption was the result of informed choice or critical exploration of alternative models). However, we concluded that this model does not and cannot offer either encouragement to or scope for the kind of continuous, critical and rigorous debate over curriculum issues which our discussion of knowledge and values had led us to claim that there should be.

In particular we noted that it offers no scope for consideration of the purposes for which particular subjects or bodies of knowledge-content might have been included in the curriculum or require of us that we be clear about, and openly declare, the reasons we have for including them. Nor did it allow us to take account of the children themselves and the impact of this process of transmission on them. We concluded, therefore, that what rendered this model of curriculum planning inadequate was its lack of awareness of and inability to cope with several other major dimensions of the educational debate, in particular the purposes, the aims, the objectives of educational planning and the principles upon which such planning might be undertaken. These we recognized had been emphasized in two other models of curriculum planning and it is to an examination of these that we turn in the next two chapters.

3

CURRICULUM AS PRODUCT
AND EDUCATION AS INSTRUMENTAL

We saw in Chapter 2 some of the difficulties which follow in the wake of
attempts to begin curriculum planning from a consideration of the nature of
knowledge or of the culture of society and thus to make questions about the
content of the curriculum the first and most important problem to be faced.
The suggestion was made there that, while issues of curriculum content
cannot be ignored, they should not be regarded as having a prior claim to our
attention. We noted too that a major inadequacy of that approach is that it
ignores several other important dimensions of the curriculum debate and of
curriculum planning.

It was pointed out there that, as a result of a growing awareness of this
inadequacy, there have been many attempts in recent years to encourage a
recognition of these other aspects of the curriculum and to suggest, in
particular, that a consideration of its purposes, its aims and objectives might
be a more appropriate starting point, that this might be a more suitable
planning model. We noted too that others have suggested that the consideration of the principles underlying the processes of education might be a
better basis for planning, and thus yet another model has emerged.

In fact, once we acknowledge that curriculum content cannot of itself be
the first consideration, that some justification of the choice of such content is
required, we have to recognize that the emphasis in curriculum planning
must be placed elsewhere and that questions of content become secondary
to questions about purposes or principles. Furthermore, such differences of
emphasis will lead to the generation of different planning models.

It is to an exploration of the first of these alternative approaches to planning that we turn in this chapter, to an examination of that planning model which begins from the prespecification of curriculum objectives. For this appears currently to be the model which is in fashion, often in conjunction with the content model, and yet it is clear that not everyone who wishes to advocate its use is fully aware of its implications.

One preliminary point must be made before we begin this exploration. It must be stressed again that, as we saw in Chapter 1, the question of the suitability and the characteristics of planning models is as relevant to the individual teacher in the planning of his or her own work as to a development team concerned to plan a national curriculum project. The question whether educational planning should begin from a consideration of its content, its objectives or its underlying principles is an important issue for every teacher, not least because of the pressures he or she may face to adopt a model which is favoured by someone else. The truth of this will not need to be emphasized to those teachers and student teachers who have wrestled to meet demands for the prestatement of lesson objectives from tutors, headteachers, advisers or inspectors.

For it is also the case that many of those external pressures on teachers, which, as we also noted in Chapter 1, have grown dramatically in strength in recent years, have taken the form of requiring them to state the objectives of their teaching and/or to keep records of what they have done in terms of prespecified objectives set either by themselves or by others. The most recent publications on curriculum emanating from Her Majesty's Inspectorate, those in the *Curriculum Matters* series for example, all place great emphasis on stating the objectives (along with the content) of the school subjects they are concerned with. And it is clear that a similar approach has been adopted, or perhaps again uncritically assumed, by those who have framed the new National Curriculum, and is reflected in what have emerged as the agreed, or at least approved, attainment targets and the assessment procedures to be imposed when that National Curriculum becomes fully operative. In short, people outside the schools, including it would seem most of those in the Inspectorate, appear to be making unquestioningly the tacit assumption that this is the only model one can adopt for curriculum planning.

At the same time, there are still those who positively eschew such an approach. The Humanities Curriculum Project, for example, took this line and, indeed, its Director, the late Lawrence Stenhouse, suggested that prespecification of objectives is not appropriate within the humanities generally (Stenhouse, 1970). Interdisciplinary Enquiry (IDE), as propounded by Goldsmiths' College Curriculum Laboratory, also deliberately and consciously rejected an objectives approach (James, 1968), regarding it as unsuitable to attempt to state in advance what the result of pupil inquiry should be.

Furthermore, it has been argued (Blenkin and Kelly, 1981, 1987; Kelly, 1981) that planning through the prespecification of curriculum objectives is inappropriate, not to say inimical, to that educational tradition that has emerged through the 'progressive' movement and has developed in some British primary schools, especially those concerned with the very young child. External pressures for this kind of planning, however, are to be felt as much in that sector of schooling as elsewhere. It thus becomes particularly important for teachers to sort out the issues that are involved if they are to be able to respond to such pressures appropriately and not merely by yielding to them. It was for this reason that a detailed discussion of this problem was undertaken in *The Primary Curriculum* (Blenkin and Kelly, 1981, 1987), and readers of that book will recognize in what follows much that was included there.

THE GROWTH OF THE OBJECTIVES MOVEMENT

A concern with curriculum objectives has been one of the most striking features of the recent move towards deliberate curriculum planning to which we also referred in Chapter 1. Statements of objectives were, for example, the starting points for many curriculum projects developed under the aegis of the Schools Council, and we have witnessed a growing pressure on teachers to pay due regard to them in their planning.

The impetus for this came initially early in this century from those who were impressed by the progress of science and technology and believed that the same kind of progress might become possible in the field of education if a properly scientific approach were to be adopted there also. As is so often the case, the origins of this movement can be traced to the United States; in the United Kingdom it is a much more recent phenomenon.

The tone of this movement was set by one of its earliest proponents, Franklin Bobbitt, who expressed great concern at the vague, imprecise purposes he felt characterized the work of most teachers, announced that 'an age of science is demanding exactness and particularity' (Bobbitt, 1918, ch. 6; Davies, 1976, p. 47) and suggested that teachers be required to write out their objectives in clear, non-technical language that both pupils and their parents might understand. He also distinguished between what he called 'ultimate' objectives, those for the curriculum as a whole, and 'progress' objectives, those for each class or age group.

The cry was taken up by others. In 1924, for example, Werrett Charters attempted a 'job analysis' of teaching and offered a method of course construction based on this kind of approach. His suggestion was that we first determine what he called the 'ideals' of education, then identify the 'activities' that these involve and finally analyse both of these to the level of 'working units of the size of human ability' (Charters, 1924; Davies, 1976, p. 50), those small steps that need to be mastered one by one. In this way the curriculum could be reduced to a series of working units and its whole structure set out on a chart or graph.

Thus, early pioneers of the movement, like Bobbitt and Charters, gave it from the beginning a scientific, behavioural, job-analysis flavour, their general purpose being to introduce into educational practice the kind of precise, scientific methods that had begun to yield dividends in other spheres of human activity and especially in industry.

The spread of interest in testing that was a feature of educational development in the 1930s can be seen as another aspect of this same movement. For the link between the prespecification of objectives and the testing of performance has long been a close one, and that it continues to be so is apparent from the emphasis on attainment targets, allied to assessment procedures, within the new National Curriculum in the United Kingdom.

This link was made quite explicit in the work of the next major exponent of the objectives approach, Ralph Tyler. For Tyler's original aim was to design scientific tests of educational attainment and his solution to this problem was to suggest that this could be done most readily and easily if a clear statement had been made of the kind of attainment that was being aimed at. If course objectives had been formulated and those objectives defined in terms of intended student behaviour, that behaviour could then be evaluated in the light of those intentions (Tyler, 1932; Davies, 1976).

This provided the foundation upon which Tyler was later to base what has come to be regarded as the classic statement of the objectives approach to curriculum design. In a book in which he expresses alarm at the level of generality he claims to have detected in teachers' responses to questions about their work, he sets out the four questions which he says must be faced and answered by curriculum planners. Those four questions, as we saw in Chapter 1, are concerned with the purposes, the content, the organization and the evaluation of the curriculum (Tyler, 1949).

The next milestone was reached in 1956 with the publication by Benjamin Bloom and his associates of their *Taxonomy of Educational Objectives Handbook I: Cognitive Domain*. For this introduced a new dimension into this form of curriculum planning with its division of objectives into three categories or 'domains' – the cognitive, the affective and the psychomotor – and at the same time it offered the most detailed and ambitious classification of objectives in the cognitive domain that had yet been attempted. This was matched by the publication in 1964, under the editorship of D.R. Kratwohl, of a second handbook that offered a similar classification within the affective domain.

It was some time before the work of either Tyler or Bloom began to have any real impact but by the mid-1960s their influence was beginning to be felt not only in the United States but in the United Kingdom too, and, in an article published in 1969, Paul Hirst made the same kind of claim that we should begin our curriculum planning with a statement of our objectives, arguing, as we saw in Chapter 1, that not to do so is to transgress a basic principle of rationality, since, in his view, an essential feature of any rational activity is that it be goal-directed.

At the level of educational practice, little interest was initially shown in this style of planning. Some response to the early promptings of Bobbitt, Charters and others can be seen in the planning of vocational courses but that was as far as things went. One reason for this may well have been the wordy and jargon-ridden nature of most of what was written about it. But at least two other reasons have been posited (Hirst, 1969). One is the fact that at secondary level that obsession with subject content which we examined in Chapter 2, reinforced by the demands of largely monolithic examination syllabuses, rendered it unnecessary for teachers ever to think about what their purposes or objectives might be. The second is the suggestion that at primary level the 'romantic' or 'progressive' movement, in particular because of its emphasis on 'child-centredness', also had the effect of deflecting attention from a clear formulation of objectives. Paul Hirst explains this as an obsession with methods or procedures but it has also been interpreted, as we saw in Chapter 1 (Blenkin and Kelly, 1981, 1987), as the result of a concern with education as a process of development and this, as we shall see in Chapter 4, has very different implications. At all events, although teacher trainers demanded from their students, and inspectors from their probationer teachers, and even some headteachers from all their staff, lesson notes that began with a clear statement of the aims and objectives of their lessons, few responded to such requests with any degree of clarity or effectiveness and the practice was not taken seriously by any who were engaged in the realities of teaching.

The statement of clear course objectives, however, was a major feature of most of the curriculum projects that emerged during that period of widespread innovation that followed the establishment of the Schools Council in the United Kingdom in 1964, and this was a key factor in the growth of interest in this approach to curriculum planning that came in the 1960s. The allocation of public money (although never a large sum) to curriculum development on this scale brought with it the requirement that a proper account be given of how that money was being spent. For this reason, as well as for considerations of a purely educational kind, evaluation was a central concern of most new projects from the outset, and in those early years a proper evaluation was interpreted as requiring a clear statement of goals, aims, purposes, objectives.

It was through the work of the Schools Council, therefore, after a long and interesting history, that the concept of curriculum planning by objectives finally entered the consciousness of the practising teacher. And so, when in the late 1970s, as a result of several factors of a largely political kind which we will explore more fully in Chapter 6, pressures began to be felt by teachers to plan their work more carefully and precisely, it was to this model that they were inclined and, indeed, encouraged to turn (Blenkin, 1980).

This approach to curriculum planning, however, requires more careful analysis than most teachers were able to give it, and it is to that kind of examination that we must proceed. Before we can do so, however, it will be helpful to try to pick out the major characteristics of this approach.

THE MAIN CHARACTERISTICS OF THE OBJECTIVES APPROACH TO CURRICULUM PLANNING

Linear and hierarchical sequencing

We might begin this exploration by noting a generally accepted distinction between objectives and aims (Taba, 1962). Aims are usually seen as very general statements of goals and purposes. Such aims by themselves, however, have often been regarded as too general and lacking in specificity to provide clear guidelines for planners or teachers, so that curriculum planning has been seen as a process of deriving more precise statements of goals from these general aims; these more precise statements of goals are normally termed objectives. Indeed, some writers have even suggested that we should recognize three or more levels of specificity (Kratwohl, 1965): general statements of goals that will guide the planning of the curriculum as a whole, behavioural objectives derived from these which will guide the planning of individual units or courses, and a third level of objectives appropriate in some cases to guide the planning of specific lessons; to use Wheeler's terms, 'ultimate', 'mediate' and 'proximate' goals, the last providing specific classroom objectives (Wheeler, 1967). This, as we saw earlier, is the kind of structure that was envisaged by the early pioneers of the movement, and the important point to note is that this approach to curriculum planning assumes that education must be planned in a step-by-step linear manner. It is in fact an attempt to translate into classroom terms

that linear step-by-step process which behavioural psychologists have discovered to be the most effective way of conditioning animals – dogs, cats,
rats, pigeons and so on.

It is important to stress at the outset that only through this kind of linear
and hierarchical scheme can one make any real sense of the distinction
between aims and objectives, in short, that it is of the essence of the aims and
objectives model of curriculum planning. For this reason those many
proposals which seek to use these as planning devices but do not wish to
embrace – at least explicitly – the kind of linear, hierarchical approach to
educational planning which is their inevitable concomitant run immediately
into serious conceptual muddles and, as a direct consequence of this,
practical confusions; for they have no other conceptual base for distinguishing between aims and objectives. As we shall see later, this was a
difficulty many of the early Schools Council projects fell into. More topically
– and less excusably since the lessons of the Schools Council's experience
were there to be learnt from – this is also a fundamental weakness of all the
publications in the current HMI *Curriculum Matters* series. A linear and
hierarchical structure is essential to the aims and objectives model of
curriculum planning. If one is not prepared to accept that and all that follows
from it, there is no basis for distinguishing aims from objectives and thus no
reason or justification for the adoption or the advocacy of this model.

The term 'objective' might of course be used to mean merely any 'goal' or
'purpose' (although, in view of the specific meaning we have just seen it has
come to have in discussions of education and curriculum planning, such a
usage would seem less than helpful). There is nothing fundamentally wrong
or mistaken in such a usage. However, the attempt to distinguish 'aims' and
'objectives' implies that these terms denote different kinds or levels of
educational goal or purpose, so that to make this distinction reflects either a
clear acceptance of a hierarchy of goals, and thus of the objectives model
and all it entails, or a disturbing failure to achieve conceptual clarity over
what one's planning model really is. For, if there is a distinction between the
two concepts, it can consist only of their hierarchical relationship with each
other.

The classic statement of this kind of hierarchy of goals is to be found in
Bloom's taxonomy of educational objectives (Bloom *et al.*, 1956; Kratwohl
et al., 1964). That the notion of the hierarchical nature of the interrelationship of these objectives is fundamental, is apparent from the gradation
of objectives in the cognitive domain from the acquisition of the knowledge
of specifics, through such higher-level cognitive abilities as classification,
comprehension, application, analysis, synthesis and so on to the making of
evaluative judgements. Similar gradations are offered within each of the

categories, comprehension, for example, being broken down into translation, interpretation and extrapolation.

However, Bloom also offers us another distinction within this range of objectives since, as we have seen, he divides them into three clear domains: the cognitive, the affective and the psychomotor – the head, the heart and the hand. Thus he is suggesting that in framing our objectives we need to be clear not only about the sequential nature of the activity but also about the different categories of behaviour we might be concerned with. For the cognitive domain is defined as comprising 'objectives which emphasize remembering or reproducing something which has presumably been learnt, as well as objectives which involve the solving of some intellective task for which the individual has to determine the essential problem and then reorder given material or combine it with ideas, methods or procedures previously learned' (Kratwohl *et al.*, 1964, p. 6). The affective domain, we are told, comprises 'objectives which emphasize a feeling tone, an emotion, or a degree of acceptance or rejection' (op. cit., p. 7). Finally, the psychomotor domain consists of 'objectives which emphasize some muscular or motor skill, some manipulation of material and objects, or some act which requires a neuromuscular coordination' (ibid.).

Thus these two dimensions which Bloom and his associates offer us enable us to prespecify our objectives at varying levels of specificity in order to outline in great detail the kinds of behaviour which are the objectives of our curriculum. We are offered a hierarchy of goals, of 'intended learning outcomes' defined in terms of the kind of behaviour the pupil is intended or expected to display through his or her thoughts, actions or feelings if we are to be able to claim that our objective has been achieved. It is easy to see why this approach has proved, and continues to prove, so attractive to some curriculum planners.

Conversely, however, it is when we are offered this kind of highly detailed statement of how a curriculum is to be planned in terms of objectives that we begin to see what it is that other people have found unacceptable in this approach, or at least we begin to become aware that it is not such a straightforward matter as it may at first have appeared to be.

The results of Bloom's work, therefore, have been twofold. On the one hand, recent years have seen a proliferation of curriculum projects which have begun with detailed statements of their objectives, an increasing, although largely uninformed, use of the term in official publications, such as the HMI *Curriculum Matters* series (DES, 1984a, 1985a, b, c, d, 1986a, b, 1987b, c), and ever more frequent demands on teachers from advisers, HMI and others for statements of their teaching objectives. On the other hand, we have also witnessed a developing movement away from the idea of prespecified curriculum objectives, a reaction against what has begun to appear to some as an undue limitation on the scope of the teacher and, indeed, of education.

A good example of the former would be the elaborate table of objectives given by the Schools Council's Science 5–13 Project team (Schools Council, 1972) which begins by listing nine broad aims focused on the central goal of developing an inquiring mind and a scientific approach to problems and then proceeds to break these broad aims down into a detailed list of shorter-term behavioural objectives, grouped in such a way as to be closely linked to the children's stages of conceptual development. Thus at the second part of Stage 1, the early stage of concrete operations, the broad aim of developing interests, attitudes and aesthetic awareness is broken down into four objectives:

> Desire to find out things for oneself
> Willing participation in group work
> Willing compliance with safety regulations in handling tools and equipment
> Appreciation of the need to learn the meaning of new words and to use them correctly.
>
> (Schools Council, 1972, p. 60)

A further example, taken from the field of primary education, is even more directly derivative of Bloom's taxonomy. For the Schools Council's Aims of Primary Education Project divides its aims into those related to intellectual, physical, spiritual/religious, emotional/personal and social/moral development and then divides these different kinds of aim on a second axis into those 'to do with knowledge, skills and qualities' (Ashton, Kneen and Davies, 1975, p. 13). Thus again the interrelationships of objectives are seen as essentially hierarchical and all learning is viewed as a linear activity. There are many examples of this kind of approach to be found among the schemes for the teaching of reading that teachers have been offered in recent times and, in particular, among the more sophisticated 'reading workshops' or 'reading laboratories' designed for use with pupils in junior schools and middle schools, or in the lower classes of secondary schools. The Kent Mathematics Project is also an example of the use of this model in the teaching of mathematics.

Every one of the HMI publications in the *Curriculum Matters* series has adopted a similar approach. Thus *Mathematics from 5 to 16* (DES, 1985) divides its objectives into 'five main categories' (p. 7) – facts, skills, conceptual structures, general strategies, personal qualities. It then proceeds to break these categories down into more specific objectives, the category 'facts', for example, being refined into Objective 1, Remembering terms; Objective 2, Remembering notation; Objective 3, Remembering conventions; Objective 4, Remembering results.

These are all examples of the fashion which has developed, too often without any really critical reflection, for assuming that the statement of objectives is the only starting point for curriculum planning. They are all, incidentally, also good examples of the difficulties people experience when they attempt to translate such a model into the realities of curriculum planning and practice and of the confusion and muddle with which such attempts are usually beset. For all of them, as may be apparent even from the brief examples given here, slide from aims to objectives to content to procedural principles and back again as though there were not deep conceptual differences between these and the different approaches to educational planning and practice they give rise to, and especially as though, what is obviously and sadly the case, their authors have no appreciation or understanding of those deep conceptual differences.

This is a point which we will take up later. The main thing to be emphasized here is the linear nature of such planning schemes, the difficulties of which we will also explore later. One major feature of the model, then, is its concern to impose a linear, hierarchical structure on all educational planning. And even the most cursory reading of these examples will make immediately apparent some of the difficulties that have been identified in this kind of approach to curriculum planning and will explain why other projects, notably the Humanities Curriculum Project and the Bruner-sponsored project, 'Man: A Course of Study' (MACOS), deliberately eschewed the idea of prespecifying their objectives.

Objectives as behavioural

A further important characteristic of this view of curriculum planning is that the objectives it requires us to prespecify are clearly and unequivocally behavioural. Tyler, for example, tells us that 'the most useful form for stating objectives is to express them in terms which identify both the kind of behaviour to be developed in the students and the context or area of life in which this behaviour is to operate' (1949, pp. 46–7). Bloom calls them 'intended learning outcomes' and says that they are to be defined in terms of the behaviour the pupil is intended to display through his or her thoughts, actions or feelings. Mager (1962, p. 13) says, 'A statement of an objective is useful to the extent that it specifies what the learner must be able to *do* or *perform* when he is demonstrating his mastery of the objective.' And Popham (1969, p. 35) tells us that 'A satisfactory instructional objective must describe an observable *behaviour* of the learner or a *product* which is a

consequence of learner behaviour.' The observable behaviour might take
the form of something like 'skill in making impromptu speeches or performing gymnastic feats' (ibid.). Products might be an essay or 'an omelet from
the home economics class' (ibid.).

This being so, 'a properly stated behavioural objective must describe
without ambiguity the nature of learner behaviour or product to be measured' (op. cit., p. 37). For example:

> When given a description of a research design problem, the student can select
> correctly from the twenty statistical procedures treated in class that one which is
> most appropriate for analyzing the data to be produced by the research.

> Having been given a previously unencountered literary selection from
> nineteenth-century English literature, the student will be able to write the name
> of the author and at least three valid reasons for making that selection (ibid.).

The Schools Council's Aims of Primary Education Project offers the same
kind of definition, declaring that 'if the teacher's aims are to help guide his
practice, then they should be expressed in behavioural terms. That is to say
that they should state what the child will actually be able to do when the aim
is achieved' (Ashton, Kneen and Davies, 1975, p. 15). This concern with
observable changes of behaviour is also apparent in some of the forms of
record-keeping that have recently been urged upon primary teachers.

A more recent publication which stresses the behavioural nature of its
objectives is the Further Education Unit's *Vocational Preparation* (1981,
p. 39), which tells us that 'the prescribed objectives are described in terms of
a combination of observable performances to be expected of students and
learning experiences to which they should be exposed'. (Note the running
together of objectives and content – how can a learning experience be an
objective?)

Another recent example is to be found in – of all places – a set of
recommendations to teachers for implementing pastoral care. Here we are
told (Raymond, 1985, p. 254): 'Objectives have to be written in a manner
which describes what pupils do in a selection of situations. These are known
as behavioural objectives.' And again, in the context of personal development, we read (Baldwin and Wells, 1980, p. xv) that 'objectives for personal
development should state the type of behaviour to be observed'.

Again, the important thing to recognize is that the notion of behaviour
modification is essential to this model of curriculum planning. There may
well be areas, such as that of vocational training, where this is entirely
appropriate. Whether it is appropriate to all forms of educational planning,
and especially to pastoral care or personal development, is questionable, as
we shall see, but that is not the issue here. For the time being, we must

merely note that to adopt this as the model for all educational planning – an adoption which, as we have seen, is implicit in the assumption of a conceptual distinction between aims and objectives – is to be committed to the idea of education as the modification of pupil behaviour, whether one defines what one means by 'objectives' in behavioural terms or not, or, indeed, even if one does not bother to offer a definition at all.

The focus of this approach to educational planning, then, is essentially on the modification of pupil behaviour, and the success of such a curriculum is to be gauged by an assessment of the behaviour changes the curriculum appears to have brought about in relation to those it was its stated intention to bring about. Thus, for example, within the testing procedures in the new National Curriculum in the United Kingdom, the records of achievement for school leavers 'will have an important role in recording performance and profiling a pupil's achievements across and beyond the national curriculum' (DES, 1987a, p. 12).

Value neutrality

A final feature of the behavioural approach to curriculum planning that we must note is that, like all scientific approaches to the study and planning of human activity, it endeavours to be value-neutral. Bloom's taxonomy, for example, has been criticized on these grounds, since it is not based on any clearly worked out concept of education (Gribble, 1970). However, this is not a criticism that he or any of the others would accept as valid, since they are concerned only to present teachers and curriculum planners with a scheme or a blueprint for them to use as they think fit; it is not their concern to tell them how to use it. They regard education as a matter of changing behaviour but they do not accept responsibility for questions about what kinds of behaviour education should be concerned to promote or what kinds of behavioural change it should be attempting to bring about. They maintain their scientific stance, therefore, and leave it to the persons using their scheme to make the decisions about how it should be used. Thus this approach deliberately sidesteps the most difficult and intractable problem that faces curriculum planners – that of deciding what kinds of activity shall be deemed to be educational. And in itself, like the content model we explored in Chapter 2, it can offer no help or guidance with this aspect of educational decision-making. This must be regarded as a very serious disadvantage in this model as a basis for *educational* planning, and it may explain why most of those who have promoted the model (as opposed to those who have merely accepted and attempted to use it uncritically) have been inclined to use the word 'instruction' for what they are concerned to

plan rather than the much more pregnant term 'education'. As a model for
instructing people, it may well have much to recommend it; as a model for
educational planning, as we shall soon see, it is seriously flawed.

ARGUMENTS FOR THE USE OF OBJECTIVES

These, then, are the major features of this approach to curriculum planning.
We must now consider briefly the main reasons why some people have been
and still are concerned to urge it upon curriculum planners. There would
seem to be four of these, which we might call the logical, the scientific, the
politico-economic and the educational arguments for the use of objectives.

The logical argument we have already referred to in considering the case
put by Paul Hirst. Briefly, it claims that part of what it means for an activity
to be rational is that it should be directed towards some clear goal or
purpose. If education is to be regarded as a rational activity, therefore, it
must state its goals or purposes. If it does not, then, as both Tyler and Hirst
have argued, it becomes literally aimless. Another way of putting this is to
accept the analysis made by Israel Scheffler (1960), Richard Peters (1967b)
and others of teaching as an intentional activity and to claim that we should,
therefore, acknowledge and state the intentions of our teaching. How can
one teach, it is asked, if one doesn't know what one is doing it for. The power
of this argument is difficult to deny, although it is not regarded even by its
proponents as leading necessarily to the use of objectives of a strictly
behavioural kind.

Thus, although it has been offered as such, it does not strictly constitute an
argument for the aims and objectives model of curriculum planning. For to
say that our educational planning must have purposes is not to say that those
purposes must then be broken down into that linear hierarchy of behavioural objectives we have seen to be essential to this model. And, as we shall
see later, to suggest that we need different kinds of objectives for educational planning is not to offer a modification of this model but rather to offer a
model which is completely different. The lack of recognition of this crucial
point is at the root of that failure to offer a satisfactory basis for distinguishing the concept of an aim from that of an objective which we noted
earlier characterized some of the Schools Council's projects, such as the
Science 5–13 Project and the Aims of Primary Education Project which we
looked at briefly earlier, and which continues to be a major feature of those
recent HMI pronouncements on curriculum in the *Curriculum Matters* series
to which we have also referred.

The second main kind of argument which has been offered in support of
this planning model is the scientific argument, on which we have also

touched briefly. This represents an attempt to bring into the practice of education some of the precision, accuracy and technological efficiency that is admired as the key to advances elsewhere and thus to render it more 'respectable'. This was clearly the major motivation of the early exponents of this view and the application of scientific method to the study of human performance and achievement in industry by men such as Frederick Taylor obviously aroused the interest and enthusiasm of certain educationists of his day (Davies, 1976). This argument also gained force from the predominance of behavioural psychology within educational theory in the 1920s and 1930s. For the main impact of behavioural psychology on education theory, if its effects are not modified and tempered by the application or acceptance of other disciplines and other considerations, is to reduce it to scientific analysis of an essentially means–end kind and to advocate this sort of approach to educational planning.

The politico-economic case is made at a rather more mundane level but it is one that is becoming increasingly influential through such developments as the new National Curriculum, so that both its existence and its effects must be clearly recognized. Fundamentally, what it claims is that most educational provision is made at the expense of the taxpayer and that most curriculum development is financed in the same way, so that the taxpayer is entitled to a clear statement of what his or her money is being spent on and thus of what it is intended should be achieved by it. More significantly, perhaps, it is argued that there must be a careful evaluation of the effectiveness of measures that are taken in schools or at other levels of curriculum planning in order to ensure that public money is not being wasted and that the country is not being deprived of the talents and skills its economic welfare requires of its citizens. Such evaluation, it is felt, can be made properly only if it is based on a clear statement of intentions. Thus the effect of current attempts to monitor standards in the United Kingdom and to raise the level of teacher accountability is to push teachers towards the prespecification of their objectives (or to prespecify their objectives for them), just as the need for evaluation to demonstrate that the taxpayer was receiving value for money pushed most of the early Schools Council projects towards the same curriculum model.

Lastly, some reasons that might be described as educational have been advanced in support of the prespecification of curriculum objectives. Again, however, they make the assumption that evaluation requires such prespecification. Thus it has been argued by Hilda Taba (1962) that objectives must be prespecified because this is crucial for evaluation and that evaluation in turn is crucial for effective teaching, the continued presence of certain subjects on the curriculum and for curriculum development itself. 'It is well known', she tells us (op cit., p. 199), 'that those things that are most clearly evaluated are also most effectively taught.' She also advises us that 'it is difficult to defend the "frills" from current attacks because attainments other than those in "essentials" are not readily demonstrable . . . With a clearer platform of objectives and more adequate evaluation data, both the necessity and the efficacy of many aspects of the school program would be vastly more defensible' (ibid.). Lastly, she claims that this is essential for the continued development of the curriculum since we can change it effectively only if we obtain appropriate data concerning its effects. 'Evaluation thus serves not only to check the hypothesis on which curriculum is based but also to uncover the broader effects of a program which may serve its central purpose well, but may, at the same time, produce undesirable by-products' (op. cit., p. 315).

This emphasis on evaluation and the assumption that it can take place only if objectives are clearly prestated is typical, of course, of an approach to education whose base is essentially psychological. It is important to note, however, that studies of curriculum evaluation (MacDonald, 1973; Hamilton, 1976), as we shall see in Chapter 7, have demonstrated that it is possible to evaluate a curriculum whose objectives have not been clearly stated in advance. Indeed, it might be argued that those very educational advances that Taba is concerned with are better promoted by the use of more sophisticated forms both of evaluation and of planning.

The case for the prespecification of curriculum objectives, then, is a powerful one, although perhaps only if one is prepared to accept those assumptions which we have seen underpin it. Many of the objections to it, however, are equally cogent. It is to a consideration of these that we now turn.

SOME PROBLEMS PRESENTED BY THE OBJECTIVES MODEL

We must begin by noting that this approach raises some fundamental theoretical issues concerning the nature of education and also concerning the nature of human beings. For the most fundamental criticism that has been levelled at this approach to curriculum planning is that its attempt to reduce education to a scientific activity, analogous to the processes of industry, commits it to a view of humans and of human nature that many people find unacceptable and even unpalatable. For to adopt this kind of industrial model for education is to assume that it is legitimate to mould human beings, to modify their behaviour, according to certain clear-cut intentions without making any allowance for their own individual wishes, desires or interests. Like the materials upon which the industrial worker operates, children's minds are to be fashioned by teachers according to some preconceived blueprint.

This kind of view also requires us to accept that human behaviour can be explored, analysed and explained in the same way as the behaviour of inanimate objects, that it can be studied scientifically by methods similar to those used by the physical scientist or even the biologist and that it can be explained in terms of causes rather than purposes, by reference to external forces acting on the individual rather than internal drives and choices of a personal kind. Fundamental to the view, therefore, is a psychological theory of a behaviourist kind and it is with behaviourist psychology that the movement has been associated from the start. In fact, most of its theoretical proponents have been psychologists rather than educationists or teachers. We shall see later, when we look more closely at current government policies for the school curriculum, that these too are based on the same kind of scientist view of humanity and society and on the assumption that one can study both, and thus make one's educational prescriptions, in a pseudo-scientific manner.

This passive model of humans is endemic to the theory and it is thus not acceptable to those who take the view that the individual is to be regarded as a free and active agent, responsible for his or her own destiny and who, as a direct consequence of this, believe it to be morally wrong to deny him or her that responsibility and freedom by attempting to mould his or her behaviour to suit the ends of someone else. Such a process, they argue, is indoctrination rather than education and thus to be deplored.

It is for this reason that it has also been attacked as being based not only on an inadequate and unacceptable model of the individual but also on an equally unsatisfactory concept of education, or perhaps on no concept of education at all. For those who have attempted to disentangle the concept of education from other related concepts such as training, instruction or indoctrination have done so by drawing attention to certain features of education that are not necessary parts of these other processes and, indeed, are sometimes explicitly excluded from them (Peters, 1965, 1966). Pre-eminent among these features is that of individual autonomy without a concern for which, it is argued, no process of teaching can be called education. Such a view of education clearly entails the kind of active model of humans we have just been discussing and precludes an approach to educational planning that begins from a clear idea of the kinds of behaviour modification that teachers are to try to bring about in their pupils.

In this context, it is interesting to note again how many of the books and articles written to promote an approach to educational planning through the prespecification of objectives contain the word 'instruction' in their titles or use that word to describe the kinds of teaching they have in mind. It is also interesting to consider the examples that they give, since most of them are of a relatively simple, instructional kind.

We thus have a model for curriculum planning which is based either on no concept of education at all or on one which lacks all subtlety and sophistication, for it sees the process of teaching merely as the transmission of predetermined knowledge-content chosen in pursuit of certain predetermined objectives. It thus makes no allowance for the subtleties which anyone who has any direct experience of education can readily recognize in any teaching/learning process worthy of the name of education. Education is, or can and perhaps must be, more than mere instruction or mere learning. This model of curriculum planning is based on a concept of education which cannot accommodate these further dimensions of the educational process, and thus, in the eyes of many people, on no concept of education at all.

There are several further aspects or consequences of this which we must explore in greater detail. First, we must consider the implications of the instrumentalism which is an essential and ineluctable part of this model. Second, we must note the charge that it leads not only to a view of teaching as mere instruction or the transmission of knowledge but that, beyond this, it adds to that content or transmission model the idea that we must select our content or knowledge in order to bring about certain predetermined behavioural changes, to achieve some kind of behaviour modification, so that in effect it leads us inevitably to a view of teaching as a form of indoctrination. Third, we must question the linear approach to teaching and learning which it assumes, the 'Thirty-Nine Steps' model of educational planning, much favoured by behavioural psychologists and also by politicians and others who see education from the outside and have inevitably a somewhat simplistic view of it. We must also note the muddle that the attempt to adopt this model usually leads to, especially noticeable in the *Curriculum Matters* series of documents to which we have already referred more than once, when people adopt or advocate the model without full appreciation of what it entails and thus find themselves unable to abandon those dimensions of the educational process they continue to regard as important despite the fact that their adopted model will not admit of them, or, alternatively, attempt to fit their own educational ideals, or concept of education, into a model not designed to accommodate them. And, lastly, we must note the restrictions which this approach places on both teacher and pupil in the educational situation. We will now consider all these issues in turn.

Consider the endemic instrumentalism of this model. There is nothing illogical or incoherent in seeing schooling in instrumental terms, in terms of what it is *for*; this view has a long history and most parents would no doubt still share with Mr Tulliver of George Eliot's *The Mill on the Floss*, at least in part, the ambitions he harbours for his son Tom's schooling. 'I want him to know figures, and write like print, and see into things quick, and know what folks mean, and how to wrap things up in words as aren't actionable. It's an uncommon fine thing, that is . . . when you can let a man know what you think of him without paying for it.' If this is how one sees schooling and how one wishes to plan the curriculum, one is quite entitled to that view. The point here is not necessarily to condemn such a view as, first, to emphasize that it is endemic to the objectives model of curriculum planning, that the adoption of that model commits one to that view of schooling, that it necessitates planning the curriculum in terms of its end-products, and, second, to draw attention to some of the things that this position implies.

It implies, first of all, a rejection of other concepts and dimensions of teaching and schooling which some would claim would make them more worthy of being described as 'education'; it requires us to settle for something considerably less than many would wish to see and/or get from an *education* system. For a major feature which it has been claimed must be present if an act of teaching is to be properly described as educational is that pupils must be engaged in it for its own sake. This is sometimes expressed by saying that it must be a process of initiation into activities that are intrinsically worthwhile (Peters, 1965, 1966). Whether such activities can be accurately defined or identified is, as we saw in Chapter 2, a difficult question. What is apparent, however, is that in a properly educational process the teacher must view the content of his or her teaching as being of value in itself and his or her intention must be to persuade his or her pupils so to view it. For if its justification lies in what it leads to, if, in short, the process is an instrumental one with ends or purposes outside itself, then, as we have seen, we would more naturally refer to it as 'training' or 'instruction'.

This illustrates either that the concept of education implicit in this model lacks this dimension that Richard Peters and others wish to give it or that the model lacks any concept of education at all. For if one of the things that characterizes education as opposed to other activities that involve teaching and learning, such as training or instruction, is that education is essentially concerned with activities whose value is intrinsic to them, such a notion of education is clearly at odds with the idea of activities planned according to extrinsic behavioural objectives, goals extrinsic to the activity itself. John Dewey first drew our attention to this feature of education when he asserted that education can have no ends beyond itself, since it is its own end. This view has subsequently been developed more fully by Richard Peters (1965, 1966, 1973a) who claims, for example, that 'to be educated is not to have arrived at a destination; it is to travel with a different view. What is required is not feverish preparation for something that lies ahead, but to work with precision, passion and taste at worthwhile things that lie at hand' (Peters, 1965, p. 110). On this kind of analysis not only does the notion of prespecified behavioural objectives run counter to the very concept of education but the broad aims of education must also be seen from a different perspective, not as what education is *for* but as what it *is*, so that to assert that education is concerned with the development of personal autonomy, understanding, a cognitive perspective, a recognition of the value of certain kinds of activity and so on is not to state extrinsic goals for education so much as to identify features that should characterize any process that is to be described as educational, a point we will pick up again in the next chapter.

Another way of expressing this is to say that on this kind of analysis education contains a value element, a commitment to the intrinsic worth of certain kinds of activity, and that this element is essential to it. Any approach to educational planning that ignores this element, that sets out deliberately to be value-neutral, as we have seen the behavioural objectives approach does, must be inadequate as a basis for the planning of activities which are educational in the full sense. Such an approach might be quite satisfactory for the planning of schemes of training or instruction, and this would explain why, as we suggested earlier, its main impact at the practical level has been on the planning of vocational courses. But for those activities that most teachers would wish to argue constitute the education they offer their pupils, the things they would claim were for their 'personal development' rather than for their vocational advancement, those things whose presence on the curriculum would be justified in educational or intrinsic terms, the model is quite inadequate. In fine, while the concept of an *instructional* objective is not difficult to grasp, that of an *educational* objective would appear to have no substance at all and to be, in fact, a contradiction in terms.

There is a further, important implication in this and that is that it must lead to the emergence of a society which has never learned, except perhaps by accident, to value things for their own sake, a society in which utility is the sole concern, a society in which all are absorbed only by the means of existence and never by a consideration of its ends. This approach to educational planning has wide-sweeping implications not only for education itself but for the nature, and indeed the future of society and for attitudes to human life and existence (MacIntyre, 1964). Confucius once said, 'If you have twopence to spend, you should spend a penny on bread and a penny on a flower, the bread to make life possible, the flower to make it worthwhile.' The objectives model can offer no help or guidance with the second element of that advice. Its adoption as the planning base must therefore imply that its users have no interest in this aspect of human existence or, more likely, that they have not recognized the full implications of the model they have adopted. It must be emphasized, then, that the model must lead to an instrumental view of schooling and that it cannot accommodate, and thus offers no basis for, planning any other form of educational provision.

The next major difficulty of the objectives approach to curriculum planning follows naturally from this. Once we adopt a model that allows us to see content as instrumental, we immediately risk slipping into some kind of indoctrinatory process, as an examination of Plato's theory of education will again quickly reveal. For there are many areas of the curriculum which involve content of a kind which is highly controversial and to approach these areas with a clear prespecification of intended learning outcomes in behavioural terms is to abandon education altogether for what must be seen as a much more sinister process. In the teaching and learning of music and the fine arts the prime concern is to elicit an individual response from the pupil; it is clearly not appropriate to decide in advance what that response should be (Eisner, 1969). 'How can you put on the blackboard the mysterious internal goal of each creative person?' (Pirsig, 1974). In literature too the whole purpose of introducing pupils to great literary works is lost if it is done from the perspective of intended learning outcomes (Stenhouse, 1970). Again that purpose is to invite the pupil to respond in his or her own way to what he or she is introduced to. To approach a reading of *Hamlet*, for example, in any other way is either to reduce it to an instrumental role, as we have just seen, designed to promote an understanding of words, poetic forms, even philosophy, or to attempt to impose one's own moral and aesthetic values, one's own subjective interpretation of the play and response to it on one's pupils. If appreciation of literature or any of the arts means anything at all and has any place in education, it cannot be approached by way of clearly prespecified objectives.

This is one of the major reasons why the Schools Council's Humanities Curriculum Project deliberately eschewed any kind of statement of objectives and, indeed, went so far as to make teacher neutrality its central principle. Being concerned to introduce older pupils in secondary schools to some of the controversial issues that face modern society, such as relations between the sexes, living in cities, war and so on, and being of the opinion that these are issues upon which a number of different value stances can be taken with equal validity, it recognized that the involvement of pupils in these issues could not be undertaken justifiably with clear objectives as to what the outcome of their learning and discussions should be, but only according to certain procedural principles designed to allow them to reach their own informed opinions on them. To do anything else would be to indoctrinate rather than to educate.

This has also led some people to reject the behavioural objectives approach to the planning of the curriculum for children with special needs (Goddard, 1983). It is perhaps in this field that the model has been adopted most readily and extensively and in its starkest form. Indeed, in this kind of context the notion of 'behaviour modification' seems to have been adopted with few qualms, and there has been little objection to the view that in the case of children with special needs or learning difficulties it is not only acceptable but even necessary to concentrate all one's attention on modifying their behaviour and improving their performance of certain kinds of behavioural task. Thus Wilfrid Brennan (1979, p. 97) tells us that 'clarity of terminal and intermediate objectives in the curriculum is seen as essential if the teacher is to use the total learning situation in order to continuously "shape" [note the metaphor] the development of the pupil', and we are also told (Leeming et al., 1979, p. 68) in relation to the education of children with special needs that 'the only way we can hope to change children and know we have succeeded, is to change their behaviour. This is the basis for the use of an objectives approach to the curriculum.' However, if this approach leads, if only in certain areas of the curriculum, to forms of indoctrination, if it treats human beings as passive recipients of experiences intended to bring about behavioural changes felt to be desirable by others, if it denies the notion of learning for learning's sake, then it is at least as unsatisfactory as the sole approach to the teaching of children with special educational needs as it is in the case of other pupils. And it is right that Alan Goddard and others should be insisting that there be more to the education of such children than that, that 'what we often want to teach is not behaviour, neither can it be reduced to behaviour' (Goddard, 1983, p. 272 – referring to Swann, 1981). Indeed, it is difficult to see the point of the Warnock Report's (DES, 1980) recommendation for the integration of pupils with special needs wherever possible into ordinary schools and classrooms on any other grounds – unless of course behaviour modification is to be the aim for all pupils.

We must also note the criticism that this approach is based on an inadequate view of the learning process. There are several aspects of this. In the first place, the hierarchical form of the relationships between objectives that is characteristic of taxonomies such as that of Bloom (1956) does not reflect the realities of the learning process. The linear model that it assumes, which attempts to break down all learning into a step-by-step procedure, is not suitable for most of the learning that goes on in schools. We do not acquire knowledge and then, at some later stage, attain understanding; the two must go hand in hand. Real learning is developmental rather than linear. The acquisition of knowledge or the transmission of knowledge-content may be linear processes (although even here such a view does not acknowledge the complexities and the subtle differences in children's learning patterns, since it allows adjustments only for different rates of learning); the development of understanding certainly is not; it is a far more subtle process and much more likely to be brought about by some form of what Jerome Bruner has termed a 'spiral' curriculum, where one returns to concepts at ever higher levels of understanding, than by a 'Thirty-Nine Steps', linear and hierarchical set of offerings. Any view of the learning process that does not recognize this must be regarded as too simplistic to serve as a basis for any but the most unsophisticated of teaching activities.

To look at this form a different point of view and in more detail, the real thrust of this criticism is that the relationship that exists between educational objectives is too complex to be reduced to an unsophisticated model of this kind, which sees that relationship as a hierarchy of simple to ever more complex objectives (Hirst, 1975). The relationships existing between the many things that teachers are endeavouring to achieve with their pupils are far more complicated than such a model supposes.

A good example of this is the suggestion often made by the advocates of this approach, and which is implied by all the assertions we hear about the need for the teaching of 'the basic skills', that we ought to set about teaching these skills before we attempt more sophisticated forms of teaching and learning; in short, that our approach to teaching and learning should be not only linear but also hierarchical. The teaching of basic skills, even those of a psychomotor kind, cannot be separated out from other kinds of goals without risking the loss of that essential ingredient of education that we must also be concerned with. It is possible to teach basic skills in an instructional manner – the basic skills of reading, for example, of using a saw or a wood-chisel, of drawing straight lines or circles and many others – and in this area the use of the behavioural model has appeared to be successful. The wide adoption and evident commercial success of 'reading workshops' and 'reading laboratories' provide ample evidence of this. However, if we do not at the same time have clearly in mind the educational dimensions of the activities we are engaged in, then, while our efforts might well result in highly skilled performance at the behavioural level, they are likely to result in our achieving little beyond that and may even be counterproductive to any further attainment and, indeed, to education itself. For, as the Bullock Report (DES, 1975) pointed out, it is possible to help pupils to a high level of reading performance and at the same time to kill or to inhibit any love or appreciation they may have developed for the written word. Indeed, as the

Report also pointed out, even that high level of skilled performance itself will be short-lived. There are more 'non-readers' about than those who merely cannot decipher the symbols of the written word. This is a major danger of attempts to measure standards of attainment in schools in terms simply of performance or behaviour. It is thus a danger not only of the objectives model of curriculum planning but also of those popular, public and political demands for improved standards in the 'basic skills' which have this kind of simplistic model of education at their tap-root.

Furthermore, that division of objectives into domains, which we saw to be a major feature of Bloom's taxonomy, or into the categories or spheres offered by the Aims of Primary Education Project (Ashton, Kneen and Davies, 1975) is an attempt to create distinctions that are unrealistic in practice and untenable in theory. For it is not possible to envisage an educational activity that concerns itself only with certain cognitive or intellectual goals without simultaneously involving affective or emotional considerations and probably the development of psychomotor skills too. Indeed, we have been arguing that it is of the essence of an educational activity that it should be concerned not only to develop cognitive abilities but at the same time to promote a recognition of the intrinsic value of the activity and a feeling for those standards of truth and beauty which are an essential component of what it means to have knowledge and to be educated (Pring, 1971). For how could one attempt to ensure that 'the child should be able to read with understanding material appropriate to his age group and interests' (Ashton, Kneen and Davies, 1975, p. 17) without, at the same time, endeavouring to see to it that 'the child should be developing a personal appreciation of beauty in some of its forms, both natural and artistic' (op. cit., p. 19) and that 'the child should find enjoyment in a variety of aspects of school work and gain satisfaction from his achievements' (op. cit., p. 21), not to mention that 'the child should be happy, cheerful and well balanced' (ibid.)? Conversely, how can one hope ever to achieve these affective goals if one has largely to ignore them when setting out to attain the former 'aims related to intellectual development' (op. cit., p. 17)?

Every activity in which a pupil engages will have a range of purposes both within and between the three 'domains'. This is brought out very well in the general statement of the traditional objectives of craft teaching offered by the architects of the Schools Council's project, 'Education through the Use of Materials', as 'developing motor skills, such as sawing, planing and filing, and appreciation of design and craftsmanship in furniture and engineering, with all the satisfaction that attainment in these activities can bring to some pupils and which for so long have been the "bread and butter" activity of the workshop' (Schools Council, 1969, p. 10). The Science 5–13 Project too has stated quite clearly that 'a teacher will have many objectives for her children in mind at any one time, and in general there is potential for working towards several objectives through any one activity' (Schools Council, 1972, p. 32). Thus, in practice, every activity will embody a range of objectives, involving 'some intellective task', 'a degree of acceptance or rejection' and probably 'some manipulation of materials and objects' too.

It is perhaps because of this inevitable interrelatedness of all aspects of learning in any fully educational process that so many of those who advocate or attempt to use this model in an educational context slip very quickly into serious forms of conceptual confusion and thus into offering practical advice which is at best highly muddled and confusing. We have already noted the predilection of the HMI *Curriculum Matters* series for the prestatement of teaching objectives. All the documents in that series adopt this approach and style with no apparent regard for possible differences between subjects or for the problematic nature of this model. None acknowledges that there are different models or approaches which might have been adopted; none attempts or offers any kind of justification for the model used. One can only assume that this is because their authors are not aware that one might approach curriculum planning in any other way or of the many inadequacies of the approach they have chosen or fallen into. As a result, they all reveal a disturbing confusion between a concern for the subject-content of their prescriptions, the desire to organize it in a linear and hierarchical fashion by the clear prespecification of objectives and a lingering desire for the kind of educational justification which might come from a view of their subject as an 'area of experience' with something to offer to children's development above and beyond the transmission of the knowledge-content itself.

All this reveals a failure to appreciate the deep conceptual issues which underlie the differences between these approaches. This comes out perhaps most clearly in that failure to distinguish conceptually between aims and objectives, to which reference has already been made on more than one occasion. In several of the booklets it is not made clear – and it is certainly not easy to divine – what the conceptual difference is between those things which are stated clearly as 'aims' and those which are called 'objectives'; yet the distinction is made very positively and it is clearly intended to be significant. One, *Home Economics* (DES, 1985d), states first its aims, then 'some principles of teaching home economics' (op. cit., p. 2) and then its objectives. Again, no attempt is made to distinguish these concepts or to demonstrate their different contributions to curriculum planning. The 'main objective' for seven-year-old pupils is declared (op. cit., p. 7) to be 'to start to lay the foundations of knowledge, attitudes and skills, which will be the basis for later, more formal work in home economics', a very general goal which could as easily be an aim or a principle. The section on objectives (op. cit., pp. 6 ff.), however, is clearly concerned primarily with content, since it begins by stating that 'the content of home economics courses may conveniently be categorised in three main areas . . .' This section goes on to list not only the prescribed content of home economics teaching but recommended methods too, so that its objectives are expressed largely in terms of content and methodology. The publication on Geography (DES, 1986b) also resolves the problem of distinguishing aims and objectives by expressing its objectives in terms of subject-content and methodology. The objectives of health education are expressed in the form of syllabuses for the primary and the secondary phases of schooling (DES, 1986c). In *Craft, design and technology from 5 to 16* (DES, 1987c) we are offered a series of 'aims' which might well be interpreted, and would be unexceptionable, as the kinds of procedural principle which might underlie a process or a developmental approach to curriculum planning in this area, or which might be seen as an explication of the contribution of craft, design and technology to those 'areas of experience' which were suggested by an earlier HMI publication, *Curriculum 11–16* (DES, 1977c). However, it then proceeds to translate these into statements of skills and knowledge-content and into shorter-term objectives. In short, like its fellows and predecessors, it reveals little or no understanding of the complexities of curriculum planning or of the deep conceptual differences between planning models, and thus offers a conceptually confused, and hence practically confusing, set of recommendations to teachers. This is particularly disappointing in an area of the curriculum where more progress has been made than in most towards explicating the subject in procedural terms and thus towards establishing a coherent planning base (Kelly *et al.*, 1987).

Throughout this series, which has been offered to the profession as what the covering letters have described as a 'contribution to that search for greater clarity and definition about the 5–16 curriculum which was one of the themes in the Secretary of State's speech to the North of England Conference' and as reflecting 'HMI thinking about the curriculum over recent years', the same kinds of conceptual muddle are glaringly apparent. Nor is this to be allayed or offset by the proviso stressed at the beginning of several of these booklets, that 'it is essential that this document should be read as a whole, since all sections are interrelated. For example, the list of objectives must be seen in relation to the defined aims and to what is said about the principles of teaching and assessment.' To read something as a whole is not to give it a coherence it does not have, nor is such coherence achieved merely by asserting the need to read it as a whole. Rather the coherence should be demonstrated and the interrelationships claimed should be explicated; and to do this a good deal of conceptual clarification would need to be undertaken.

In most cases it does seem that the conceptual confusion arises from a desire to embrace the rhetoric of a 'progressive' approach to educational planning and the vocabulary of the increasingly fashionable process model, which we shall explore in Chapter 4, while at the same time advocating the more politically acceptable and 'hard-headed' view of education as instrumental and as primarily directed towards economic success. Or perhaps it reflects a conflict between the vestiges of a concern with education in the full sense and the realities of political expediency. Or again it may result from an unwillingness to acknowledge all the inevitable implications of the instrumental, economic, political view. Whatever the reason, it leads to a highly confused and unsatisfactory set of prescriptions for educational practice.

The final criticism which has been levelled at this planning model and which we must note here is the charge which Charity James (1968) made that this approach restricts the freedom of both teacher and pupil. For both will be inclined to see the objectives as fixed or given, just as secondary teachers tend to see examination syllabuses as immutable, so that not only will they concentrate on what must be rather simple instructional goals, they will also lose the opportunity to play an active role in the educational process, a process which, it is claimed, is fully educational only if both teachers and pupils are active within it. Thus it is argued that the prespecification of intended learning outcomes to an educational process denies autonomy not only to the teacher but also to the pupil and anything that does not take account of the incipient and developing autonomy of the pupil cannot be accurately described as educative (Pring, 1973). The curriculum on this view must be seen as the dynamic interaction of teacher and pupil and this cannot be promoted by a scientific, 'industrial' model requiring careful preplanning of outcomes. If education is seen as a continuous, ongoing, open-ended activity, the idea of constant modification and reassessment must be endemic to it, so that any approach to planning an educational activity that starts with a clear specification of objectives will be based on a misunderstanding of what an educational activity really is. Every act of education takes place in its own individual context (Sockett, 1976a) and thus cannot be predetermined. Education is an art as well as a science and far too complex and sophisticated an activity to be elucidated in terms of this kind of simple model.

This view of education as an ongoing, open-ended process, subject to constant reassessment and modification as a result of pupil–teacher interaction is supported by the practical experiences of many teachers. We noted earlier that teachers and student teachers, even in the face of concerted pressures upon them to prespecify the objectives of their lessons, have in practice rejected this approach and we suggested that this might be seen as evidence of its impracticability. We can perhaps see now that it is precisely those teachers who are concerned to offer something that goes beyond mere training or instruction who have found this model impossible to use. The realities of the teacher's task are too complex to be met by an approach like that of the industrial planner. This has been reinforced by the experience of many of those curriculum projects that have attempted to use this kind of model, such as the Schools Council's project, 'History, Geography, and Social Science 8–13' (Blyth, 1974) and the Nuffield 'A' level Biology Project (Kelly, P. J., 1973). For even when sets of objectives are presented to them in clear terms, teachers do find it impossible not to modify them continually in the light of the experiences that they and their pupils have from the moment the work begins. As John Dewey once pointed out, objectives have a tendency to change as you approach them. It is thus not bloody-mindedness on the part of teachers that causes them to cannibalize what they are offered; it is a realization that, if they do not make this kind of constant adjustment, the goals of their teaching will remain at a simple level and that which is truly educational will be at risk. It is here that the practitioners may fairly claim to have been ahead of the theoreticians. It is here too that the most serious threats are posed by the growing pressures on teachers from outside the school, and especially by the simplistic, objectives-based pre-scriptions of the National Curriculum and its supporting documentation.

One major reason, then, why some people have recently wished to argue against the prespecification of objectives is the conviction that education is, or can be, a more sophisticated activity and curriculum planning as a result a more complex process than this simple theoretical model suggests. This is a point we have noted several times already. And, to foreshadow what we shall discuss in greater detail in the next chapter, what teachers need is a set of principles which will guide them in making the minute-by-minute decisions which this complex process requires.

Any model we adopt for curriculum planning must allow for the personal and professional autonomy of the teacher. If we do not allow for this, we create constraints on the activity of teachers and their scope for exercising their professional judgement on the spot. This is clearly a very real danger with too simple an objectives model.

SOME ATTEMPTED MODIFICATIONS

The problems presented by this curriculum planning model, then, are serious and cast major doubts on its efficacy as a tool for educational planning at any level. Several attempts have been made, therefore, to modify it in ways which might preserve the emphasis on stating the purposes of our planning while avoiding the difficulties we have just noted.

Other forms of objectives

The first such attempt has argued that it is not the specification of objectives in itself which causes the troubles we have listed but rather a misunderstanding as to the kind of thing an educational objective is (Hirst, 1975). In short, it is said that we must look for another model for curriculum objectives, since the behavioural model of curriculum objectives is unsatisfactory. First, it is unsatisfactory precisely because it is behavioural and, therefore, loses sight of the fact that educational objectives must of their very nature be concerned with much more complex forms of 'personal and mental development' (Hirst, 1975, p. 15). Second, it is based on a misunderstanding of the relationship between objectives. Third, it leads to a view of curriculum planning as a kind of engineering or computer programming which fails to understand how curriculum objectives come to be framed. Lastly, it operates at too general a level, assuming that curricula can be planned in a Utopian, *carte blanche* manner rather than recognizing that curriculum development must be seen as a piecemeal activity taking place in specific contexts (Hirst, 1975).

Thus, it is not the idea of having a purpose to our planning that is at fault. It is the way in which we view that purpose and its relations to the activities that will embody it. Given that the engineering or computer-programming model is inadequate, it is argued that we must set about the search for a more suitable model rather than reject the idea of specifying objectives altogether.

On the other hand, it is difficult to know what an educational objective would be if it were not to be seen as a statement of the intention to change or modify behaviour, unless it were a general statement of principle, a long-term aim. Any short-term goal must be expressed in terms of the behaviour changes we hope to bring about. Certainly the only way in which we could measure the achievement of a short-term goal would be by examining the behaviour of our pupils. Thus, even if we attempted to express the goals of a lesson in terms of *educational* objectives, such as 'to develop habits of inquiry', rather than tight *behavioural* objectives or 'intended learning outcomes', our intention would still be to change behaviour and our success or failure must still be evaluated by observation of pupil behaviour. Any short-term goal, therefore, must be behavioural in nature.

This suggested modification, however, draws our attention to the fact that the problem centres on the manner in which we translate long-term goals or aims into the realities of short-term practice. The essence of the aims and objectives model, as we have seen, is the particular distinction which it makes between aims and objectives – a distinction we have also seen is persistently ignored or unappreciated by those who continue to use these terms as distinct concepts without recognizing or explaining the conceptual difference between them. For the distinction made in this model is not merely between long- and short-term goals; it lies much more significantly in the fact that the latter are *derived* from the former, and together they create a linear, step-by-step hierarchy of goals. An objective such as that we have just instanced, 'to develop habits of inquiry', is not an objective in the sense in which that term is used and understood by those advocating a proper objectives model; it is much more like what such a person would call an 'aim', a long-term goal (since, apart from any other consideration, it is clearly not something anyone would expect to achieve in a single lesson, or even in a week of lessons), just as we have seen the 'objectives' of many Schools Council projects and of the HMI's *Curriculum Matters* series are.

What is implied in this suggestion of Paul Hirst's (1975), then, is that this kind of aim, far from being translated into a hierarchy of short-term objectives, should be seen by teachers as an underlying principle against which they should undertake their detailed planning and make the minute-by-minute decisions that successful classroom practice requires. It thus offers us not so much a modification of the objectives model as a pointer to the advantages of that process model of curriculum planning, which the next chapter will explore. It also identifies the source of that conceptual confusion which it has been suggested has bedevilled all those curriculum pronouncements and prescriptions which have seized upon the terms 'aims' and 'objectives' without understanding the distinctive concept and view of curriculum they encapsulate.

Different models for different areas of curriculum

A second attempt to resolve the problems of the objectives model has taken the form of suggesting that we should examine each area of the curriculum separately on the assumption that different subject areas or curriculum activities will require different approaches to their planning.

This argument has taken two main forms. The first has distinguished the teaching of science and mathematics from teaching in other areas of the curriculum and has proposed that, while the prespecification of objectives would appear to be inappropriate in the latter context, the teaching of 'factual' material in 'linear' subjects like mathematics, where a clear progression of step-by-step learning may be discerned, does lend itself to clear statements of sequences of intended outcomes. Certainly, it is the case that most of the examples used by those who have wished to argue the unsuitability of the objectives model have been derived from humanities subjects. The most cogent and often quoted example is that used by Lawrence Stenhouse (1970) in the attack he mounts on the objectives model, the example, which we noted earlier, of the teaching of *Hamlet*.

This case against the prespecification of objectives in such contexts would appear to be irrefutable and it is not difficult to appreciate its force in relation to all those subjects that comprise the humanities. However, is it possible to approach the teaching of mathematics and the sciences differently? Some have certainly felt that it is and in practice a good deal of the teaching of these subjects can be seen to reflect an acceptance of the validity of this model. This is particularly true of some of the schemes for the teaching of mathematics in the primary school, such as Fletcher Mathematics and the Kent Mathematics Project, to which we referred earlier. We have also noted already the degree of preoccupation with curriculum objectives shown by the team associated with the Science 5–13 Project.

It has been argued, however, that this distinction between the humanities and the sciences is difficult to maintain. For it is difficult to sustain the view that science is value-free and that it is not, therefore, subject to the same problems as the humanities subjects. In particular, it has been suggested that nothing could be more unlike true scientific method or inquiry than to begin an experiment with a clear statement of what one intends to prove by it (Sockett, 1976a), that the old-style 'required-to-prove' approach to the teaching of science indicates a misunderstanding of the nature of scientific exploration and is unlikely to promote an appreciation of what science truly is. For this reason, although, as we have said, the prespecification of objectives played a major part in the evolution of the Science 5–13 Project, those objectives on examination prove, as we have seen, to be rather more loosely framed than at first sight they appear to be, and in practice they have been used to support an approach to the teaching of science in the primary school that is enquiry-based. This is even more apparent in the work of the follow-up project, 'Learning through Science' (Richards, 1979). Similarly, there is no evidence to support the assumption that an understanding of the logic of mathematics will best be achieved if mathematics is experienced in a logical sequence. In the case of both subjects, it would seem again that the model is appropriate only if we see the teaching of them in terms of the transmission of knowledge and skills. The development of understanding here as in all areas of teaching requires a more sophisticated teaching and planning model.

It becomes increasingly clear, then, that in all areas of the curriculum, if our concern is with education and we wish to distinguish this from instruction, training and other teaching activities, one of the things we must do is to eschew the prespecification of objectives.

It is this that has led some to propose a different kind of division of curriculum activities, a separation of those whose justification is clearly educational from those which are equally clearly instrumental, forms of training for which statements of intent are not only acceptable but even necessary. Some support for this view comes from the fact we have already noted that the most widespread practical use of systems of objectives has occurred in the area of vocational preparation and training. Certainly, in such contexts the content of what is taught is clearly chosen on instrumental grounds, so that most or all of the objections that have been raised would seem not to be applicable. In teaching someone to drive a car, for example, it would be foolish not to have a clear idea of one's goals, expressed in quite explicit and clearly sequenced behavioural terms – 'he or she shall be able to bring the car to an immediate halt when confronted by an obstruction, human or material' and so on.

However, while this is undoubtedly a proper and acceptable approach to the teaching of 'basic skills', it is not as easy to identify and single out these skills in the context of schooling as many theorists appear to believe and, as we have just seen, serious dangers lurk in those attempts to make this kind of distinction within the school curriculum. There is a growing body of evidence that to attempt to break down any of the complex human activities into which schools and teachers are concerned to initiate pupils into hierarchies of sub-skills, as the objectives model requires, or even as this kind of modification of it would encourage us to do, is to put at risk the more important aspects of those activities or the longer-term goals of teaching them. Written language, for example, is 'far too complex a system for any simple description in terms of a build up of sub-skills to account for it', so that 'if we try to offer a logically pre-programmed sequence of knowledge we simply interfere with the sense-making opportunities which real reading and writing offer to the learner' and 'any attempt to make learning literacy easy by offering only parts of the whole experience is almost certain to violate the meaningfulness of normal written language' (Money, 1988, p. 142). And, in mathematics too, it has been suggested (Metz, 1988, p. 187) that 'an emphasis . . . on applying rules in a step-by-step manner ignores not only the need to make general sense of a situation first, but also the importance of reflecting on any solution obtained after the rules have been applied'. Education is far too complex a process to be broken down in this kind of way.

'Instructional' and 'expressive' objectives

Elliot Eisner's (1969) suggestion that we distinguish between 'instructional' and 'expressive' objectives can be seen as an attempt to combine both the solutions we have considered. For it attempts both to offer an alternative model of an educational objective, in the way that Paul Hirst (1975) suggested, and to recommend that we approach the planning of different parts of the curriculum in different ways. For Eisner, an 'instructional' objective is a behavioural objective of the kind we have been discussing. An 'expressive' objective, however, does not specify an outcome of instruction in behavioural terms. 'An expressive objective describes an educational encounter. It identifies a situation in which children are to work, a problem with which they are to cope, a task in which they are to engage; but it does not specify what from that encounter, situation, problem, or task they are to learn . . . An expressive objective is evocative rather than prescriptive' (Eisner, 1969, pp. 15–16).

Eisner gives as examples of expressive objectives:

1) To interpret the meaning of *Paradise Lost*,
2) To examine and appraise the significance of *The Old Man and the Sea*,
3) To develop a three-dimensional form through the use of wire and wood,
4) To visit the zoo and discuss what was of interest there.

(op. cit., p. 16)

He goes on to suggest further that it is this kind of objective that teachers have more often than they have instructional objectives of a behavioural kind and that this is particularly so in 'the most sophisticated modes of intellectual work' (op. cit., p. 17).

It is this kind of thinking that lies behind those statements of objectives offered by several Schools Council projects which we noted earlier were not strictly behavioural in form but appeared to be seeking a more satisfactory educational basis. It is also another way of attempting to express as objectives those complex forms of development of which Paul Hirst speaks. This in turn reflects the thinking of many teachers who, while acknowledging the difficulties created by attempts to specify the goals of their teaching in narrow behavioural terms, feel it quite appropriate to speak of the 'broad aims' of education.

It is clear that both Eisner and Hirst are endeavouring to avoid defining an educational objective in instrumental terms because they are aware of the fundamental contradiction that that entails. However, if that contradiction is fundamental, it cannot be resolved by seeking different kinds of objectives for educational activities; it can be resolved, as we saw earlier, only by replacing the notion of 'aims and objectives' with something entirely different. This, in effect, is what Eisner's notion of an expressive objective actually does. For, as the examples given clearly show, it does not provide us with a set of objectives so much as an aim to be expressed in terms of procedures or principles. It is misleading to use the term 'objective' with its connotations of extrinsic purposes to denote a notion whose central concern seems to be with processes. This is a point we shall return to in the next chapter.

Objectives as provisional

A fourth kind of solution has emerged from the practical experience of a number of curriculum projects that we have already briefly referred to. A number of project teams have discovered that no matter how carefully their objectives have been framed they quickly come to be modified by teachers in the light of the experience and feedback they begin to receive as soon as they begin to implement the project. They have thus come to realize that the objectives they framed would have to be regarded as tentative and open to constant modification and adjustment. Those, for example, who were associated with the Schools Council's project, 'History, Geography and Social Science 8–13', came to recognize that they must regard their objectives only as 'provisional' (Blyth, 1974) and those concerned with the Nuffield 'A' level Biology Project came to describe their objectives as 'mutable' (Kelly, P. J., 1973). This view not only reflects more nearly the practical realities of the classroom and of teacher behaviour and experience, it is also closer to what we really mean by scientific exploration which, as we pointed out earlier, is characterized not by possessing a clear idea of where it is going but rather by being hypothetical, open-ended and subject to constant modification. This development is reflected in the practice of some local authorities of offering curriculum 'guidelines' to their teachers rather than statements of objectives, although it is sometimes the case that these guidelines are so tightly framed that their point is lost and their impact on the curriculum continues to be restrictive.

Such an approach is also supportive of the development of the curriculum, since it allows for the kind of continuous change and adjustment that the notion of development entails. It thus recognizes that in education 'objectives are developmental, representing roads to travel rather than terminal points' (Taba, 1962, p. 203). It also acknowledges the force of one of those criticisms levelled by Paul Hirst at the behavioural objectives model of educational planning, namely that it assumes that curricula can be planned in a Utopian, *carte blanche* manner rather than recognizing that curriculum development must take place in a specific context and must be seen as essentially a piecemeal activity (Hirst, 1975).

It is for this reason that we are now being encouraged from a number of sources to adopt a much more flexible approach to the framing of objectives so as to avoid a tight computer-programming approach to pupil activities. It has been suggested, for example, that we should begin by stating course objectives but that we should avoid the temptation to frame them in highly specific behavioural terms and that we should not be afraid to state long-term objectives, since many important educational outcomes may not be achieved except after many months or years of effort (Hogben, 1972).

A recognition of the developmental nature of educational goals leads also to a willingness to accept unintended learning outcomes (Hogben, 1972) and it is further suggested that we be on the alert for these and that we do not reject or discourage them merely because they do not conform to our prestated short-term goals.

In short, we should regard our objectives, certainly those of a short-term variety, as provisional, mutable and subject to modification in the light of the continuous experience both of ourselves as teachers and of our pupils once a course or piece of work has got under way.

This solution, however, although commending itself in many ways, not least in its obvious reflection of the actual practice of teachers and other curriculum planners, suffers from one major theoretical weakness which must render it, in the long term, an inadequate basis for satisfactory curriculum planning. For, apart from the fact that it embraces an instrumental model of education, the problems of which we have already discussed, its fundamental weakness is that it advises and encourages us to change and modify our objectives and to accept learning outcomes from our teaching which we did not intend to bring about, without offering us any criteria by which we can make judgements about the desirability of such changes and modifications or of these unintended outcomes. If we change our objectives or accept the validity of experiences or learning we did not intend or foresee, and if at the same time we do not accept the validity of all such changes or outcomes, we do so only because we have some criteria of judgement against which we can assess these unexpected and unplanned events. If this is so, and logically it must be, then it is these criteria which are, or should be, the real bases of our curriculum planning, and not our initial, mutable, provisional objectives, which must be seen as essentially second-order considerations. Until we get to grips with those basic principles, both our theorizing and our practice will continue to be muddled.

In fact, a common difficulty evinced by all the proposed solutions we have so far examined is that, while ostensibly seeking new models of educational objectives or attempting to identify areas of the curriculum where existent models might apply, they have all failed to realize that all educational planning must begin from a consideration of its basic principles or of the processes it is concerned to promote.

Indeed, this is a basic weakness of the objectives model itself. For, in rejecting, as we have seen it does, all responsibility for those value choices which are essential to education, it refuses to offer us any basis upon which we can even make a selection of the objectives we are to aim for. Nevertheless, as we shall see when we come to discuss the problems of curriculum evaluation in Chapter 7, even those who advocate this approach recognize that it is necessary for evaluative procedures to ask questions not only about the effectiveness of a programme in attaining its objectives but also about the desirability of the objectives themselves, to provide data for their subsequent modification. The model itself, then, draws our attention to the fact that educational planning must begin from considerations which are logically prior to statements of its objectives.

It is for this reason that others have recently stressed the need to begin educational planning from statements of principles rather than goals, assertions of the value positions that are to act as a base for all subsequent decisions. And it is to a consideration of this third approach to educational planning that we turn in our next chapter.

SUMMARY AND CONCLUSIONS

We have in this chapter examined in some detail the objectives model of curriculum planning. We began by tracing its history and suggesting that it can be seen as the result of a desire to make the practice of education more 'scientific' and thus as an effect of the influence of psychology, especially that of the behaviourist school, on education theory.

We then tried to pick out the essential characteristics of this view and, in doing so, we laid particular stress on the fact that those systems of objectives that have been proposed are behavioural, hierarchically structured and value-neutral. We next suggested that support for this approach to curriculum planning came not only from those who wished to make education more scientific but also from those who felt that in order for it to qualify as a rational activity it needs to have clear goals of some kind, from others who have felt that they could see advantages of an educational kind in it and, most recently, from politicians and others who have seen this as the only way of evaluating what schools and teachers are doing and testing their effectiveness and efficiency.

Having thus outlined the case for this model of curriculum planning, we then considered some of the criticisms that have been levelled at it. Most of these seemed to focus on the claim that both in theory and in practice to approach education in a manner that regards it as an instrumental activity is to lose one essential ingredient that makes education what it is, namely a process whose justification must lie within itself. Thus we saw that the critics of the objectives model base their attack mainly on the fact that it treats education as instrumental and, as a corollary of doing so, often adopts a passive model of human beings, the model that is at the root of behavioural psychology. We saw too that in practice this leads to teaching that is better described as instruction or training or even indoctrination than education and that it places constraints on both teachers and pupils that inhibit that freedom of interaction some have claimed to be central to the educative process.

We also considered some attempts which have been made to offer what might be regarded as modified versions of this model or to ensure that curriculum planning should satisfy the requirement of being a rational activity, at least in the sense of being goal-directed, while not at the same time being either unduly restrictive or completely instrumental. It was suggested, however, that a major weakness of these alternative forms of the objectives or product model of planning was that again they fail to offer us any assistance with the value issues which are central to educational decision-making, in short, that they provide us with schemes for curriculum planning but not the principles upon which this might be based. They reflect that narrow, mechanistic approach to curriculum which we suggested in Chapter 1 is restricted and restricting both of curriculum planning and curriculum study.

The concern throughout has been not so much to argue against the use of this model – indeed, it has been stressed that it is one completely logical and coherent way of approaching the planning of school provision. Rather, the intention was to point up what is implied by the adoption of this model in an attempt to ensure that those who do adopt it or who advocate its adoption are fully aware of what that means.

In particular, an attempt was made to reveal some of the limitations of the model, to point out that, at best, it is a mechanical model for the implementation of curricular policies but can offer no assistance with the framing of those policies, in fact, to suggest that there is, or can be, far more to education than is encompassed, or even dreamed of, in its underlying philosophy (if, indeed, it can be said to have one), and to demonstrate that there is at least one other model of curriculum planning which sets out to make available to us these additional potentialities of education, to enable us to plan and to structure our educational provision in a manner free of the kinds of restriction we have uncovered here. In the next chapter we turn to an exploration of the model which seeks to achieve this.

4

CURRICULUM AS PROCESS AND EDUCATION AS DEVELOPMENT

We have explored in the last two chapters the model of curriculum which would have us begin our educational planning from a selection of the knowledge-content to be transmitted and that which would start from a declaration of aims and objectives. We noted many inadequacies in both models but, in particular, the fact that neither offers any real help with that decision which must precede all others, namely the choice of content and/or aims and objectives. The content model offers, or takes as read, a number of arguments based on a view of the nature of both knowledge and culture which we suggested was far from convincing; the objectives model does not even attempt that but claims rather to be value-neutral.

In this chapter we will examine an approach to curriculum planning which endeavours to face up to this value issue as the prime concern in educational planning, which suggests that our educational purposes should be framed in terms of the processes which we regard education as able, and concerned, to promote, which advises us to select the knowledge-content of our curriculum not by reference to some supposed intrinsic value which it is claimed it has or by a reference to its assumed effectiveness in securing certain extrinsic aims or objectives, but in relation to its likely contribution to the development of the pupil, and which recommends that we see these purposes not as goals to be achieved at some later stage in the process but as procedural principles which should guide our practice throughout. All these features of this model we will consider in greater detail in what follows.

We must first note, however, that in seeking to face the value question squarely, it is a model which cannot in itself be value-free, or rather which cannot ignore questions of value or assume that these are unproblematic. There is no suggestion here that we can engage in educational planning without attending to the matter of choices, and especially to the justification of those choices, or that we can make those choices in a pseudo-scientific manner or by reference to some philosophical or epistemological theory which will offer God-given and objective answers to questions of value and of choice. Nor is there even an appeal to some kind of consensus view, whether spurious or verified, such as that which forms the only justification offered for the new National Curriculum in the United Kingdom. Rather it acknowledges that choice in any sphere will be made from one ideological position or another, so that it recognizes the necessity of setting out one's basic ideological position from the outset.

At one level we might see the process model as saying little more than that curriculum planners should acknowledge their ideological stance, whatever it is, and translate that into procedural principles which will be a constant guide to action. In short, it might itself claim value-neutrality. However, its reason for advocating this derives from a clear concept of education as something more than the mere acquisition of predetermined knowledge or the attainment of prescribed behavioural changes, so that its basic rationale is such as to make any kind of value-neutrality impossible. The addition to this model of the concept of education as development makes this plain, since this brings with it a very clear statement of educational goals, as well as a conviction that those goals can be attained in practice only if they are translated into procedural principles rather than into statements of content or of short-term objectives.

In short, this model has a clear concept of education but does not attempt to claim any pseudo-scientific or pseudo-objective status for that concept. It recognizes that no one and no discipline, despite the efforts of philosophers of education, can tell us what education *is*, but that many kinds of study can throw light on what it *can* or *might be*, what its potentialities are. It thus offers us such a view of what education might be and what, in the eyes of its advocates, it should be; and it endeavours to unpack for us what is involved in that view both in theory and in practice. In other words, its essence is a positive awareness of the ideological nature of all educational (and, indeed, all social) prescriptions, and a concern to explicate clearly its own ideology as the only basis it can see for planning education and the school curriculum in a form which acknowledges and caters for that central element of values we have noted so often already. Whereas the other models we have considered are models of curriculum *planning*, this model is also a model of curriculum, and, indeed, of education.

THE GROWTH OF THIS VIEW

The view which we are about to consider begins from the premise that the starting point for educational planning is not a consideration of the nature of knowledge and/or the culture to be transmitted or a statement of the ends to be achieved, whether these be economic or behavioural, but from a concern with the nature of the child and with his or her development.

The idea that in seeking answers to our questions about what should be taught we look to an examination of the nature of the child is not new; it is certainly not a product of the twentieth century. The revolt against the traditional view of education as concerned with the purveying of certain kinds of abstract knowledge and the development of rationality was begun by Rousseau in the eighteenth century and carried forward by other, perhaps more influential, educators, such as Froebel and Montessori, in the last century. The main thrust of that revolt was against the idea that we plan our educational practices by a consideration of knowledge or of society, and that we begin to look instead to the children who are the objects of those practices and plan according to what we can discover about them. It is for this reason that this general movement has been termed 'child-centred'.

What is recent is the rigorous examination of what this entails, since for many years, while admittedly encouraging a more humane approach to education and requiring a more careful consideration of the child's feelings and his or her reactions to educational practices, it was highly suspect theoretically, leading more to the generation of a romantic reverence for childhood than to any rigorous analysis of what education fundamentally is or should be. It is one thing to claim that education should be planned according to what we know about the nature of children; it is quite another to spell out precisely how our knowledge of children should be reflected in our educational planning. Thus some of the early theories seemed to suggest that no planning should be done at all, since they advised us to leave the child alone to develop naturally, to grow like a plant in a garden, free from the corrupting or confining influences of adults.

This lack of a properly rigorous and substantiated theoretical base for this approach to education and curriculum was also reflected in the Plowden Report (CACE, 1967); and it is probably the main reason why subsequent studies have revealed that its practice, at least in our junior schools, is not as widespread as the rhetoric might lead us to believe (Bennett, 1976; DES, 1978; Galton, Simon and Croll, 1980; Bennett *et al.*, 1984).

However, a sound theoretical base does exist and has been strengthened in recent times from two main sources. First, the pragmatist philosophy of John Dewey, which he himself applied and related quite directly to education and the curriculum, has been recognized as reinforcing this general view of educational theory and practice (Blenkin and Kelly, 1981, 1987, 1988a; Kelly, 1986), and especially, as we saw in Chapter 2, the notion that education should be seen in terms of the continuous experience of the individual, a process which 'has no ends beyond itself' and one which promotes not only the development of the individual educand, but also the evolution of knowledge and thus of human society. Second, the work which has been done in the study of children's development, especially in the cognitive sphere, by people such as Jean Piaget and Jerome Bruner, and which has been taken on in more recent times by the work of Margaret Donaldson (Donaldson, 1978; Donaldson, Grieve and Pratt, 1983), Elliot Eisner (1982) and others, as well as by Bruner's own latest work, has done much to reveal to us not only how children learn but, more importantly, how their minds develop, and has thus led to the emergence not merely of a new theory of learning but, much more crucially, of a new concept of learning, one which sees it in terms of the development of understanding rather than the acquisition of knowledge.

These developments have led to three consequences of great relevance to us here. Firstly, they have led many people to that rejection of the knowledge base for curriculum planning which we noted in Chapter 2. Secondly, they have led to the emergence of the view that educational planning must be based on clear statements of its underlying principles or of the processes it seeks to promote rather than of the goals it is concerned to attain (Stenhouse, 1975). And, thirdly, and most recently, they have led to the idea that those principles are to be found in the nature of the development of the child, that education should be seen not just as any process or series of processes but as a process of development, and that, consequently, the fundamental values of education are to be found in the nature of human development and its potentialities (Blenkin and Kelly, 1981, 1987, 1988a; Blenkin, 1988).

The first of these, the rejection of the knowledge base, we examined at some length when exploring in Chapter 2 the inadequacies many have found in the notion of curriculum as content. We need now, however, to consider the two other developments more carefully, since they constitute major elements in the case for planning the curriculum in terms of the development of the child.

CURRICULUM AS PROCESS – AIMS AND PRINCIPLES

Paul Hirst's claim (1969) that all rational activities are characterized by having clear goals or objectives has perhaps been accepted by many educationists too uncritically. For, while this may be a major characteristic of rational activity, it is certainly not peculiar to human activity, since it is quite apparent that much of the behaviour of animals is goal-directed. It is also true that much animal behaviour is characterized by the ability to generalize, since, as Mark Twain wrote, a cat who sits on a hot stove-lid will not sit on a hot stove-lid again. It is a reflection on the quality, rather than the existence, of the ability to generalize that he is able to go on to claim that such a cat will not sit on a cold stove-lid either.

What is uniquely characteristic of human behaviour and does offer a valid and important contrast with animal behaviour is that it is in many cases based on adherence to principles. Thus it might be argued that it is this feature of human behaviour which offers the most appropriate basis for planning education, so that some educationists have advised that we turn from the search for objectives of any kind and devote our attention instead to achieving agreement on the broad principles that are to inform the activity or course we are planning and in the light of which all on-the-spot decisions and modifications will be made.

Lawrence Stenhouse, for example, has suggested that 'in mounting curriculum research and development, we shall in general . . . do better to deal in hypotheses concerning effects than in objectives' (Stenhouse, 1970, p. 80). Such an approach, he is claiming, will encourage us to be much more tentative, less dogmatic and more aware of the possibility of failure and the need for corrective adjustments than statements of objectives which may lead us to feel we know where we are going without fear of contradiction. He has also suggested that we should begin by defining the 'value positions embodied in the curriculum specification or specifications' (op. cit., p. 82). Again, to do this will provide us with a clear view of the principles upon which the original planning was founded, which can act as a basis either for later changes in our procedures or for modification of these value positions themselves in the light of subsequent experience.

This is a point that Richard Pring has taken up in urging teachers and curriculum planners to seek agreement on the principles of procedure that will guide the conduct of any particular curriculum project and to concern themselves not with prespecifying goals but with statements of the norms and principles that will inform the activity of both teachers and pupils (Pring, 1973). Only thus, it is argued, will it be possible for us to reconcile the idea of rational curriculum planning with that of education as a continuous lifelong process to which terminal goals cannot be attributed.

It was on this kind of base that the Schools Council's Humanities Curriculum Project was established, making no attempt to specify learning outcomes but stating quite clearly the principles to be adhered to in the classroom. In fact this has been the practice of most curriculum projects. For where objectives are stated, these are seldom really short term, but usually have a kind of 'middle-ground' appearance and are stated in general procedural terms. In other words, they are often neither very broad educational aims nor immediate intended outcomes but rather statements of the general principles that the project team felt should underlie the work of a particular subject area. If they are to be called objectives at all, they resemble Eisner's expressive objectives rather than instructional objectives framed in behavioural terms.

What has happened, as was pointed out in Chapter 3, seems to be that many people are very confused in their thinking about objectives, so that they call what they are doing framing objectives but then proceed to make these of such a general kind that they are not objectives in the instructional and behavioural sense of the term at all, but rather expressive objectives or principles of the kind we have been discussing. Thus even the Schools Council's Science 5–13 Project, which sets out a programme of objectives with a very taxonomous look to it, is at pains at the same time to stress that all these objectives are at a level of generality such as to give both teachers and children a good deal of freedom over choices of activity, materials, experiments and so on (Schools Council, 1972). Indeed, the experience of that project points up precisely the problem we have been endeavouring to air, since its objectives could not be tightly framed without being in conflict with the enquiry approach to science that it was also at pains to promote.

We noted in Chapter 3 that most recent official pronouncements on curriculum, especially those in the HMI/DES *Curriculum Matters* series, were also inclined to offer objectives of this kind. We noted too the conceptual confusion in their attempts to divide these stated goals into 'aims' and 'objectives', suggesting that, if there is a conceptual distinction between the two terms, it can derive only from the fact that each refers to purposes of a different order and level of specificity, in other words that it implies a hierarchical and linear relationship between these different kinds of purpose. The essence of the objectives model, as we saw, is that it advocates the making of this kind of conceptual distinction and thus the establishment of this kind of linear hierarchy in which *aims* are used as the base from which more specific *objectives* are derived.

The essence of the process approach is that what is derived from what are stated as overall aims is not a series of short-term goals or objectives but rather a detailing of the principles which are inherent in those aims and which are to inform and guide subsequent practice – a breaking down of an aim such as 'the development of literary awareness' not into an elaborate series of sub-goals or objectives (beginning with something like 'performing in such a way as to indicate that he or she has mastered the uses of the letter "a" '), but into a clear listing of what literary awareness means, what its essential elements are, what its constituent processes are, so that we can plan the work and the activities of pupils throughout in the light of the principles these give rise to.

Thus the model allows us to have our goals, purposes, intentions, aims as educators but frees us from the necessity of seeing these as extrinsic to the educational process and from the restrictions of having only one, step-by-step, predetermined route to their achievement. It allows us to have our content, but frees us from the need to select this by reference to anything other than the principles inherent in our aims or purposes. It thus enables us to focus attention on developing the understanding of the pupil rather than on the transmission of predetermined content or the achievement of pre-stated behavioural changes. And it provides us with a firm and clearly articulated base from which to make all the decisions that curriculum planning and educational practice require of us.

Most people do seem at root to accept that an educational curriculum must be viewed in terms of processes rather than simply content or be-havioural outcomes. One might express this by saying with Richard Peters that it is the manner rather than the matter of learning that we must look to in defining an educational activity (Peters, 1965). It is clear that even those theorists who have expressed very positive views about the content of the curriculum have at heart been more concerned with the processes of development they felt or assumed such content would promote rather than with that content itself. It is plain that Plato's advocacy of mathematics, science and dialectic was at least as much a result of his concern for the kinds of intellectual abilities they would engender in those exposed to them as of any intrinsic merits he saw in the activities themselves. It is also clearly the case that Paul Hirst's (1965) recommendation that education involves initiation into the discrete forms of knowledge or understanding he posits is prompted at least as much by the forms of rational thinking he feels they promote as by their intrinsic value, the ability to think scientifically, for example, being what the notion of education requires rather than the mere display of certain behaviours recognizable as the regurgitation of statements of scientific 'fact'. It is this too that Alfred North Whitehead (1932) was drawing our attention to when he spoke of education as 'the art of the utilization of knowledge' rather than the acquisition of 'inert ideas'. And, of course, it is this that Dewey is stressing when he asserts that all knowledge is to be seen as the developing experience of the learner.

It all comes down to the same thing fundamentally, namely that education and, therefore, the curriculum have to be planned in the light of those processes they are seen to comprise rather than in terms either of the subject-content it is claimed they should contain, or include, or a set of behavioural outcomes they are designed to promote or achieve. Aims and processes cannot be separated; the aims are reflected in the processes and the processes are embodied in the aims. As Dewey said almost a century ago in his 'educational creed', 'the process and the goal of education are one and the same thing'.

The difficulty arises when the framing of short-term goals is seen as a tight deductive process from these broader statements of aims, processes or principles. It is the relation of our short-term objectives to these longer-term aims that is the crucial issue. The model that is unacceptable for all the reasons we have listed at length is that which offers us a hierarchy of goals, beginning, for example, with the *ultimate* goals of all education, deriving from these *mediate* goals for different stages of learning, deducing from these *proximate* goals for shorter-term activities and finally drawing from these specific classroom *objectives* (Wheeler, 1967). This kind of deductive process becomes almost inevitable when one calls these broad statements of intent 'aims' and then derives shorter-term 'objectives' from them; and it is important to recognize why they are to be seen clearly as generating principles rather than objectives, as well as why this approach to curriculum planning is different from, and indeed incompatible with, an approach through the prespecification of aims and objectives.

The answer to these questions is to be found in the difference, which is more than a semantic one, between a principle and an aim. For an aim can be seen as extrinsic to the activities which constitute the attempt to attain it, while a principle is integral to those activities. An aim can be viewed as something which will be attained at a later stage in the process, while a principle must be seen to be present at every stage. Thus a teacher of young children who regards literary appreciation as an aim of education, if persuaded to adopt an objectives model and thus to see this aim as extrinsic, will be encouraged to view his or her task as 'preparatory' and to approach the teaching of reading as if it were merely a step on the road to that extrinsic goal, and so may adopt methods of teaching, perhaps unduly emphasizing the 'basic skills', which may even turn out to be counterproductive to its attainment, while one who sees it as a principle will be concerned to ensure that it should inform even the earliest steps of linguistic development. For the same reason, ideas such as those of autonomy, freedom of thought, critical awareness and all those other qualities we might include in a definition of what it means to be educated, are of as much concern to teachers in nursery schools as to those in universities. In short, the adoption of a principle ensures that the end justifies only those means which are compatible with it.

It is because aims have been seen as extrinsic by most of those concerned with major attempts at changing the curriculum in recent years that they have been tempted into proceeding to deduce from these aims more specific teaching objectives. It is because they have done this that teachers have felt the need to modify and change those objectives, as well as to accept the educational validity of some of the learning outcomes which were unintended. Where teachers have done this, however, they have usually done it in response to and in accordance with principles which they have felt to be embodied in the broader aims. It would avoid much confusion at all levels of both theory and practice if this were acknowledged, the status of such principles as the essential starting point of educational planning recognized and the principles themselves clearly articulated. Another way of putting this was once suggested to me by a friend and colleague, HMI Roger Shirtliffe, who suggested the acceptance of the maxim of the artilleryman, that if the aim is good enough the objectives are destroyed.

A further point should also be noted. If we are clear about the model of planning we are using, this will have a reciprocal effect in that we will also be clearer about our educational purposes or goals. Our view of these purposes will itself be affected, modified and changed by the way in which we plan to develop and use them – whether by deriving short-term objectives from them or translating them into principles of procedure. For this will indicate to us whether our aims are themselves to be expressed in terms of content or extrinsic goals or processes – subject-content or behavioural changes or the development of competencies. The model we adopt, then, will not just offer us a mechanism for translating aims into practice, it will influence the aims themselves from which we begin, it will reflect a particular concept of education and it will be the product of the underlying ideology of the planner. In short, every planning model, whether or not it claims to be value-neutral, has a built-in ideology, an inherent concept of education, which those who adopt or advocate it must recognize.

In summary, let us note that education must of course have aims. Much depends, however, not only on what those aims are but also on how they are conceived, whether as extrinsic or intrinsic to the educational process itself. Even more crucial is how these aims are translated into practical planning, whether they are seen as the source of working principles of a procedural kind or of a hierarchy of short-term sub-objectives. It is also vital to note that these two approaches are quite different from, and indeed incompatible with, each other. To offer educational and curricular prescriptions which do not clarify which of these two approaches they are recommending, or which, worse, like the HMI *Curriculum Matters* series, offer a mishmash of the two, is to do the opposite of 'contributing to the search for greater clarity and definition' in relation to the curriculum debate and, more seriously, to deny teachers the advantages of clear advice and a conceptually sound base for the realities of their practice. Teaching is of itself a complex activity, so that teachers should be excused the added complexities of having to cope with incoherent sets of curriculum guidelines.

The process model, then, does not suggest that in educational planning we should take no account of outcomes or products, and it is certainly not advocating that we should not have clear aims. It does propose, however, that in both the planning and the execution of an educational curriculum the major emphasis should be on the processes of development it sets out to promote, so that, if it can be said to be concerned with products or outcomes, these will be defined in terms of intellectual development and cognitive functioning rather than in terms of quantities of knowledge absorbed or changes of behavioural performance.

This takes us to that other point which we noted earlier when tracing the growth of this approach to educational planning – the idea that not only should our planning begin from statements of the procedural principles which are to underlie our practice but, further, that these principles should be derived from the view that the prime concern of the educational process is with human development.

EDUCATION AS DEVELOPMENT

Our first criticism of the objectives model of curriculum planning was that it assumes a passive model of the individual and feels it right and proper to regard education as concerned to mould the behaviour of children according to certain predetermined goals or blueprints. This must be the case with any approach to education whose prime concern is with extrinsic goals, unless, of course, those goals are set – as they seldom are in schools – by the person being educated.

The central feature of the developmental planning model is that it begins from the opposite view of human nature, of human development and of human potentiality. It sees the individual as an active being, who is entitled to control over his or her destiny, and consequently sees education as a process by which the degree of such control available to each individual can be maximized.

All the fundamental, underlying principles of the developmental model derive from this basic position, which, as was pointed out earlier, is offered not as a scientifically demonstrable theory but as the value position which its advocates adopt and which they recognize the right of others to reject, provided that they appreciate to the full what it is they are rejecting.

To begin with, if one takes this kind of view of the individual, a central feature of one's educational theory and practice must be with the development of the child's growing ability to act autonomously, so that the promotion of autonomy becomes a major principle of one's educational practice. It should be noted that this is not now being offered as a 'truth' deriving from a philosophical analysis of the concept of education, as it has been by some philosophers of education, such as Richard Peters (1965, 1966). For the conceptual analysis of the philosopher can produce neither 'truths' nor consequent prescriptions for action; it is 'words about words', an exploration of what words mean and no more than that. The case for autonomy here is rather that it is a logical consequence of the value position from which we started, the idea of the individual as an active being responsible for his or her destiny. For one cannot coherently take that view of the individual and then argue that education must be some form of moulding or indoctrinatory process.

Several further points follow from this commitment to autonomy. To exercise autonomy, people need a range of consequent capabilities. Autonomy is not merely a negative concept signifying a claim for freedom from constraints; it is also a positive notion implying the development of those capacities which will, or can, enable one to make the personal choices, decisions, judgements that autonomous living implies, and give one as much genuine control over one's destiny as is possible. Thus, to become as fully autonomous as possible as a human being, one needs to develop the greatest possible depth and breadth of understanding, one needs the capability to look critically at the world, one needs to develop the ability to make up one's own mind about the many aspects of that world. These, then, become further procedural principles to underpin our educational planning; and, again, these are not qualities whose educational justification is to be found in an analysis of the concept of education; they are necessary and logical consequences of our view of the individual.

It is for this reason that John Dewey stressed the importance of experience as the only route to anything one could describe as education – 'not knowledge but self-realization is the goal' (Dewey, 1902); that the Hadow Report (Board of Education, 1931, p. 93) claimed that 'the curriculum is to be thought of in terms of activity and experience rather than of knowledge to be acquired and facts stored'; and that present-day advocates of this approach, with the advantage of recent work in the field of developmental psychology, speak of 'active learning' as opposed to the mere learning of 'facts'. Thus education is seen as a process of growth, as the developing experience of the individual and a further procedural principle emerges by reference to which we may plan our curriculum and, perhaps more impor- tant, evaluate its effectiveness – the degree to which it supports this kind of continuous experiential and active learning.

It must follow next that this must be an individual matter. It is a nonsense to assume that this kind of active learning can be promoted in all pupils by exactly the same kind of educational diet, as provided, for example, by the new National Curriculum. This is why the advocates of this view have constantly stressed the necessity of taking into full account the needs and the interests of individual pupils (Wilson, 1971) and developing their experien- tial learning from those, of building the educational experience of each child on what that child brings to school with him or her. This is also a way of ensur- ing that the curriculum does not become the vehicle for the imposition on the child of knowledge and values which are alien to him or her (Keddie, 1971).

To all these general principles can now be added refinements of a much more detailed kind. The work of Jean Piaget (1969) drew our attention to certain important qualitative differences between the thinking of the child and that of the mature adult. This view has been refined extensively by others subsequently working in this field, especially in relation to its 'stage theory', since it has more recently been argued that what Piaget described as stages of cognitive development and suggested all must pass through in an invariant sequence if they are to reach full intellectual maturity, are rather to be seen as modes of thought or representation, all of which persist into adulthood. The important point to be emphasized here, however, is that, whether they are stages through which we must pass or modes of thought we must learn to work within, if we are to pass through them or acquire a facility within them, we will need the right kind of educational provision. Intellec- tual maturity does not just happen in the way that, at least to a very large extent, physical maturity does. There are many physically mature adults, including some who are drawing their pensions, who have never reached Piaget's final stage, that of 'formal operations', when ideas can be handled conceptually rather than only in concrete form, or have never acquired a facility with what Jerome Bruner called the 'symbolic' mode of representa- tion. Such people remain forever cognitively and intellectually stunted, and thus deprived of much of the richness life can offer to those who are helped to this level of mature thinking. They are also, perhaps more crucially, extremely limited in relation to the kind of human autonomy we suggested earlier is essential to a fully human form of existence. Thus we begin to see further, more detailed principles emerging as the basis for our educational planning and practice, principles deriving from a concern for what has been called 'the growth of competence' (Connolly and Bruner, 1974).

Once started on this train of deduction, we can go on to derive many more principles which will reflect in greater detail that basic value position from which we started. We can see, for example, how the rather simplistic notion of cultural transmission can be, indeed must be, translated into the rather more complex and sophisticated idea of access to a critical understanding of aspects of the culture in which one lives and is growing up, as well as to the important notion which Bruner also offers us of 'cultural amplifiers'. We can see how the similarly simplistic notion of instruction in various bodies of knowledge-content can and must become the more subtle notion of the selection of knowledge-content in terms of the promotion of that growth of competence, and, indeed, the achievement of greater control over the circumstances of one's life. And so we might go on. Nothing we deduce, however, will take us in any way beyond what is implicit in our basic notion of the individual as an active, autonomous being. We must also remind ourselves of the point made in the last section, that we can bring about this kind of development only if we see all these principles as ever present in the educational process and not as end-states to be achieved at some later date.

One final point needs to be made. The autonomy from which we begin is essentially a moral autonomy, since the making of autonomous decisions and judgements must imply the making of autonomous moral choices. This is why the final stage of moral development was seen by Piaget, and later by Laurence Kohlberg (1963), as the stage of autonomous moral thinking. Thus this model is not only able to cater for the moral dimension of education, indeed the whole affective dimension, in a way that others cannot (Kelly, 1986), it specifically requires of us that we face up to the idea that education is moral development, that it is thus also social development, in fact, that it must embrace the whole spectrum of affective development, and that it cannot be viewed solely in terms of cognitive or intellectual growth. Recent work in developmental psychology has highlighted the crucial importance of the social context for cognitive development itself. And Elliot Eisner has claimed with some conviction that, if development is the concern, the cognitive forms of development cannot be isolated from the affective, since 'there can be no cognitive activity which is not also affective' (Eisner, 1982, p. 28). There are many dimensions to human experience and, as Eisner (1985, p. 240) also suggests, 'the very existence of such varieties should be clue enough that they perform important functions in helping us grasp concepts of the culture in which we live'. Any form of education which ignores these affective aspects of experience, as Eisner claims schooling in western cultures does, is limited and diminished. The developmental model of curriculum regards this affective dimension as a central feature of that form of human development which it is being claimed education should be concerned to promote.

Thus the developmental model of curriculum planning goes beyond the process model in that it not only advises us to base our planning on clearly stated procedural principles rather than on statements of content or of aims and objectives but, further, it suggests that we should look to a particular view of humanity and thus of human development as the source of those principles. Further still, it would claim that this is the only view of education one can take if one sees the individual in this light, so that to reject this view of education is to reject also the view of the individual upon which it is based. Unlike the objectives model, it thus offers us an overtly stated value position from which to make our subsequent educational judgements and decisions and, unlike the content model, it encourages us to see that value position as itself problematic rather than assuming or claiming some pseudo-scientific or epistemologically objective status for it. In this way it promotes not only a particular model for educational planning but also, and perhaps more crucially, the idea that there must be continued debate about and consequent development of that model. The very notion of change, development, evolution is built into it and must therefore discourage the kind of dogmatic prescriptions we have seen emerging from other sources based on other models.

Clearly, however, as a model for educational planning, it has attracted its critics, more perhaps than either of the models we considered in earlier chapters. This may be due, at least in part, to its having lacked the kind of clear and cogent articulation it might have been given. Nevertheless, criticisms of it abound and we must now turn to a consideration of the most prominent of these.

SOME CRITICISMS OF THE DEVELOPMENTAL MODEL

In so far as this model has grown from theories variously described as 'progressive' or 'child-centred' or even as 'process', it has met with a good deal of criticism over the years. To some extent, what has now emerged has done so in response to these criticisms, so that some of them may no longer display any real cogency. It is important, however, that we consider what some have seen as weaknesses in the model, if only to be able to appreciate why certain aspects of it are often currently emphasized.

Particular attention has been focused on concepts such as 'needs', 'interests' and 'growth', which we have seen are central to this view of education and curriculum, as well as on the concept of development itself, and we must consider briefly some of the debate which has centred on each of these concepts in turn.

Needs

The idea that we should begin our curriculum planning by attempting to discover what children need is attractive. The use of children's needs, however, as a criterion of choice for planning their education has been seen by some as fraught with difficulties (Dearden, 1968, 1976; Wilson, 1971). In the first place, the argument that we can resolve questions of what anyone ought to have by reference to what they are seen to need involves an illicit process from 'is' to 'ought' which can never constitute sound reasoning and which, amongst other things, begs a good many moral and social questions. For it may be claimed that the whole fabric of society is held together by the ability of most people to go without some of the things they might feel they need in the interests of social cohesion.

Second, as many writers have pointed out, 'needs' is a value term and thus cannot of itself offer us a firm criterion of choice between needs. There can be and are many differing views and opinions concerning what children need or what any particular child needs, ranging from those of the child himself or herself to those of the politicians responsible for the public funding of the educational system. Each individual or group will assess such needs in terms of further criteria that will constitute a particular ideology, a particular view of the goals or principles of education.

In short, the term 'need' does not offer us a straight objective description of certain features of human nature that we can use as a basis for planning any kind of social or educational provision. At all but the very basic levels it is impossible to distinguish what we need from what we want or, worse, what someone else thinks we ought to want or ought to have. We must still choose between the things that people need or think they need; and again the notion of need in itself will not provide us with the criterion by reference to which we can make such choices.

The notion of 'needs' in itself, it is claimed, cannot resolve our problem, since some further basis is required from which we can evaluate both the competing needs and the different interpretations that will be offered.

However, this is one of those criticisms which it was suggested earlier have led to those recent modifications of this view which we have noted. The crux of this criticism is that the concept of 'need' offers us no help with the value issue of deciding what criteria we should or can appeal to in evaluating between needs. We have seen, however, that the main point of the developmental view has been to face that value issue, and the notion that education is, or should be, about individual development is designed to make very plain the criteria we should appeal to in evaluating children's needs. For it advises us that the main needs we are to be concerned with are the child's developmental needs, the provision of whatever experiences seem most likely to promote his or her educational development in accordance with those principles we began to unpack in the previous section. It offers us a criterion not unlike Dewey's notion of the 'experiential continuum', suggesting that the needs we should take most account of are those whose satisfaction is most likely to lead to continued growth and development.

While the notion of 'needs' in some absolute sense, then, offers us little or no help with educational planning and is thus quite properly criticized, that of 'developmental needs' is very different, and is not open to the same kinds of criticism. For it leaves us in no doubt which of the child's needs have relevance for his or her educational provision and which, therefore, we as educators must give priority to.

We will find ourselves coming to a similar conclusion when we look at that other related concept which has attracted the attention of the critics, the notion that the child's interests should form the basis for his or her education.

Interests

It is partly because of the difficulties people have found in the concept of 'needs' that we have been offered a second device by which it is suggested we can implement at a practical level the idea that education should be based on the nature of the child – a recommendation that we should base our decisions concerning the content of the curriculum on a consideration of the interests of the child. Briefly, it is suggested that we plan our curriculum not in the light of what we think to be the nature of knowledge or by reference to what appear to be the requirements of the society or culture in which we live, but in response to what we can find that is actually of interest to the children themselves.

At one level such an approach has obvious advantages. For there is no doubt that children do work better and learn more effectively when they are interested in what they are being required to do. Conversely, a lack of interest in the work teachers require of them is responsible for the failure to learn and the ultimate alienation and disaffection of many pupils. Every good teacher appreciates this elementary fact of child psychology and all teachers endeavour to make their lessons, and the work in which they are engaging their pupils, interesting in as many ways as possible. Again we note, therefore, that this kind of approach will lead to an improvement in our methodology; we will be better teachers for taking account of children's interests in planning how we will present our material to them.

Interpreted in this way, this approach to educational planning through a consideration of children's interests is no more than a methodological device for improving our teaching of what we want them to learn, by making them interested in what we feel they should be interested in or by starting from their interests and leading them on to what we want them to do.

However, there is a further and deeper level at which we have been offered this idea of children's interests as a basis for our curriculum planning. It has been suggested (Wilson, 1971) that we should actually decide on the content of our curriculum by reference to the interests of children and that we should plan our work, not in order to use these interests to achieve our own purposes but to help the children to pursue their interests more effectively and with more discrimination and to organize their experiences in such a way as to extend and deepen those interests and gain a clearer view of their intrinsic value.

If education is concerned with activities that have an intrinsic value rather than with those that are instrumental to the achievement of ends beyond themselves and if, as we have argued, it is not possible to identify certain activities as being characterized in some way as having this intrinsic merit, then we must accept that intrinsic value, like beauty, is to be found not inhering in objects or activities but in the eye of the valuer, that those activities that are intrinsically valuable are those that the children do actually value in themselves and that, as a result, a curriculum can be truly described as educational only if its content consists of those things that children value and through the pursuit of which their development will be promoted.

In brief, then, it is argued that a consideration of the interests of children is central not only to an effective methodology but also to the educational content of our curriculum. It is further argued that only an approach such as this will enable us to avoid the problems that arise when a curriculum is planned by reference to other considerations and, as a result, lacks relevance, becomes reified and leads to the total alienation of pupils from their education.

What is being recommended here is very clear. If we are to avoid all the ills that are said to follow for many pupils when teachers or others decide for them what they shall learn and thus impose their values on them, we can do this only by letting them decide what the content of their education will and should be by revealing to us what they are interested in. There are, however, several difficulties with this view and we must consider some of these now.

In the first place, the identification of children's interests is not the straightforward matter it may appear to be at first glance (White, 1964, 1967;

Wilson, 1971). Distinguishing an abiding interest from an inclination, a passing whim or a temporary fad, even at the conceptual level, is not easy and clearly we must first know what sorts of thing interests are if we are to use them as the basis of our curriculum planning.

But even if we sort that question out there still remain many difficulties in actually recognizing what we are looking for and identifying children's interests. It is clearly not enough to think only in terms of what children enjoy doing since pursuing an interest is not necessarily always a pleasurable activity, as I have often found as I have worked on this book. Some interests which people pursue with enormous devotion and enthusiasm are of a kind that appear to be characterized mainly by being 'nice when you stop'. Nor is it merely a matter of asking children what their interests are, since they cannot always tell us, and their behaviour can often be misleading, an appearance or show of interest not always being a reliable indication of the existence of a real interest in the full sense.

Thirdly, we need to know more than we do about the origins of children's interests and we need to give some thought to this before too readily accepting them as the basis of their education. A child whose home background is a very limited one is unlikely to have a very wide range of interests and we may not be doing him or her the greatest of favours by underwriting those limitations. For all children there are likely to be areas of understanding they will miss if we attend only to what they are already interested in and, even though the dangers of reification and alienation will immediately again rear their heads, there will be occasions when teachers will need to stimulate interests in children where they do not already exist. If this is not so, we run the risk of depriving some children of large areas of experience that they might otherwise have profited from. If, on the other hand, this is so, then again the presence or absence of an interest will not in itself constitute the central criterion for deciding whether a particular activity or body of knowledge should be included in our curriculum or not.

The same difficulty also arises when we consider the question of selection of interests. It is likely to be the case that some of children's interests will appear to be of a trivial kind, unless we define interest in such a way as to exclude all such. Certainly not all interests will appear to be equally valuable or important and some may even seem to require discouragement on moral or social grounds. In this context we are always given the example of the child whose interest lies in pulling wings off insects – I have never met this child myself, although I have often wanted to – and clearly in such cases the interest is not to be encouraged on the mere grounds that it is an interest. Furthermore, every child will have many interests and it will not be possible, even if it were desirable, for him or her to pursue them all, so that again choices need to be made among these interests and decisions taken as to which of them should be developed.

Again, therefore, we need some criterion of choice other than the fact that certain interests are believed to exist. As we have seen already, to say that education should be 'child-centred', in whatever sense we use the term, cannot be to be advocating complete freedom of activity for the children and, if the teacher is to play any part at all in the child's education, he or she must select the activities that he or she will encourage and promote. He or she must also decide on the directions in which he or she will promote them since there are countless ways in which an interest can be developed and not all of them will appear equally valuable or desirable.

Again, we see that it is the value issue which is being regarded as the stumbling-block, the question of the criteria of judgement we are to use in selecting the content of our curriculum, even if it has been conceded that this should be chosen from among the interests displayed by our pupils. Again, however, we might note that this kind of criticism, while it might have had some cogency when directed at earlier theories, loses some of its force when we add the idea of education as development to the mix. For again the thrust of that is to suggest that the central criterion of choice among children's interests is the degree to which their pursuit is likely to enable us to promote their continued development along the lines we set out earlier.

It is at this point that some of the theorists who have taken this kind of view introduce into the debate the notion of 'growth', suggesting that the ultimate criterion we should appeal to in making a selection among both the interests and the needs of pupils is to be found in the idea that the main function of education is to promote their continuous growth.

Growth

Much the same debate has arisen, however, from attempts to explicate the demand that we base our curriculum planning on a consideration of the nature of the child by reference to the idea of growth. For the idea of growth in itself is of little real help to educationists since what they really want to know is how, when and where they might be justified in interfering with that growth. Similarly, analogies drawn from gardening are not very helpful since the main need of the gardener is to know when to interfere with the natural development of his or her flowers, tomatoes or hops. The notion of growth in itself, it has been argued, cannot enable us to distinguish education from maturation and, therefore, cannot provide us with any of the criteria we are looking for (Dearden, 1968).

To speak of guided growth, as, for example, John Dewey does, would appear *prima facie* to beg the question or at least to do no more than push the question one stage backwards. For we now have to ask what criteria we should appeal to in deciding how to guide children's growth. Again we see that the idea of growth is helpful to us in reaching decisions about appropriate methods in education, since it suggests that these should be such as to ensure that the development of children involves fundamental and permanent changes and that their learning should not be superficial, that it should not consist of 'inert ideas' (Whitehead, 1932) that remain as outward manifestations rather than becoming inner transformations, but should involve understanding and knowledge in the full sense.

Some choice must be made, however, of the particular kinds of learning and understanding we are to help children to acquire, so that again we see it is not sufficient even to define growth in terms of guided growth towards understanding. Nor does the notion of guided growth help us in decisions of content. The idea of guidance in itself implies direction; a guided activity is an activity with an end or aim in view. However, neither the notion of growth nor that of guidance can, it is claimed, in itself offer answers to this question of direction.

Dewey's own answer to this problem is an interesting one. He is aware that growth must be directed and he is also aware that this implies the existence of some kind of goal. On the other hand, his view of knowledge, as we saw in Chapter 2, will not allow him to produce any theory that implies that teachers, parents, adults generally or even society as a whole have the answers to this question of goals, since, as we have seen, for him knowledge must be allowed to develop and evolve and this cannot happen if the knowledge of one generation is imposed on the next, no matter how gently this is done. His answer is to assert that the only criterion we can use in attempting to evaluate one kind of activity, one body of content, one set of experiences in relation to others is an assessment of the extent to which each is likely to be productive of continued experience and development. Thus he speaks of an 'experiential continuum' (Dewey, 1938, ch. 3) which is for him the essence of education as a continuous lifelong process and which offers us the principle by which we can reach decisions concerning the content of each child's curriculum, that principle being always to choose that activity or those experiences likely to be most productive of further experience. 'The educative process is a continuous process of growth, having as its aim at every stage an added capacity of growth' (Dewey, 1916, p. 54). And, furthermore, 'the criterion of the value of school education is the extent in which it creates a desire for continued growth and supplies means for making the desire effective in fact' (op. cit., p. 53). Thus he offers us the notion of development, rather than those of needs, interests or growth, as the ultimate criterion of educational choice.

There is a good deal that is of value in this concept of the teacher as one who keeps constantly open the options available to each pupil and tries to ensure continuous development and progress, forever widening horizons and steering pupils away from any experience that will have the effect of closing them down. The idea is an attractive one and as a principle to underlie all of our educational practice it would appear to be of great importance.

As a practical criterion by which we can pronounce upon the competing claims of different activities or bodies of knowledge for inclusion in a curriculum, however, it does not take us very far, as any teacher will know. Furthermore, it does not help us to decide whether or how this continuous process is to start, what experiences we are to offer pupils initially to get them started or, perhaps more important, which experiences we should steer them away from. We still require a framework of values to enable us to make choices among the many possibilities that exist for pupil activity both at the beginning of and throughout this process of education by means of continuous and productive experiences. There are many directions in which growth can be guided and many of these will be as productive and as praiseworthy as one another, just as there are many different ways in which I can train up the roses in my garden. We still need to be able to assess which of these directions is the most appropriate or likely to be the most prolific, and the idea of continuous development offers little if anything more than the idea of continuous growth itself. It will not provide us with the practical answers we need.

However, this approach to the debate does have the merit of directing our attention towards the object of the educational process, the child himself or herself. It also leads us again to ask whether we might not find more satisfactory answers to some of the fundamental questions of education by looking at it as a process or a series of processes rather than by concentrating our attention on its intended outcomes, its end-products or its content.

Again, however, what it lacks, as the critics have rightly indicated, is the value-base which will provide us with criteria of choice, a basis on which to decide on appropriate directions into which we might guide children's growth. Again, therefore, it might be claimed that the notion of education as development meets many of these criticisms and fills this crucial gap by offering us the basic values upon which a more positive theory might be built. For its view is that guided growth means growth directed towards the attainment of those competencies we discussed earlier, towards the maximization of potential, towards the achievement of the highest possible levels of functioning – cognitive, affective, psychomotor and, above all, human and moral.

If the notion of development does solve, as is being claimed, many of the difficulties which people have seen in some of the other major elements of this view of education and model of curriculum planning, there are those who have claimed that the concept of development itself needs to be analysed and explored rather more closely than the advocates of this view may have analysed and explored it hitherto. We must look finally, therefore, at what might be implied or involved in such a demand.

THE CONCEPT OF DEVELOPMENT

It should be pointed out first that it is not the intention here to discuss those criticisms which have been directed at the idea of education as concerned with some kind of natural development or maturation, the 'non-interference' view which is a major feature of Rousseau's philosophy and which has led to those *laissez-faire* approaches to teaching and those unstructured forms of learning which have been advocated by some proponents of 'child-centredness' and rightly criticized as being diametrically opposed to anything one might term 'education'. It will be clear from what has been said already that the concern here is essentially with *guided* development.

It is worth noting secondly that a major reason for this is that education cannot be planned without some reference to development, that 'formal education cannot take place without the adoption of some stance towards development' (Blyth, 1984, p. 7). Formal education cannot be conceived in any way other than as some kind of guided development. The key issue is thus the nature of that guidance. We have noted before that even content-based approaches to education have some notion of development at their base. Certainly, objectives-based approaches to curriculum are concerned to bring about certain changes in pupils' behaviour and performance, in short to develop them in certain ways. One of the strengths claimed for the developmental view of education and the process model of curriculum from which it is derived is that they both accept this as the essence of education and thus as the only logical starting point for educational planning.

The next point to be made is that, as what has just been said reveals, one can take many different views of the kind of development one is endeavouring to promote. It is thus at this point that the critics have directed their attention, pointing out that 'development' is a value-laden, normative concept, that it can mean many things to many people, or even all things to all people. There are two major aspects of this criticism we need to note.

The first is that discussions of development, particularly those which have been critical of the concept as a basis for educational planning, have tended to see it as a process leading to some kind of end-state. Thus there has been discussion of the concept of development as an aim of education (Kohlberg and Mayer, 1972), some at least of the problems of which disappear if, as was suggested earlier, we view it not in terms of extrinsic goals but of intrinsic guiding, or procedural, principles. The mistake is, as Dewey (1916, p. 50) puts it, that 'growth is regarded as *having* an end, instead of *being* an end'. We must note too that central to this concept of education as development is Dewey's notion that education is a continuous lifelong process which has no ends beyond itself but is its own end, so that it must be stressed again that to speak of education as development is to view it as a process and to focus attention on the intrinsic features of that process rather than on clearly defined extrinsic aims or goals.

We must note further that for some this concept of an end-state to human development has been interpreted in the form of some notion of the ideal or perfect human being. This is perhaps most obvious in Plato's discussions of education and of society, but it is no less significant, even if it is less overt, in modern versions of philosophical rationalism (Kelly, 1986). If we have some concept of human perfection, as rationalism clearly has, we must see education as a process by which people can be led towards this state. It is perhaps worth noting too that, on this view, childhood is regarded as some kind of imperfect and inferior form of existence, from the inadequacies of which children are to be liberated, as from the 'original sin' of Christian theology. The view of education which is being explicated here, however, as we have seen on several occasions, begins from a rejection of this notion of human perfection, regarding it in fact as a quite meaningless concept, since it is a view which rejects that rationalist epistemology which is essential to such a concept. Again, therefore, it must eschew the notion of an end-state to the process of development, since its basic epistemological stance renders such a notion illogical. On the other hand, as we have also seen, it is an approach which is predicated on a view of the child's thinking as being qualitatively different from that of the adult, so that it must see the educational process as concerned to liberate children from the limitations imposed by these early and primitive levels of cognitive functioning. To say that, however, is not to say that it is a process directed towards some definable end-state; it is merely to say that its concern is with the enhancement of capability, the extension of the individual's powers, competencies and, in general, control over his or her environment and, indeed, destiny.

This takes us naturally to the second major aspect of this criticism. For this concept of the end-state of development has led some critics into the value issue. Thus, Paul Hirst and Richard Peters ask:

> What, too, at the human level, corresponds to the mature oak-tree or elephant which represents the end-state of plant or animal development? Does not human life offer a great variety of possibilities of development? And do not these depend partly on cultural pressures and partly on individual choice – factors which do not apply at the plant or animal level? And is not our conception of such an end-state irredeemably valuative in nature?
>
> (Hirst and Peters, 1970, p. 45)

Their own answers to these questions are of course to be found in their adherence to that rationalist epistemology which they also espouse. On their view, only certain kinds of development are appropriately fostered by education, namely the development of those God-given forms of rationality of which they also speak. Thus, for them, education is not just any kind of development; it is the development of the rational mind along all of the several dimensions of rationality they claim to have identified. And their criticism of the concept of education as development stems from the fact that in itself it appears not to go as far as they would want it to go in identifying the particular kinds of development it is concerned with.

It will be plain, however, from what has already been said in this chapter, that the notion of education as development it has been concerned to analyse and explicate is one which recognizes only too clearly the need to be quite specific about the forms of development it is concerned with, and thus the value positions implicit in its stance. A major difference, however, and one which reveals the heart of the problem, is that while Hirst and Peters, and indeed the whole band of rationalist philosophers of education, have sought to answer these questions through their analysis of the nature of knowledge, an analysis whose weaknesses we identified in Chapter 2, those who are currently offering this as a theory of education and as a model for curriculum planning are doing so on the basis of explorations of the nature of children's thinking, of aspects of their cognitive development and an analysis of the nature of human cognition.

The contribution of developmental psychology to educational theory has been seen, again especially by those whose prime concern has been with the knowledge-content of education (Lawton, 1975), as primarily, perhaps solely, methodological, offering advice, especially through its (now largely outmoded) stage theory of cognitive development, on *how* we might best promote children's knowledge and understanding in the major areas which rationalist epistemology has attempted to identify. The central point of the developmental view of education, however, is that it shifts the focus of attention from the knowledge-content to the child's levels of cognitive functioning. Thus, while it might accept the view that education should set out to promote scientific thinking or understanding and mathematical thinking and understanding, it is the thinking and the understanding which are its central concern, not the mathematics or the science. It thus stresses the need for teachers to understand how these forms of thinking and understanding can be developed rather than to possess themselves vast stores of mathematical or scientific knowledge. Its central concerns are with the development of the child's intellectual capacities, with what we saw earlier has been called the 'growth of competence' (Connolly and Bruner, 1974), so that it offers not merely a new methodology but a whole new concept of education.

Development is thus not the vague concept its critics have claimed; nor are its advocates unaware of the need to specify very clearly their value stance, the forms of development they are concerned to promote. These can be specified with increasing clarity as a result of the recent work of developmental psychologists (Donaldson, 1978; Wells, 1981a and b; Donaldson, Grieve and Pratt, 1983; Tizard and Hughes, 1984) and of those curriculum theorists who have been attempting to translate this work into curricular terms (Eisner, 1982; Blenkin and Kelly, 1987, 1988a; Blenkin, 1988). They can be clearly seen to include development through all the stages of cognitive functioning or command of all the modes of representation which this work has identified; they embrace development of the ability to operate on all dimensions of human functioning – moral, social and affective as well as cognitive; they include a facility for thinking within whatever forms of understanding we might identify – mathematical, scientific, historical and so on – provided that we appreciate that the significant differences are those in the thinking processes themselves not in the knowledge-content towards which they might be directed; and they can be seen to add up to a deliberate process of maximizing the individual's powers and widening his or her horizons in the interests of the greatest possible enrichment of experience and control over one's destiny, placing, as the Hadow Report, *Infant and Nursery Schools* (Board of Education, 1933), suggested, 'less weight on the imparting of an ordered body of knowledge and more on the development of the child's innate powers'.

This concept of development, then, while it can be, and in some discussions clearly has been, vague and thus unhelpful in educational planning, need not be so. Recent work in fact is enabling us to be increasingly clear and specific about what it does entail. And the fact that it is a concept which is manifestly value-laden is offered by its advocates as a positive strength, rather than a weakness, since it acknowledges the value-laden nature of the educational process itself and seeks neither to avoid the implications of that, as the objectives model does, nor to resolve it by an appeal to some highly problematic notion of the God-given status of certain kinds of knowledge, like the content model. It is thus seen by its advocates as offering a more satisfactory, and certainly more honest, basis for curriculum planning, since it requires that we analyse and make quite explicit what our educational ideology is rather than pretend that we do not have one.

The process/developmental model of curriculum planning, therefore, has the merit of taking account of all the many dimensions of education and curriculum – purposes, principles, values, content. It thus may be seen to have certain advantages over the other models which, as we have seen, emphasize one or another of these features but cannot effectively embrace them all.

It also has the merit of offering a theoretical model which might be recognized as reflecting more accurately, and thus supporting more constructively, the realities of educational practice. For teaching, especially that which purports to be educational, cannot often be undertaken by reference merely to its subject-matter. And only seldom, and then at very low levels, is it a linear, step-by-step process. It requires the making of day-to-day and even minute-by-minute decisions; it is a complex process of interaction between teacher and taught. It thus needs a planning model which will ensure that those interactions reflect the complexities of the sophisticated goals from which it starts. This the translation of those goals into procedural principles offers to teachers in a way that the attempt to reduce them to ever more simplified objectives can never do.

It has been said that this approach to education is idealistic and, indeed, unrealistic. It is, however, no more idealistic than those notions of education as initiation into intrinsically worthwhile activities which we have noted on several occasions. And if it requires of teachers higher levels of professional performance, so be it. There are many teachers who are already doing a most effective job in implementing this kind of curriculum, perhaps especially in some of our nursery and first schools. And if we are right in suggesting that it reflects more closely the actualities of most teachers' practice, to adopt it fully requires little more than that they reflect more deeply on that practice and the theoretical considerations which underpin it. In fact, a further merit of this model is that it demands what Lawrence Stenhouse (1975, p. 123) called 'an evaluative response', suggests 'a further possibility which I shall call here *the research model*' (ibid.) and takes us towards his notion of 'the teacher as researcher' which we shall look at in more detail when we consider strategies for curriculum change and development in the next chapter. Education is a complex undertaking. It is all too often viewed in simplistic terms by those outside the school. If teachers themselves shy away from its complexities, then all is certainly lost.

CURRICULUM PLANNING MODELS

Now that we have considered the main features of the three models of curriculum planning we have identified, it might be worthwhile to attempt briefly to pull some general points together.

First of all, let us note that we have here three different approaches to the question of the purposes of education – one which sees these in terms of the acquisition of knowledge, whether seen as intrinsically valuable or as economically useful, a second which has no kind of view of what the aims of education are or should be but offers us a mechanism for achieving those we have decided to pursue, and a third which puts to us the notion of education as the promotion of human development. The last two offer us also a methodology, the aims and objectives model advising us to break down our aims (once we have decided on them) into a series of sub-aims or objectives, the process model suggesting that we would be better advised to translate our aims into procedural principles by reference to which we can undertake both our preplanning and our practice.

The underlying differences between these models, then, and the reasons for their differing recommendations are to be found in their approach to the question of what education is, their concept of education. The first sees it either in terms of initiation into bodies of knowledge deemed to be intrinsically worthwhile or as the acquisition of useful knowledge. The second has no concept of education at all but attempts to maintain a value-neutral stance. And the third has a concept of education as a process of continuous growth and development, which can be promoted only through adherence to certain clearly articulated principles of procedure and practice.

Each offers us too a distinctive view of the role of content in the curriculum and quite different criteria for the selection of curriculum content. The first sees the role of content as central and finds the criteria of selection in the content itself – either its presumed intrinsic value or its usefulness. The objectives model places its aims and objectives first and offers these as the criteria for selecting content, suggesting that we select that content which seems to be most likely to help us to achieve our objectives. The process model requires us to select that content which will promote the processes or the forms of development which are its concern and to make such selection in the light of the procedural principles derived from these.

The next point we should note is that, since these models are based on quite different views of the purposes of schooling, quite different concepts of education, and quite different notions of the role of subject-content in the curriculum and the basis for selecting this, as well as offering quite different schemes for educational practice, it is important that anyone undertaking curriculum planning should be absolutely clear about the fundamental conceptual differences between them. We have already noted the failure of the HMI/DES *Curriculum Matters* series of publications (DES, 1984a, 1985a, b, c, d, 1986a, b, 1987b, c) to recognize the important differences between the concepts of 'aims', 'objectives', 'principles' and 'processes' or at least their failure to achieve clarity in their own use of these terms. It is worth noting also here the tendency of those documents to see those differences they do recognize as being merely methodological. Thus the authors of *Curriculum Matters 2* (the only non-subject-specific contribution to the series, to which one might look for some understanding of general curriculum issues) view approaches to the primary curriculum not as reflecting a different concept of education and its purposes, that concept, for example, which is encapsulated in the Plowden Report (CACE, 1967), but merely as a different method of achieving the goals of transmitting predetermined knowledge-content, telling us that 'parts of the programme for the younger children may be organised through carefully planned activities, such as domestic role play and the use of constructional toys, within which desired knowledge and understanding can be developed' (op. cit., p. 8). It would seem clear from this that a major reason why this series attempts no justification or explication of whatever its model of curriculum is and why it also reveals such conceptual muddle is that its authors do not recognize the existence of different concepts of education but only of different methodologies.

This complete lack of conceptual clarity and the failure to recognize the fundamental distinctions we have seen to be crucial to productive curriculum planning come out most clearly in the following passage in which notions of aims, objectives, content, intrinsic value, development and others are hopelessly interwoven:

> The criteria for selecting content should be in the aims and objectives which the school sets for itself. That which is taught should be worth knowing, comprehensible, capable of sustaining pupils' interest and useful to them at their particular stage of development and in the future. It should be chosen because it is a necessary ingredient of the areas of learning and experience or because it has an important contribution to make to the development of the concepts, skills and attitudes proposed.
>
> (DES, 1985c, p. 37)

It must be stressed, then, that adequate curriculum planning requires a full recognition of the deep conceptual differences between these approaches to education and curriculum and of the fundamentally different forms of practice they lead to and demand.

It follows from this that curriculum planners must not only recognize the need to make informed choices between these alternative approaches, they must also have clear reasons for the choices they make and they should be prepared to make these reasons plain. It is quite unacceptable for anyone to plan a curriculum or a piece of work, at any level, without first setting out quite clearly, whether for himself or herself or for others, the curriculum model adopted and the reasons for its adoption. For, as we have seen, this choice is not only of a methodology, it involves also a concept of education, and, indeed, of humanity. It is thus inexcusable for curriculum statements and prescriptions, again like those in the *Curriculum Matters* series, which are offered as guidance to the whole educational system, to refuse or to fail to do this. All curricular recipes must be based on a clear concept of education and a clear model of curriculum planning, and they must make plain their reasons for adopting these. Otherwise, they are at best unhelpful and at worst dishonest.

The emergence of several, clearly defined approaches to education and curriculum planning, then, has offered teachers and all other would-be curriculum planners a range of choices. It has also imposed on them the consequent requirement that they consider these choices very carefully in their planning and that they have good reasons for their decisions. There is, or should be, no longer any excuse for that muddle or lack of clarity which has characterized curriculum planning and thus diminished educational practice for far too long.

SUMMARY AND CONCLUSIONS

In this chapter the attempt has been made to show how the inadequacies identified in the approach to curriculum planning from the perspective of its content, which we explored in Chapter 2, and the approach through the prespecification of objectives, which we considered in Chapter 3, have led to the emergence of a third planning model, which requires that we start with an analysis of the processes we are concerned to promote and a statement of the procedural principles which are to inform all our practice if we are to succeed in promoting them.

At one level, it may be possible to regard this model as also being value-neutral, as offering us a blueprint for whatever processes we might decide to promote. Its essence, however, or its first premise, is a very clear and specific concept of education, as a process by which the individual is to be assisted towards the highest levels of autonomous human functioning, so that at root it is not value-neutral but rather reveals a very positive ideological stance, and offers a clear basis from which all its procedural principles can be derived. This, we saw, is claimed by its advocates to be one of its major strengths, since, they claim, education itself is not a value-neutral process, so that curriculum models based on the idea that it is, or can be, as well as those based on some spurious notion of the objectivity of educational values are at best unsatisfactory because they do not grasp the ideological nettle, or at worst dishonest because they pretend it is not there to be grasped.

We then went on to see how, in more recent times, this notion of curriculum as process has progressed into the idea of education as development, a concept which it has become increasingly easy to explicate quite specifically in terms of the aspects and dimensions of human development, in both the cognitive and the affective fields, which have been dramatically revealed by recent research in developmental psychology and by the application of that research to studies of the curriculum.

We looked also at some of the criticisms which have been offered of this view, especially those focusing on what have been seen as its major concepts – needs, interests, growth and development itself. An important and common thread running through these criticisms is that these concepts are normative, that they are value-laden. It was suggested again, however, that the advocates of this view would see that as a strength rather than as a weakness, and that the essence of their view is that all educational planning is by definition normative and value-laden, that it is all ideological, and that, this being so, the only satisfactory starting point for such planning is in a clear and honest statement of the norms, the values, the ideology from which it is being undertaken.

It is also claimed that it is a model which reflects more appropriately the actualities of the teacher's task and role in relation to the education of pupils. For it allows for the interactive nature of the educational relationship in a way that the other models cannot – not least by providing the teacher with a clear set of principles as a basis for the making of day-to-day, minute-by-minute professional judgements, rather than offering a rigid syllabus of content to be transmitted or a fixed hierarchy of objectives to be achieved. This is a point which takes us naturally into an exploration of the strategies of curriculum planning and change which is the subject of the next chapter.

5
STRATEGIES FOR CURRICULUM CHANGE AND DEVELOPMENT

We have noted in the earlier chapters of this book that if curriculum development is to be promoted and if curriculum change is to be effected, a good deal of attention must be given to the choice of a suitable theoretical model for curriculum planning and, in particular, to some important questions about the kind of emphasis which can or should be placed on the selection of curriculum content and the use of curriculum objectives. In later chapters we will also note the account which must be taken of a vast range of constraints and influences which together provide the context within which curriculum change and development must occur. This chapter will address itself to questions concerning the possible strategies which might be employed for changing the curriculum, the techniques which have been or may be used in attempts to bring about curriculum change or to accelerate and smooth the path of curriculum development.

First of all we will look at the role of national agencies in curriculum development. This will be done through a review of the work of two such agencies – the Schools Council, which, until its demise in 1984, was for twenty years the major national agency for curriculum development in the United Kingdom, and the Department of Education and Science's Assessment of Performance Unit (APU), which has recently been attempting to take on that kind of national role. Secondly, we will explore some of the problems of disseminating curriculum innovations, by looking at some of the models of dissemination which have been either postulated or employed and by considering their relative effectiveness. And thirdly, since this kind of exploration must lead to a questioning of the role of a centralized agency in curriculum development, since in fact the main lesson to be learnt from a study of dissemination techniques is that local initiatives have always been more effective than national projects in bringing about genuine change, we will examine the theory and the practice of school-based curriculum development, and the associated concepts of 'action research' and 'the teacher as researcher'.

NATIONAL AGENCIES FOR CURRICULUM DEVELOPMENT

The Schools Council

It was suggested in Chapter 1 that planned curriculum development, at least at the level of secondary education, is a relatively recent phenomenon, that the 'unplanned drift' (Hoyle, 1969a), resulting from the product of external pressures, which characterized such change as the curriculum once sustained, was replaced by attempts at deliberate planning and curriculum construction only in the late 1950s and early 1960s. This was largely as a result of a concern felt throughout the western world that it might be falling behind in the race for technological advancement.

In the United Kingdom that period saw the beginning of a number of attempts to change the curriculum, supported in some cases by the injection of money for research from such bodies as the Nuffield Foundation, until all these threads were drawn together by the establishment in October 1964 of the Schools Council for the Curriculum and Examinations, whose brief was 'to undertake research and development work on the curriculum, and to advise the Secretary of State on matters of examination policy' (Lawton, 1980, p. 68). It was to be funded jointly by the Department of Education and Science and the local education authorities. It is worth noting also, that its constitution implicitly endorsed the idea of teacher control of the curriculum, in that teacher members formed a majority on virtually all of its committees.

Once established, the Council began its task by identifying its major programmes of work, and, in doing so, it directed its attention towards six main areas of interest: the primary school curriculum, the curriculum for the early leaver (the Newsom Report (CACE, 1963) had just recommended the raising of the school leaving age to sixteen), the sixth form, the English programme, GCE and CSE examinations and the special needs of Wales.

It is clear that from the very outset the duality of the role given to the Council – its responsibility for both curriculum development and the public examination system – was a major factor in determining its policies and its actions. For its task was to maintain a balance between two potentially conflicting elements of the education system (Becher and Maclure, 1978). There is no doubt that these two must be planned in phase, not least because, as we shall see when we consider in Chapter 6 some of the external constraints on curriculum planning and development, the public examination system is probably the most influential of these. For the same reason, however, it is apparent that the Council's inability to bring about significant changes in the examining system severely limited its effectiveness in promoting curriculum change. For its advice on examinations was never taken seriously by the Department of Education and Science, as is demonstrated by its many unavailing attempts to bring about significant changes in the system of public examinations for sixth forms (Schools Council, 1978a, 1979), and its attempts to introduce a common system of examinations at sixteen-plus (Schools Council, 1971a, 1975b), a change which was only recently given official sanction and was implemented through the General Certificate of Secondary Education in 1988.

As a result, this dual role also determined the major flavour of its work at least during the first ten years of its life. For, like the examinations system, its work was largely subject-based and this made it difficult for it to respond to changes of focus within the curriculum. In particular, it led it to adopt a differentiated approach to curriculum planning which was rightly criticized as based on a particular and erroneous view of educational knowledge (Young, 1973). For, while it could be claimed that it was at its most influential in recommending changes in the curriculum for the less able pupil in the secondary school – its ROSLA programme – it must also be recognized that its influence here often took the form of advising schools to offer such pupils a different curriculum, consisting largely of low-status knowledge and little else (Kelly, 1980a). In fairness, it must be conceded that, while such criticism was quite justified, its errors in this area were due to ignorance and inexperience rather than to sinister intent; it must also be acknowledged that one or two projects, such as the Humanities Curriculum Project (Schools Council, 1970), realized the errors of these ways and attempted to avoid them. It must be stressed, however, that this trend in its work was the very natural result of both the subject-based approach which a monolithic examination system dictated and the greater ease with which the curriculum for the less able 'non-examinable' pupil could be changed, precisely because it is, or was, largely unconstrained by the demands of public examinations.

A second criticism which was prompted by this subject-based approach was directed at the failure of the Council to view the curriculum as a whole and to plan curriculum development as a totality. Again, one must recognize that its attempts to do so, by first changing the examination system to make this possible, were frustrated by the unwillingness of outside bodies to accept the changes proposed, as, for example, in the case of the attempts to broaden the sixth-form curriculum which were embodied in the proposals for N and F level examinations (Schools Council, 1978a). One must concede also, however, that even in the area of the primary school curriculum, where comparable constraints did not exist and where tradition might be said to favour the idea of total curriculum planning, the main influence of the Council led to a move towards a more subject-based approach and away from rather than towards the planning of the curriculum as a whole (Blenkin and Kelly, 1981, 1987). The current emphasis on the need for 'balance' in the curriculum can be seen as a direct result of the failure to achieve this kind of total planning and of the completely unbalanced curriculum experienced by many pupils in the upper reaches of the secondary schools which it has resulted in (DES, 1979). Again, it would be unfair to lay this charge entirely at the door of the Schools Council or to fail to acknowledge that its procedures must be seen largely as the product of its dual brief. Its contribution to this trend, however, must be recognized.

A third aspect of the work of the Schools Council which attracted criticism was the encouragement it offered to most of its projects to adopt an objectives-based planning model. Again it might be claimed that this was an inevitable consequence of its parallel concern for examinations. It must also be conceded that this was understandable in the context of the general climate existing at the time when it was established. Whatever the reasons, however, it is clear that from the beginning the Council was concerned not only that, in order to demonstrate its proper use of public funds, the work of all its projects should be evaluated, but inclined also to the view that this could best be done, perhaps could only be done, if they began by making clear statements of their objectives. There were, of course, notable exceptions to this general trend, among which again was the Humanities Curriculum Project (Schools Council, 1970), but these exceptions merely prove the rule and there is no doubt that as a whole the Schools Council added its weight to that growing trend towards regarding this as the only proper basis for curriculum planning, a trend which we both noted and vigorously questioned in earlier chapters. The link between the prespecification of objectives and the evaluation of the curriculum we will explore more fully in Chapter 8; we must merely note here that the Schools Council can be criticized for lending its general support, at least in its early years, to the view that this link is non-problematic, although this must be offset by a recognition of what some of its projects contributed to the opening up of this issue.

Lastly, we must note that a further major criticism was directed at the methods of dissemination adopted by many of the Schools Council's projects. Again, we will look at the problems of the dissemination of curriculum innovation later in this chapter. We must comment here, however, that on the evidence of its own Impact and Take-Up Project (Schools Council, 1978b, 1980) the work of the Council was less effective than one would have hoped and that this was to a large extent attributable to the forms of dissemination it adopted, particularly in its early years, or to its failures to pay adequate attention to the problem of dissemination. This criticism too is easily made from hindsight and its approach here should perhaps be seen as typical of, if not inevitable in, the context of the first ten years of its work. However, it must also be seen as contributing to the growing criticism of that work, and as a factor in its ultimate demise.

The force of most of these criticisms was recognized by those responsible for the work of the Council, so that its later years saw new trends arising from the emerging inadequacies of the old. There was a broadening of scope, for example, which saw some projects extending their sphere of interest down the age range and a general move towards seeing the curriculum as a whole. There was also a development away from the starkest forms of objectives-based planning, as more sophisticated forms of evaluation were developed. The emergent problems of dissemination, too, led to a greater concentration on the idea of supporting local, school-based initiatives.

However, it is quite clear not only that the early patterns and structure adopted by the Schools Council influenced curriculum development generally but also that they acted as a continuing constraint on its own work and thus inhibited these later developments (Blenkin, 1980). It is equally clear that they provided ammunition for those who argued that a teacher-controlled Schools Council had failed to make a significant impact on the curriculum of the schools. It might be claimed that the success of the Schools Council is to be judged not by its direct influence on curriculum change but by the contribution its work made to promoting debate about the curriculum, to extending awareness of the complexities of curriculum planning and to creating an interest and concern for curriculum issues among teachers. But the influence of the Council's work on general development in both the theory and the practice of curriculum change, while it may be very extensive, is difficult, if not impossible, to quantify, while its failure to achieve direct changes through its own projects was manifest from the evidence of its own Impact and Take-Up Project (Schools Council, 1978b, 1980). Its attempts to learn from the inadequacies of its earlier practices, then, were thwarted not only by those practices themselves but also by the strength they added to the case of its opponents.

These criticisms of the achievements of the Schools Council under a system of teacher control, then led, first, to its reconstitution. For the move to reduce the teachers' control of the curriculum, which we will explore in Chapter 7, gained strength from the criticisms by outsiders of its work (Lawton, 1980), and also from the economic stringency which led to the availability of less money for curriculum development. Thus the main thrust of the reconstitution of the Council was towards reducing the influence of teachers in the formation of its policies and increasing that of many other bodies with an interest in education. In short, in unison with the general trends of the time, it was designed to open educational policy to public debate, and thus to bring it under the control of the administrators.

One major reason for this reorganization can be seen to be its political and economic desirability. We must acknowledge, however, that there may have been good educational reasons for it too. Many of the criticisms we discussed earlier came from within the profession and their strength has to be recognized. Some kind of reconstitution, therefore, was needed and it is clear that this resulted in some important structural and policy changes.

For its research became concentrated, as one of the Council's information pamphlets issued at that time told us, in five main areas:

- purpose and planning in schools, i.e. the effectiveness of a school's staff as a professional team
- helping teachers to develop their skills
- aspects of the curriculum, including content and pupil's skills, ideas and attitudes
- the needs of particular groups of children such as those in ethnic minorities, the disrupted [*sic*] and the gifted
- fairness, accuracy and uniformity of standards across the examination system.

This led to the establishment of major programmes, one in each of these areas – Organization in Schools, Helping Teachers' Professional Development, Developing the Curriculum for a Changing World, The Needs of Individual Pupils, and Improving the Examination System.

Finally, it should also be noted that although this new constitution reduced the involvement of teachers at the top level of management of the Council, they retained a strong membership of the Professional Committee and greater numbers of practising teachers participated in the earlier development stages of curriculum projects.

It will be clear from this that many of the lessons of the early years of the Council's work had been learnt and attempts were being made to respond to the criticisms we listed earlier by putting right some of the inadequacies of the early policies which they were directed at. In doing this, however, this new policy itself raised further questions. For example, while the

importance of school-based curriculum development had come to be acknowledged, as we shall see later, it is not yet established that this is best
supported by a national development policy rather than by local agencies.
Nor is it clear that this kind of policy is the best way to raise the quality of
teachers. In fact, many doubts continue to exist about the viability of
attempts to effect changes in the curriculum by establishing some kind of
national policy, especially when the body created to do this has a role which
is merely advisory and lacks the power to implement its policies in any way.

Problems of this kind and the criticisms they led to were the major stated
reasons why the funding of the Council was withdrawn in 1984. There is no
doubt, however, that there were also significant underlying political reasons
for this action, as we shall see when we explore the political context of
curriculum change and development more fully in Chapter 6. This was
clearly a step towards the establishment of the new National Curriculum
and, in that context, perhaps the greatest significance of this action is that it
had the effect of removing the only major source of politically independent
research in education and the only politically free agency for curriculum
change and development.

Its role in curriculum development was in theory to be taken over by the
School Curriculum Development Council (SCDC), but this is clearly a
politically controlled body and has had little impact on either curriculum
development or the curriculum debate since it was established. In effect, the
role of national agency for educational research and curriculum development has since that time been taken over by the Assessment of Performance
Unit. As a branch of the Department of Education and Science, this body
too can hardly claim to be politically independent or free of political
influence, not least in so far as its policies, and indeed its publications, must
always have ministerial approval. However, it has, especially in recent
years, made significant efforts to adopt the role of a national agency for
curriculum development, so that it will be worth our while here to give some
attention to its work.

The Assessment of Performance Unit (APU)

The APU was not originally intended as an agency for developing the
curriculum in any sense. Rather, as we shall see when we consider the
build-up of political pressures on the school curriculum in Chapter 6, it was
one of the more obvious examples of the attempt to create mechanisms for
the monitoring of standards of attainment in schools. Several events foreshadowed the creation of the APU (Lawton, 1980), as we shall see, but the
intention to establish it was first announced officially in a government White

Paper in 1974, and it came into existence in the following year.

Its terms of reference made clear its role as an agency for monitoring attainment, since among those terms of reference we see 'to promote the development of methods of assessing and monitoring the achievement of children at school, and to seek to identify the incidence of underachievement'; and it is worth remembering that these continue to be its stated purposes. It was also said at the time by Rhodes Boyson that he wanted 'national monitoring to be used for firing heads and teachers' (Mack, 1976, p. 603), so that it is not surprising to learn that its birth was greeted with a good deal of suspicion and hostility, especially by curriculum theorists such as Michael Young (1976), Denis Lawton (1980) and myself in the first edition of this book in 1977.

The APU worked very hard in the early years to divest itself of this image. It stressed the complete anonymity of its monitoring exercises, which are conducted in such a manner as to make it impossible to identify individual pupils, teachers or schools. It emphasized its light sampling techniques and the fact that no child is ever exposed to a full battery of tests. It made much of the voluntary nature of its activities, children being tested only in schools to which the headteacher grants testers access. Above all, it laid no claim to any role in curriculum development; 'we are not a covert agency for curriculum development', claimed one of the administrative heads of the Unit, Jean Dawson (1984, p. 126). Indeed, the manner in which it set about its task was chosen specifically in an attempt to avoid influencing the school curriculum in any way.

Inevitably, however, the activities of a unit of this kind, especially in the light of its political origins, cannot fail to influence the curriculum, or at least the way in which teachers view the curriculum (Kelly, 1987). The projects undertaken, certainly in the early years of the APU's existence, were focused on particular school subjects, so that they had the effect of tightening subject boundaries (Hextall, 1983) and, perhaps more important, of discouraging teachers from viewing the curriculum in any terms other than those of its content, its component subjects and its 'objectives'; in short, the approaches adopted seemed to rule out any concept of curriculum as process. The choice of subjects also could not fail to have some effect. There is a strong likelihood that the subjects chosen – mathematics, language, science, modern languages and, most recently, design and technology – have gained status from being selected, so that they are given a central place by schools in the planning of curricula. Conversely, there is likely to be some loss of status for other subjects. There are even more serious implications for those areas of the curriculum or aspects of education which the APU explored and then subsequently decided, for one reason or another, that it could not, or should not, monitor – physical development, aesthetics and personal and social development. A further aspect or result of this is that the emphasis has been on cognitive aspects of the curriculum at the expense of and to the detriment of those, less easy to assess or monitor but perhaps educationally more important, affective dimensions of schooling. Finally, it is worth noting the influence on the subjects which have been monitored of the view of those subjects that is reflected in the monitoring instruments devised. Many different definitions of any subject are possible; that of the testers must be reflected in any kind of monitoring exercise or, worse, that definition which results from the inevitable emphasis on those aspects of the subject that can be tested. This lay behind Maurice Holt's criticism of the activities of the APU on the grounds that 'they are attempts to reduce a complex and ultimately impenetrable process to measurable outcomes' and that 'inevitably, these attempts present a distorted view of what they claim to measure' (Holt, 1981, p. 80).

Thus, although every attempt was made to avoid any suggestion that the Unit's work was intended to influence the school curriculum, few remained convinced that its work could be done without such influence and, indeed, some even questioned whether that work could have any point if the school curriculum were not to be affected by it (Kelly, 1987).

For these reasons, along with others, in the last few years the Unit has moved into a second phase, in which it has accepted responsibility for curriculum development and, in doing so, has attempted to broaden its conception of curriculum and thus the scope of its research and analysis. Some of the work of the science team, for example, has reflected a concern with processes rather than merely with content or skills – 'a genuine testing of scientific performance', as it has been described (Brown, 1980, p. 79). Attempts have been made too to get away from that 'distorting' practice of breaking every subject down into skills and sub-skills for monitoring, the disintegration of subjects into lists of countless 'performance indicators', and to achieve more holistic forms of testing. The English (language) team has developed quite sophisticated testing techniques, for example, to reflect its view that 'the ability to write, although dependent on separable skills, consists not merely of the mastery of techniques (such as spelling, sentence division and punctuation) but of their incorporation into a complex of cognitive and social abilities' (APU, 1982, p. 93). And the most recently created team, that established to monitor design and technological capability, has not only taken on this holistic approach and adopted a procedural definition of design and technological activity (Kelly *et al.*, 1987), it has also, because of the cross-curricular nature of its brief, found itself perforce transcending traditional subject boundaries. This in turn has led to the beginnings of some informal, or semi-formal, cross-curricular collaboration between all the subject teams. Finally, the design and technology team has also devoted some attention to the question of defining the subject or area of the curriculum it is concerned with (Kelly *et al.*, 1987), so that this too has had the effect of extending the scope of its survey to embrace conceptions of the subject as well as standards of pupils' attainment within it.

This process by which the monitoring exercise has slowly turned itself into a more widely conceived form of curriculum research has been matched by a change in the Unit's publication policy, the main purpose of which is to make its findings more readily available and accessible to teachers. Lengthy and detailed reports are now supplemented by shorter publications written specifically for teachers. Videotapes have also been produced and made available; and conferences have been organized to enable those teachers involved in APU surveys to share their understandings with others. There have also been other moves to encourage existing teams to turn attention towards a more positive research and development role and away from a single-minded concentration on the monitoring of performance. The Children's Learning in Science project at Leeds is one example of a unit whose focus is now on the development of new approaches to teaching, in the light of APU findings; and the Foreign Language survey team has also been concerned to develop test instruments which were originally generated for the monitoring exercise into materials for in-school use.

The APU itself, however, is to be allowed to wither away once existing contracts have been fulfilled, and its role will be taken over by the two bodies created by the 1988 Education Act to oversee the new National Curriculum – the School Examinations and Assessment Council (SEAC) and the National Curriculum Council (NCC).

This highlights what is perhaps the major weakness of the APU as a national agency for curriculum development. Its researches have of necessity to concentrate on assessment rather than evaluation. This is a distinction we will explore more fully in Chapter 7. We must note again here, however, that curriculum development requires that we ask deeper and more sophisticated questions about the curriculum than merely how well children are assimilating what is being offered to them or even what factors are inhibiting their assimilation of it. It requires, as earlier chapters should have revealed, that we tackle the more fundamental questions of the definition of subjects and especially of their educational validity and worth. We noted just now that, in moving into its curriculum development phase, the Unit had begun to recognize this and to attempt to broaden the scope of its surveys to include this kind of dimension. However, even more than the Schools Council was, it is tied to a subject base, and whatever it attempts must be undertaken within subject boundaries, even allowing for the fact we noted earlier that the subject boundaries of its design and technology project are very widely drawn. This problem will clearly become even more marked when its work is taken over by bodies whose central concern is with the maintenance of the National Curriculum. For that is itself defined in terms of subjects, and neither the definitions of those subjects nor the boundaries between them are now on the agenda even for debate let alone modification or development.

This suggests that we should also note here a point which we will take up in more detail in Chapter 6, and one we have already foreshadowed in our discussion of the work of the Schools Council. The APU has never been a politically independent body in the way that we saw the Schools Council once was. It is, as we have seen, the Secretary of State for Education who decides, albeit with professional advice, where its attentions should be directed – at what subjects and at which age ranges. And ministerial approval is required for all its publications. This raises a number of important questions; but what is of most significance here is that it casts doubt on the effectiveness of this kind of political agency in promoting genuine curriculum research and development – and thus the development of education itself in the full sense.

It would seem, then, that in spite of all the attempts the APU and its individual subject teams have made to overcome this, it remains essentially a political agency whose prime concern, as we shall see when we consider the political context of curriculum planning in Chapter 6, is with the control of the curriculum rather than with its development. It has not entirely changed, nor ever could it, 'from Trojan horse to angel of light' (Gipps, 1987).

This last problem is of course specific to the APU and to any other agency which lacks political independence. It was not of course a problem which affected the work of the Schools Council, so that it must not be seen as necessarily a difficulty which must face any national agency for curriculum development. One problem, however, which seems to be a general problem for any such body, which faced the Schools Council and which has been and is of great concern to the APU, and which will no doubt confront the two new National Curriculum bodies, is that of the effective dissemination of the results of work undertaken and findings obtained by research into the curriculum – whatever form that research takes and whatever those results and findings are. We must now, therefore, devote some more direct attention to this issue of dissemination.

THE DISSEMINATION OF INNOVATION

It was suggested earlier that a major reason for the failure of the Schools Council to influence curriculum change more directly and more widely was to be found in the dissemination strategies that were adopted. The dissemination of innovation is another problem that was created by that shift we have noted on several occasions from unplanned drift to deliberate planning, from random evolution to positive engineering. The essence of the change is that dissemination replaces diffusion (although the terms are not always used with meanings as clearly distinct as this). 'Once the curriculum reform movement got into "third gear" the term "diffusion", suggesting a natural social process of proliferation, gave way to the term "dissemination", indicating planned pathways to the transmission of new educational ideas and practices from their point of production to all locations of potential implementation' (MacDonald and Walker, 1976, p. 26).

The intentions behind this process were several. It was hoped that it would lead to improvements in the channels of curriculum change; there was optimism that it would accelerate the speed of curriculum change; it was expected that the quality of the curriculum would be improved; and greater cost-effectiveness was also envisaged (MacDonald and Walker, 1976).

The problems which rapidly became apparent arose from two major and interrelated sources. First, the effectiveness of this process was seen to be affected to a high degree by those many constraints which limit all forms of curriculum development. At an early stage in its existence, the Schools Council identified several of these as being particularly significant in the constraining effects they were clearly having on innovation – 'finances, staff attitude, the mobility of pupils, parental pressures, and examinations' (Schools Council, 1971b, p. 15). This whole issue of constraints on curriculum planning will be examined in some detail in Chapter 6.

The second set of problems for programmes of dissemination arose from the models of dissemination which were used, and some discussion of the models which have been identified must be undertaken as a prerequisite to examining the problems themselves.

Two major attempts have been made to identify different models of dissemination – those by Schon (1971) and Havelock (1971). These have been taken as offering the bases of an understanding of the problems of disseminating educational innovation, but it must be noted and emphasized straight away that their analyses are based on evidence culled from spheres other than education, a process whose dangers and inadequacies we have had cause to comment on in several other contexts.

Schon identifies three models of dissemination, which he calls the

Centre–Periphery model, the Proliferation of Centres model and the Shifting Centres model. It is not unreasonable to see the second and third of these as elaborations of the first and thus all three of them as different versions or methods of what is fundamentally a centre–periphery approach.

The essence of the simple Centre–Periphery approach is that it assumes that the process of dissemination must be centrally controlled and managed, that the innovation is planned and prepared in detail prior to its dissemination and that the process of that dissemination is one-way – from the centre out to the consumers on the periphery. The effectiveness of this approach depends on several factors, which include not only the strength of the central resources but also the number of points on the periphery that are to be reached and the length of the 'spokes', the distance of these points from the centre.

The Proliferation of Centres model attempts to overcome these factors, or at least to reduce their significance, by creating secondary centres to extend the reach and thus the efficiency of the primary centre. The intention is that the work of the central development team is supported and extended by local development groups. In turn, these local groups are supported by the central team through the provision not only of advice but also sometimes of courses of training.

It can be seen that the adoption of this kind of model represents an acknowledgement that attention has to be given to the process of dissemination itself and not merely to the details of the innovation to be disseminated. It has been claimed (Stenhouse, 1975) that this model reflects most clearly the realities of attempts at curriculum development in recent years in England and Wales. It is certainly true that this kind of approach has been used to some effect by a number of projects, notable among which are Stenhouse's own Humanities Curriculum Project, the Geography for the Young School Leaver project and Joan Tough's project, Communication Skills in Early Childhood. And it is currently being tried by the APU for the dissemination to teachers of its findings.

Schon's third model, the Shifting Centres model, was posited to explain the spread, witnessed in recent years, of ideas such as those of civil rights, black power, disarmament and student activism, in other words changes of values and attitudes of a more subtle and less deliberate kind. These developments are characterized by the absence of any clearly established centre and of any stable, centrally established message. Indeed, this is a model which appears to be more successful at explaining how unplanned diffusion occurs than at offering a strategy for planned dissemination. Schon believes it has potential value for curriculum change but this must be questionable, since it is a model which appears to offer no basis for the development of any specific message (Stenhouse, 1975).

Havelock's analysis of dissemination strategies can be seen as an attempt to take us beyond the notion that these must always assume a one-way, centre-to-periphery process. His Research, Development and Diffusion (R, D & D) model has many affinities with Schon's basic centre–periphery approach. For it assumes a developer who identifies the problem and a receiver who is essentially a passive recipient of the innovation developed to resolve that problem. It is a 'target system' and is regarded as the model to be adopted when large-scale curriculum change is the aim.

His Social Interaction (SI) model, however, places great stress on the social interaction between members of the adopting group. Again it is a form of the centre–periphery model; again it is a 'target system'; and again the needs of the consumer are determined by the central planner. But it recognizes that the key to the adoption and implementation of the innovation is the social climate of the receiving body and that success or failure will hinge on the channels of communication there. It thus represents, like Schon's Proliferation of Centres model, the beginnings of a shift of focus from the centre to the periphery.

It is with Havelock's third model, the Problem-Solving (PS) model, that this shift is completed. For the essence of this model is that the problem is identified by the consumer and the process of innovation is thus initiated also by him or her. The individual on the periphery is thus himself or herself active and involved from the beginning and the process is essentially one in which he or she recruits outside help. The relationship between the consumer and the external support agent is one of mutual collaboration rather than that of the receiver and the sender of a message; and the whole process is personalized to the point where it has to be recognized that this is not a model of mass dissemination, since the solution that is devised for the problem need not be seen as solving the problems of other consumers. In short, it might be fairly claimed that this is not a model of dissemination at all but rather a model for school-based curriculum development which in turn has led to an idea which goes further still, namely for the establishment of 'change agents' within the school.

It will be appreciated that there is a good deal of overlap between these schemes and models. It is not an over-simplification, however, if we suggest that the major division is between those which adopt a centre–periphery approach of central development and planned dissemination and those which encourage initiatives from the consumer and have led to the development of the notion of school-based curriculum development. The latter is a relatively new concept; the former was the strategy adopted by the early projects of the Schools Council and, as we suggested earlier, this was a major factor in its failure to influence curriculum development as directly as it was once hoped it might. For there are some problems which it might be argued are endemic to this approach and which make it quite inadequate as a device for bringing about effective curriculum change.

In particular, there is a wide gap between the ideas of a project held by its central planners and the realities of its implementation, if that is even the word, in the classroom by the teachers. The existence of this gap between policy and practice is viewed by Lawrence Stenhouse (1975) as the central problem of curriculum development and, indeed, of the advancement of education itself. Even when a project team sets out deliberately to support teachers in their own developments rather than to provide a teacher-proof blueprint (Shipman, 1972), as was the case, for example, with the Humanities Curriculum Project, the Keele Integrated Studies Project and the Goldsmiths' College Interdisciplinary Enquiry Project, the same difficulties have been experienced. It has proved impossible to get across to teachers the concept of the project, the theoretical considerations underlying it, in such a way as to ensure that these were reflected in its practice. And so a gap emerges between the ideals and the realities, a gap that in some cases is so wide as to negate the project entirely, at least in terms of the conception of it by its planners.

The main danger then becomes a possible loss of credibility for the project, a rejection of the principles behind it, if a malinformed or maladroit or even malignant implementation of it derived from lack of adequate understanding has led to disastrous practical consequences. That something has not worked leads too readily to the assumption that it cannot work, rather than to a consideration of the possibility that one has got it wrong. This has been especially apparent in the reaction of some secondary schools to the results of ill-thought-out attempts to introduce mixed-ability groupings.

Such a situation is clearly unsatisfactory since it means at one level that the sums of money spent on central curriculum development have not produced anything like adequate returns and at a further level that they can be positively counterproductive, in so far as failures of this kind can lead to an entrenching of traditional positions.

This kind of reaction, however, is easy to understand, once one acknowledges that schools are living organisms and must be helped to grow and develop from within rather than having 'foreign bodies' attached to them from without, like barnacles attaching themselves to a ship's bottom. This kind of attempt at transplantation must lead in almost every case to 'tissue rejection' (Hoyle, 1969b), and that has been the experience of all such attempts at the dissemination of innovation.

Various hypotheses have been put forward to explain the inadequacies of the centre–periphery model of dissemination. One piece of research has indicated that even where a lot of positive effort has gone into promoting the dissemination of a project to the schools, barriers to its implementation exist in both the failure of teachers to perceive with clarity their new role and also the absence of conditions appropriate to their being able to acquire such a perception (Gross, Giacquinta and Bernstein, 1971). 'Our analysis of the case study data led us to conclude that this condition could be primarily attributed to five circumstances: (1) the teachers' lack of clarity about the innovation; (2) their lack of the kinds of skills and knowledge needed to conform to the new role model; (3) the unavailability of required instructional materials; (4) the incompatibility of organizational arrangements with the innovation; and (5) lack of staff motivation' (op. cit., p. 122). The first four of these conditions, they claim, existed from the outset; the last emerged later. Nor would this seem surprising.

It has also been suggested that another major factor in the ineffectiveness of this approach to curriculum change is its failure to take proper account of social interaction theory (House, 1974). Broadly speaking, the argument is that centre–periphery approaches to dissemination in education are using the wrong model of social interaction or 'personal contact'. They are attempts at imposing a highly depersonalized model and thus they reduce the level of personal contact, leaving the teacher as a largely passive recipient of the innovation. This not only restricts the flow of the innovation but invites teachers to modify and adapt it to conform to the norms of their own group.

Another perspective on this difficulty sees these attempts to impose new ideas and approaches to curriculum on teachers as examples of the use of 'power-coercive' strategies (Bennis, Benne and Chin, 1969), attempts to bring about change or innovation by enforcement. This kind of approach is contrasted with 'empirical-rational' strategies, which attempt to promote change or innovation through demonstrations of their validity and desirability, and 'normative-reeducative' strategies, which approach the task of innovation through devices for changing the attitudes, the values and the interrelationships of the teachers and for providing them with the new skills needed to implement the change. Again, therefore, we can see that a major concern is with the quality of the social interaction within the school and with the teachers' response. We can also recognize that the contrast is between imposition, whether from an outside agency or from within the school through, for example, a powerful and strong-willed headteacher, and the involvement of the teachers themselves both in identifying the need for change and in developing responses seen by them to be appropriate to that need.

Finally, it is worth noting briefly the implications of this debate for notions of teacher professionalism or the professional concept of the teacher. It would not be appropriate here to engage in detailed analysis of the concept of professionalism or, more accurately, the several different concepts we might adopt. It is important, however, to note, not least because of the enhanced significance this has in the context of the new National Curriculum in the United Kingdom, that to adopt power-coercive strategies, to attempt to develop 'teacher-proof' schemes, to endeavour to bring about change from outside the school, is to view the teacher as a technician rather than as a professional, as an operative rather than as a decision-maker, as someone whose role is merely to implement the judgements of others and not to act on his or her own. We must note, therefore, that the difficulties of this approach to curriculum planning and innovation derive not merely from the fact that it seems to have proved ineffective in practice but also because it has serious implications for the professional standing and responsibility of teachers.

These, then, have been some of the criticisms of those early attempts at curriculum innovation and change which did not plan their dissemination but rather hoped that their ideas, once propagated, would spread with the wind, and of those which, while deliberately planning the dissemination of their ideas and materials, did so in a somewhat authoritarian manner, offering what they hoped would be 'teacher-proof' schemes and packages, and expecting teachers either to accept the imposition of these upon them or to recognize unaided their supposedly self-evident attractions.

In response to these criticisms, therefore, many devices have been used to improve the processes of dissemination both by deliberately planning it and by doing this in a manner designed to take greater account of the difficulties of ensuring proper acceptance. Most of these may be seen as indications of a move towards Schon's proliferation of centres. House (1974) recommends the creation of more incentives for local entrepreneurs, the leaders of Schon's secondary centres; he also wishes to increase the number of those participating in the exercise; and his major aim is 'to reduce political, social and organisational barriers to contact with the outside world' (MacDonald and Walker, 1976, p. 20). In pursuit of much the same goals, the Schools Council attempted to establish local development groups, to involve teachers' centres, to gain the support of local education authorities, to promote the in-service education of teachers, to mount regional conferences and even, in some cases, to involve members of the project teams in the work of the schools, as change agents working in secondary centres (Schools Council, 1967, 1971b, 1974b). Many of these devices are now being employed by the Assessment of Performance Unit.

In spite of all such developments and the use of all these detailed strategies for planned dissemination, major difficulties have continued to exist. Some of these were identified by those concerned with the dissemination of the Humanities Curriculum Project. In particular, failure to achieve adequate dissemination was attributed to difficulties in communication between the project team and the schools (MacDonald and Rudduck, 1971). It would be a mistake, however, to interpret that statement at too simple a level, for a number of features of this failure of communication have also been identified. One is the tendency of teachers 'to invest the development team with the kind of authority which can atrophy independence of judgement in individual school settings' (op. cit., p. 149). The converse of this was also observed, namely the anxiety of some teachers not to lose their own style by accepting too readily the specifications of method included in the project. Both these factors would seem to point to the need for a full and proper involvement of the teachers with the development of a project. Both of them too draw attention to the significance of House's insistence on a proper regard being paid to the different forms of social interaction.

This emphasizes the importance of the manner in which innovations are introduced. It will be clear that if an innovation is to have a chance of 'taking' in a school, it will be necessary for more to be done than the mere provision of resources and in-service support for teachers. Teachers will need to become committed to it, an ideological change will need to be promoted, if they are to be expected willingly to adapt their methods and approaches to meet the demands of the new work. This offers a far more subtle problem. It is here that the manner in which the proposed change is made becomes important. For if it is imposed by the headteacher, for example, or by powerful pressure from outside, the dictation involved will be counter-productive and will promote opposition and hostility in teachers rather than support. Not only will teachers in such circumstances not work to promote the change planned; they will quite often deliberately and actively sabotage the efforts of others. It is plain that power-coercive strategies do not bring about real or effective change.

The attitudes of staff were one of the major constraints on curriculum change that the early work of the Schools Council drew attention to. When this point was made, it was asserted that 'innovation cannot succeed unless the majority of staff are, at worst, neutral; but it was clearly important to have a majority positively inclined to curricular change' (Schools Council, 1971b, p. 15). That report went on to say that 'one solution suggested was that innovation should begin by attempting to solve existing dissatisfactions' (ibid.). This suggestion clearly points to the desirability of shifting the focus from the centre to the periphery, of adopting a model more akin to Havelock's Problem-Solving model, and of employing empirical-rational and/or normative-reeducational rather than power-coercive strategies. In fact, it would appear to indicate that artificial dissemination by donor is not as good as the real thing.

Support for this view is to be found elsewhere too. For it has further been suggested that this problem goes beyond a mere failure of communication or of the strategies employed to introduce the innovation and is in fact the result of the different views and definitions of a curriculum project that we have already suggested are taken by different bodies of people involved in it (Shipman, 1972, 1973). The question must then be asked whose definition is to be seen as valid. To speak of dissemination or implementation, of the barriers to implementation created by schools and teachers, or of the need to improve the teachers' understanding of the theoretical considerations underlying a project is to make the assumption that the planner's view and definition are to be accepted as valid. For this reason, it has been suggested that 'the process of curriculum dissemination, in so far as it assumes a stable message, does not occur. The process to which the term "dissemination" is conventionally applied would be more accurately described by the term "curriculum negotiation" ' (MacDonald and Walker, 1976, p. 43). In other words, having recognized that a gap exists between the ideals of the planners and the realities of the work of the teacher in the classroom, we should be concerned to close it by attempting not only to bring the latter nearer to the former but also by seeking to bring each closer to the other. To see the need to do this is to recognize that curriculum development is essentially a matter of local development, that it requires a form of 'household' innovation, and thus that it has to be school-based.

This leads us finally to the question of the conditions which are most favourable to the implementation of change within a school.

We have mentioned several times how crucial it is that a curriculum innovation should ' "take" with the school and become fully institutionalised' (Hoyle, 1969b, p. 230). It has further been suggested that whether this is likely to happen or not will depend on the organizational health of the institution, since only a healthy institution can readily absorb a new development. As Eric Hoyle goes on to say, 'the central problem facing the curriculum development movement is the avoidance of tissue rejection whereby an innovation does not "take" with a school because the social system of the school is unable to absorb it into its normal functioning' (op. cit., p. 231).

But what criteria are we to use to define a healthy institution? We face immediately the kinds of difficulty that surround concepts of mental health, namely those that arise from the values that must be implicit in any definition we offer. On the other hand, although much more work needs to be done in this area, there are some indications of what factors are relevant to the question of a school's ability to digest satisfactorily a curriculum innovation.

The style of the headteacher is clearly crucial, since the organizational structure he or she creates within the school will be of great significance to the reaction of teachers to proposed curriculum change (Halpin, 1966, 1967; Hoyle, 1969b). The degree to which a school is 'open' is also very important (Halpin, 1966, 1967; Bernstein, 1967; Hoyle, 1969b). The more open a school is the more likely it is to be able to absorb innovation. For an 'open' school will offer teachers a greater degree of freedom and will encourage a higher level of collaboration between them. They are thus more likely to have the confidence that change requires and to have been involved themselves in the processes of change. As we have mentioned several times, no kind of change will 'take' if it is not accepted by the teacher at the coal-face. In the last resort, therefore, his or her motivation is paramount and this is most likely to be high if he or she feels himself or herself to be completely involved and, indeed, in control of events.

In more detail, the investigation into the thirty-eight schools that were involved in the Schools Council's Integrated Studies Project based at Keele led to the following rather tentative suggestions as to the main characteristics of a school that is ready for innovation.

> The salient points are that the school which is likely to introduce and implement successfully a planned innovation would:
> - have teachers who would feed back information to the project
> - have teachers who would accumulate supplementary material
> - have teachers who had volunteered knowing that they would be involved in a lot of work
> - reorganise its timetable to provide planning time for teachers involved in innovation
> - have a headteacher who supported the innovation but did not insist on being personally involved
> - have a low staff turnover among key personnel
> - be free of any immediate need to reorganise as part of a changing local school situation.
>
> (Shipman, 1973, p. 53)

To this list one might add also a further point that emerged from an exploration of the difficulties of dissemination associated with the Humanities Curriculum Project. 'It seems that an experiment settles well in a school where teachers are confronting a problem and contemplating action. The experiment should extend the range of their strategies for dealing with the problem' (MacDonald and Rudduck, 1971, pp. 150–1). If the teachers are aware of a need, then, and the climate of the school gives them the confidence and support to experiment with possible solutions to that need, a project or a scheme has a far better chance of succeeding.

These, then, are some of the characteristics of the school as a social system that will help to decide whether it is ready for curriculum innovation or not. There are besides, of course, a good many considerations of a more practical kind relating to the geography of the school, the availability of appropriate resources and such like. In the last resort, however, it is the social climate that will be crucial and we must concentrate on this if we wish to develop strategies of curriculum change within the school.

This constitutes a further argument in favour of school-based curriculum development. For it is clear that, if the social climate of the school is to be supportive of innovation, if, to change the metaphor, the organizational health of the school is to be such as to ensure that there will not be the kind of tissue rejection we spoke of earlier, it will be necessary for the initiatives to come from within, for the process to be one of growth and development rather than of transplantation. In short, the main reason for the failure of attempts to change curricula from outside is that the dissemination model itself has been wrong, so that attention has been directed towards the development of an alternative model, and we turn again towards the idea of school-based curriculum development.

SCHOOL-BASED CURRICULUM DEVELOPMENT

It is the relative failure of external attempts at the dissemination of innovation, then, that has led to the emergence of the idea of school-based curriculum development. There is, therefore, a real sense in which this must be seen not as a form of dissemination so much as an alternative to it, although it need not be regarded as precluding the possibility that other kinds of curriculum change might be attempted at the same time. We have just noted that the failure of descending models of dissemination is in part due to the need for the social and organizational climate of the school to be such as to create the conditions for any planned innovation to 'take' in the school, and that this realization, by shifting the focus of attention from the innovation to the school, from the seed to the soil in which it is to be planted, suggests that the process must be considered first from the other end and the initiative sought in the school rather than outside it.

Several major principles are reflected in this notion of school-based curriculum development. In the first place, it is based on the beliefs that the curriculum consists of experiences and that these should be developed from the learner's needs and characteristics (Skilbeck, 1976), so that it represents a commitment to the view that educational provision must be individualized.

Second, it acknowledges that a large measure of freedom for both teacher and learner is a necessary condition for education of this kind (Skilbeck, 1976). Third, it views the school as a human social institution which must be responsive to its own environment (Skilbeck, 1976), and which must, therefore, be permitted to develop in its own way to fit that environment. Lastly, it regards it as vital to this development that the individual teacher, or at least the staff of any individual school, should accept a research and development role in respect of the curriculum (Stenhouse, 1975), modifying, adapting and developing it to suit the needs of individual pupils and a particular environment.

This philosophy, then, has provided the basis for the positive arguments which have been offered in support of this shift of emphasis. Malcolm Skilbeck, for example, argues that school-based curriculum development 'provides more scope for the continuous adaptation of curriculum to individual pupil needs than do other forms of curriculum development' (Skilbeck, 1976, pp. 93–4). Other systems are

> by their nature ill-fitted to respond to individual differences in either pupils or teachers. Yet these differences . . . are of crucial importance in learning . . . At the very least, schools need greatly increased scope and incentive for adapting, modifying, extending and otherwise reordering externally developed curricula than is now commonly the case. Curriculum development related to individual differences must be a continuous process and it is only the school or school networks that can provide scope for this.
>
> (Skilbeck, 1976, p. 94)

For these reasons, then, there has been a growing conviction that the only satisfactory form of curriculum development is likely to be school-based. Recent years have thus seen a proliferation of sub-variants of this generic concept – School-Focused Curriculum Development, School-Centred Innovation (SCI) and the Effective School Movement, for example – of supportive agencies, such as Guidelines for Review and Internal Development of Schools (GRIDS), and of consequent schemes for evaluation at this level, such as School Self-Evaluation (SEE) and School-Based Review (SBR). We must now consider what this kind of development entails.

We must begin by noting that, to meet some of the problems this approach creates, some schools have recently made senior appointments of teachers with special responsibility for co-ordinating and guiding curriculum – curriculum co-ordinators or curriculum development officers, change-agents within the school. This is a practice which has much to recommend it. It is a step towards achieving that kind of co-ordinated development across the curriculum which we said in Chapter 1 was often lacking, especially in secondary schools where the tradition has been for development to go on within individual subjects in isolation from one another. It also ensures that there is one person in the school who can be expected to attempt to organize support from outside agencies for any group of teachers engaged in any particular innovative activity. Such a person can also act as a focus for curriculum study groups in the school, an essential innovation if teachers are to be made fully aware of what is entailed in school-based curriculum development. We may note here the contribution which can be made by 'curriculum support teams' established by local authorities (Ball, 1983).

It is obviously crucial for the success of the school-based approach to curriculum development that this kind of appointment be made and that some teachers be enabled and assisted to acquire the expertise needed to take up these roles. For the difficulties which face the holders of such posts have already begun to emerge (Lee, 1977; Purcell, 1981; Ball, 1983). Their task makes it necessary for them to encroach on the preserves of other colleagues' subjects and classrooms, and often this is resented. Furthermore, this encroachment often has to be undertaken with a view to getting these colleagues to change their ways, by adopting new syllabuses or approaches to teaching, by collaborating with others or even by accepting a reduced share of the timetable. They also need to be able to back up their requests for such changes and modifications by promises of adequate financial support, and this cannot always be assured. It is already clear what a difficult and even thankless task this can be, but it is also becoming equally clear that it is a task that has to be done if school-based curriculum development is to be made to work. More teachers must be given proper opportunities to prepare to undertake this kind of task.

However, if we have been right to identify the teacher in the classroom as the hub of all this activity and the person whose role is quite fundamental and crucial, the most important need will be for adequate support for him or her. It is clear that what we are describing involves a major change in the teacher's role and there must be corresponding changes in the organization and even the staffing of schools if he or she is to have the time and the ability to respond to this.

It becomes increasingly important too for initial courses of training to have prepared them to take this central role in curriculum development. It becomes even more important, however, that they be given adequate opportunities for continuing in-service education to enable them to obtain any new skills that the innovations require and a developing insight into the wider issues of education, a deep understanding of which is vital for any kind of adequate planning, research or development.

This is why major curriculum changes such as the introduction of mixed-ability groupings in secondary schools have worked most smoothly and effectively when, as in the West Riding of Yorkshire under Sir Alec Clegg's guidance, suitable in-service courses have been available on demand and tailored not to the advisory staff's ideas of what is needed but to what the teachers themselves ask for (Kelly, 1975). It is for the same reason that where national projects have developed training courses for teachers wishing to make use of the project materials, teachers who have had this training achieve more success than those who have not (Elliott and Adelman, 1973).

In short, there can be no curriculum development without teacher development and the more teachers are to be given responsibility for curriculum development the more important it becomes that they be given all possible support of this kind. The potential of the role of the professional tutor as the focal point of this kind of teacher development, linking initial and in-service teacher education and developing contacts between the school and colleges and other institutions responsible for these courses has so far not been fully appreciated but it offers opportunities that may be crucial to school-based curriculum development (Kelly, A.V., 1973; Lee, 1977). Staff development and curriculum development must be closely linked, and it is very important that teachers be put in touch with any outside agency that can provide them with the resources, the skills or the understanding they need if they are to take responsibility for developing the curriculum.

This kind of link with central agencies is important for at least two reasons. One is that without it what occurs may well be change but will not necessarily be development or lead to improvement in the quality of education experienced by a school's pupils. There has been a tendency, in response to those difficulties of prompting innovations from outside which we noted earlier, to assume that school-based curriculum development must be worthwhile merely because it is school-based. There is, however, no guarantee of this. Engagement with outside agencies may contribute to ensuring that it is worthwhile.

Secondly, there is the related danger that, if teachers' attention becomes too closely focused on their own institutions, and their possibly narrow concerns, they may fail to address curriculum issues at an appropriate level or depth. In particular, there may be a tendency to see these issues largely in managerial or organizational or even bureaucratic terms, a tendency which has been reinforced by recent governmental policies emphasizing these dimensions of schooling. However, we have seen in earlier chapters the important conceptual issues which curriculum planning and development raise, so that we can appreciate how important it is that teachers are able to address these issues in the course of their school-based curriculum development. Again, therefore, contact with supportive and illuminative outside agencies may be crucial.

ACTION RESEARCH AND 'THE TEACHER AS RESEARCHER'

This last point takes us naturally to a consideration of the related notions of action research and 'the teacher as researcher' (Stenhouse, 1975).

Action research has been defined as 'the systematic study of attempts to improve educational practice by groups of participants by means of their own practical actions and by means of their own reflection upon the effects of these actions' (Ebbutt, 1983), and as 'the study of a social situation with a view to improving the quality of action within it' (Elliott, J., 1981, p. 1). The important aspect of this notion is that it represents a claim that the only productive form of educational research is that which involves the people actually working on an educational problem or problems and is conducted *pari passu* with the development of solutions to that problem or problems. It is a view which has developed out of a growing sense of dissatisfaction with the pointlessness of much research which has been conducted outside the field of practice and has thus produced generalized findings which it is left to the practitioner to 'apply'. This latter kind of research has often not only failed to be supportive of teachers in the development of their practice, it has sometimes even been counterproductive to that purpose (Kelly, 1981). Its inadequacies, then, are precisely those of centre–periphery models of dissemination. The notion of action research is offered as an alternative form of research and one which it is claimed should provide teachers with a proper kind of support. As Elliot Eisner has said (1985, p. 264), 'what . . . we need if educational research is truly to inform educational practice is the construction of our own unique conceptual apparatus and research methods'.

The first aspect of this approach to research is that it requires the teachers themselves to be actively engaged in the activity. They must be constantly evaluating their work, critically analysing it with a view to its development and improvement. It is this feature which brings in Lawrence Stenhouse's associated notion of 'the teacher as researcher' (Stenhouse, 1975). 'The ideal', said Stenhouse, 'is that the curricular specification should feed a teacher's personal research and development programme through which he is progressively increasing his understanding of his own work and hence bettering his teaching' (op. cit., p. 143). 'It is not enough', he adds later, 'that teachers' work should be studied: they need to study it themselves' (ibid.).

Several further issues arise as a result of adopting that basic position. It is clearly vital, if teachers are to develop and if the quality of their work is to improve, that they engage in this kind of continuous evaluation of their work. Indeed, it might be argued that this is a *sine qua non* of teaching, certainly of good teaching, and that it is something that all teachers naturally do. It must be said, however, that not all teachers do it well. School-based curriculum development, as was suggested earlier, is not necessarily good just because it is school-based; and similarly teachers' own evaluations of their work are not necessarily sound and productive merely because they are their own evaluations. Teachers can be, and should be, assisted to develop the skills and techniques needed for proper and effective self-evaluation, as we shall see in Chapter 7. And there will always remain that psychological difficulty which makes objective self-evaluation difficult in any sphere.

Thus questions now arise about whether there is a role for an external figure or figures in action research and, if there is, what that role is and who this external figure or figures might be.

These were among the questions addressed by the Ford Teaching Project. We shall examine in Chapter 7 the attempts of that project to support teachers in developing the skills needed to make reasonably objective appraisals of their own work, to engage in 'research-based teaching'. We shall see the emerging notion of a process model of evaluation, of evaluation as action research. One of the main purposes of the Ford Teaching Project was 'to help teachers by fostering an action-research orientation towards classroom problems' (Elliott and Adelman, 1973, p. 10). This was offered as an alternative to the model of action research in which researchers from outside come into the classroom and work with the teacher. It was felt that this kind of relationship erodes the teacher's autonomy and that if this is to be protected he or she must be enabled to take responsibility for his or her own action research as part of his or her responsibility for his or her own curriculum development (Elliott and Adelman, 1973). This the Ford Teaching Project attempted to encourage.

What about the curriculum developer, then? Is there a place for a professional curriculum developer if curriculum development is to be school-based or in action research? It is still not clear what role there is for the outside expert. This was a second-order action research project for the Ford Teaching Project team. At the same time as helping teachers to develop the ability to engage in their own 'research-based teaching', they wanted also to explore how best this kind of teaching might be assisted from outside.

The logic of the Ford Teaching Project's approach would seem to be that, once teachers have acquired a research-based teaching orientation as part of their basic weaponry, the need for outside support will disappear, so that perhaps the role of the curriculum developer is to be seen as provisional only, his or her services being needed only until such times as teachers themselves have acquired the necessary skills.

Two questions, however, must be asked before we too readily accept such a view. In the first place, we must ask how far the average teacher is likely to be able to develop the abilities this will require of him or her. Apart from the problem of adding yet another chore to an already heavy task, we shall see in Chapter 7 that it was not easy for the Ford Teaching Project team to develop in teachers the detachment and the security of confidence necessary to be able to make reasonably objective appraisals of their work, although the team did express optimism on this point.

Secondly, however, we must also ask whether there will not always be a need for someone to come from the outside to take a detached view of what is being done, to suggest possible alternatives and to ensure that all the necessary questions raised by attempts at curriculum planning and development are addressed and not, as we saw earlier is the danger, only those of a managerial or organizational kind. Few of us cannot profit from this kind of second opinion. Perhaps this is to be seen as a function of teachers from other schools as part of the process of moderation that should be an essential element in all assessment procedures. But there may also continue to be a need for someone acting as a professional consultant, a role that members of the advisory services should perform.

We noted earlier that the ideas of school-based curriculum development and of action research, as well as generating the change-agent within the school, have also given birth to various forms of 'curriculum support team' (Ball, 1981, 1983a, b). In fact, we have already seen the emergence of two quite different models of such curriculum development, the one relying on initiatives and support from within, the other responding to such from outside. We noted earlier that the provision of such support became a major focus for the work of the newly reconstituted Schools Council and it is also the case that some local authorities have created their own curriculum support groups.

It is also clear that the role of such support groups is not always an easy one (Ball, 1981, 1983a, b). To some extent they exist to respond to and support changes initiated within a school and this is not in itself necessarily a difficult task. Their main function, however, certainly at local authority level, is to prompt changes in schools which do not initiate these for themselves and this is obviously a much more difficult and sensitive task, one which can make that of the internal change-agent appear by comparison a pleasant sinecure.

We examined earlier in this chapter the conditions which appear to be most conducive to curriculum development within a school, the factors which contribute to its organizational health. It has been argued (Shipman, 1973) that if a school possesses all those characteristics there is hardly any point in getting it to change. Certainly, it would seem that change in such a school might be left to internal processes. However, for those schools which do not enjoy these advantages, strategies must be developed for bringing about both the qualities that will make curriculum development possible for them and that curriculum development itself. In short, it is necessary to go beyond Havelock's Problem-Solving model of change by identifying the problem for the consumer when he or she appears to be unable to recognize it for himself or herself. In cases of this kind the external curriculum developer or support team has a major role to play and it is clear that it is not an enviable one.

Perhaps there is still a role then for the wandering expert in curriculum development. If there is, and only subsequent research and continuing experience will answer that question for us, it is likely that that role will be to provide teachers with expert advice and the detached appraisal they cannot provide themselves and not to arrive hawking his or her own pet project, cobbled together in a place somewhat removed from the realities of any particular group of classrooms. His or her job will be to follow and serve the teachers rather than to lead them into his or her own new pastures. He or she can only support curriculum development; he or she will no longer attempt to direct it.

The question whether there is a proper role for the external curriculum developer, however, is so closely linked to that of the role of the external curriculum evaluator that we must delay any further discussion of it until we consider more fully in Chapter 7 the wider questions of curriculum evaluation. It also, of course, raises important political questions about the control of the curriculum which we shall also take up in subsequent chapters.

SUMMARY AND CONCLUSIONS

This chapter has attempted to explore some of the issues that are raised by questions about how the curriculum changes and especially how it can be changed.

We began by looking at the work of the Schools Council as a major national agency within the United Kingdom for curriculum development. An attempt was made to trace the development of its work and some of its major characteristics and the conclusion reached was that, although its indirect influence on curriculum change through its contribution to the continuing curriculum debate has probably been very great, its direct effect on the school curriculum has been disappointing.

We next examined the work of the Assessment of Performance Unit and noted its recent attempts to take on the role of national agency for curriculum development. It was suggested that its political roots and its continued political allegiances make it difficult, and probably impossible, for it ever to become a source of genuine curriculum development and that, in particular, its primary concern with the assessment of pupil performance must always inhibit its progress towards any broader form of curriculum research.

In the case of both the Schools Council and the APU, it was suggested that a major reason for their lack of direct impact on the curriculum was to be found in the problems encountered in the dissemination of curriculum innovation. Discussion of the major models of dissemination which have been identified suggested that there may be certain problems endemic to any centre–periphery approach and that the models that seemed to offer most hope of success are those whose attention is focused on the schools themselves and which, therefore, perhaps are not models of dissemination as such at all.

One reason why this kind of approach appears to be more successful is that it takes full account of the organizational health of the school and recognizes that this is the most crucial consideration in the planning of curriculum change. It thus points again to the idea that effective curriculum development can be based only on initiatives that come from within the school, that if curriculum innovation is to be curriculum development in the full sense it must be school-based.

The chapter then turned to an examination of some of the advantages, disadvantages and problems of this device for changing the curriculum, concentrating in particular on the demands it makes on the expertise and skill of teachers and the question of the appropriate kind of outside assistance they need to meet these demands. The related notions of action research and 'the teacher as researcher' were also considered, and towards the end of this discussion it began to emerge that the ability of teachers to promote the development of the curriculum clearly depends on their ability to evaluate its effectiveness and that here again the question of what kind of external help they need is crucial. Curriculum development and curriculum evaluation are integrally linked together; the role of the teacher in the one cannot be properly debated except in association with the issue of his or her role in the other; the possible role of the external agent in the one is also clearly bound up with the role such a person might play in the other.

Strategies of this kind for curriculum change and development, therefore, are closely linked to issues of curriculum evaluation, so that it would be logical and natural to move in the next chapter to an exploration of evaluation theory. This, indeed, was the sequence followed in the first two editions of this book. Recently, however, the kinds of development we have been exploring in this chapter have become much more directly subject to external influences, especially of a political kind, so that, as we shall see later, it is the political rather than the educational aspects of educational evaluation which are now to the fore. It thus becomes necessary, before we consider the theory and the practice of curriculum evaluation, to explore those political influences and pressures so that we can see more clearly the effects they have had, and continue to have, both on the ideas of and strategies for curriculum change and development we have examined in this chapter and on those associated elements of evaluation theory which have been growing side by side with them and to which we shall return in Chapter 7.

There is a further reason for moving next to a consideration of the political context of curriculum planning and development: it creates many constraints of an indirect kind which not only influence but must be taken fully into account in planning curriculum development. In school-based curriculum development, in particular, account must be taken of what has been called (Ball, 1987) 'the micro-politics of the school'. No discussion of strategies for curriculum change and development, therefore, would be complete without further exploration of the factors which must influence and constrain all such strategies. It is to such an exploration that we turn in the next chapter.

6

THE SOCIAL AND POLITICAL
CONTEXT OF CURRICULUM
PLANNING AND DEVELOPMENT

Up to this point we have discussed curriculum planning and development as though they go on in a world populated only by teachers and other educationists. And so, that discussion has proceeded on the basis of two unwarranted assumptions. The first of these is that influences outside education have not been important in affecting what is taught in schools and that curriculum development has been entirely a matter of careful planning on the part of the professionals. Secondly, we have assumed that, so long as we take full account of the practical implications of the plans we make for the curriculum, there will be no significant gap between the theory and the practice of curriculum development, between the designing of curriculum programmes and their realization in practice. With these assumptions we have looked at several models of curriculum planning and we have considered some of the theoretical and practical difficulties that arise over the framing of purposes or principles, the choosing of appropriate content and the setting up of adequate procedures for implementation.

We suggested in Chapter 1, however, that this was only one aspect of curriculum change and development and that there were many other factors at work of which we must take full cognizance. We have also hinted throughout that there is a very wide gap between what is planned and what actually happens, between the official and the actual curriculum, between the ideals and conceptions in the minds of the curriculum planners and the realities of the outcomes of these in the classroom. This gap is due, at least to some extent, to the external pressures which form the context of the teacher's work.

We must now, therefore, give due consideration to these two important aspects of curriculum change by looking at the other pressures that are at work, the other influences, both direct and indirect, overt and covert, deliberate and incidental, that play their part in curriculum change and development.

THE INEVITABILITY OF THE POLITICAL DIMENSION OF EDUCATION

It is worth noting first of all that education is essentially a political activity, that the education system is the device by which an advanced society prepares its young for adult life in the society, a formalization of the role played in primitive societies by all or most of the adult population. The political context, then, is a major element in any scheme or system of education, and one without reference to which such a scheme or system cannot be properly understood.

It is for this reason that most of the major educational theorists or philosophers have also been, or even have primarily been, social and political philosophers. Plato, for example, offers us his theory of education only in the context of his political theory, introducing his whole discussion of education with the words 'These are the kinds of people our guardians must be. In what manner, then, will we rear and educate them?' Clearly, his main concern was with the social or political function of education; and we must note that this has been true also of many of the major figures who have followed him – Locke, Rousseau, John Stuart Mill, Dewey and so on.

Indeed, we must recognize that no one's view of education can be fully understood in isolation from his or her political persuasions, since such views must reflect the moral and social values of their adherents. And, as we shall see shortly, it is not possible to achieve anything like a proper understanding of the history of education except in the context of the political climate prevailing at any given time or period.

It is for this reason that many have stressed the political importance and significance of schooling. At the practical level, this is reflected in the importance attached to schools and teachers in revolutionary times and by totalitarian governments. Control of the school system has been seen as a close second in terms of importance to control of the media of communication in most revolutions; and it has also been a major concern of leaders of major national movements, such as Lenin and Hitler. In this connection, it is worth noting that the idea of a national curriculum which was mooted in the United Kingdom in the 1930s was rejected at that time because it smacked of totalitarianism. We should also note the interest in education which has long been shown by religious bodies. It would be a mistake to assume that such interest has always been prompted by charitable intentions and never by a desire to propagate particular religious creeds and tenets. Few can be unfamiliar with the Jesuits' claim about what can be achieved through control of the early years of schooling.

At the theoretical level, this has been most clearly reflected in recent developments in that area which has come to be known as 'the politics of knowledge' and most obviously in the claim of major international figures such as Paolo Freire and Ivan Illich that society should be 'deschooled' so that its young citizens should not be subjected to a process of socialization, or even indoctrination, by those in power.

Education and politics, then, are inextricably interwoven with each other, so that one cannot productively discuss curriculum issues in a political vacuum.

DIRECT AND INDIRECT POLITICAL INFLUENCES

It is important, however, to distinguish direct political intervention from influences of an indirect, less overt and possibly less effective kind. It is also important to differentiate direct intervention in issues of the organization of schooling from intervention in the curriculum itself.

Until recently, political intervention in the work of schools in the United Kingdom had been confined to the former, to organizational changes. The state has pronounced, and indeed introduced legislation, on the establishment of compulsory schooling, on the progressive raising of the minimum school leaving age, on access to grammar schools and support for children granted such access, on the provision of secondary education for all and, more recently, on the provision of this through the creation of comprehensive forms of secondary schooling. All these organizational changes do, of course, have implications for the school curriculum, but it has been left to teachers and other educationists to draw these implications, and, on occasions (as with the raising of the school leaving age in 1972), money has been made available to help teachers and others to explore the curricular consequences of the legislation. There have been no direct injunctions, however, in relation to the school curriculum (except for the requirement of the 1944 Education Act for the regular provision of religious education for all pupils).

As a result, the development of the curriculum has been left to influences of an indirect kind. Thus one can identify in the development of education in the United Kingdom a number of competing influences. In particular, one can see a conflict or tension between political/economic forces and idealistic or philosophical theories. One can recognize the influence, on the one hand, of notions like that of a 'liberal education' and 'progressivism' and, on the other, that of a concern with the inculcation of 'the basic skills'; one can see tensions between liberalism and vocationalism, between egalitarianism and élitism, between the Crowther Report's two purposes of education – education as a national investment and education as the right of every child (CACE, 1959). One can see the emergence of the three distinctive curricula of tripartism and the contrasting view that all pupils should have access to the same kinds of educational provision. And one remembers Raymond Williams's (1961) view of the three main general influences on the development of education in the United Kingdom: that of the 'old humanists', concerned with the transmission of the traditional cultural heritage; that of the 'industrial trainers', who looked to education for little more than a trained workforce; and that of the 'public educators', who sought a new form of curriculum to reflect the philosophy of mass education.

At the level of the actual or received curriculum one can see an uneasy compromise, a complex interweaving of all these influences of a kind that can hardly be satisfactory because of the manifest incompatibilities of some of these views. One can also see that the degree to which the more liberal, idealistic influences prevail or predominate depends to a very large extent on the degree of freedom enjoyed by teachers in curricular matters, since teachers have on balance tended to choose their profession because of certain ideals they hold about children, people and human potential, their salary scales having always been such as to provide ample evidence of their total lack of economic awareness.

THE SOURCES OF THESE INDIRECT INFLUENCES

These influences on the curriculum and on teachers' attitudes and approaches to their task originate from many different sources. One major source of such influence over many years has been those official reports which successive governments have commissioned. There is no doubt that the report of the Hadow Committee on Primary Education (Board of Education, 1931) played a major part in the development of the view of education, at least for the primary age range, as 'activity and experience' rather than as 'knowledge to be acquired and facts stored', or that this view was strongly reinforced by the Plowden Report in 1967. Subsequent evidence, such as that of the ORACLE team (Galton, Simon and Croll, 1980), may have shown that this approach is not as widespread in practice as was once thought, but this in itself is further evidence of the range of competing influences on teachers, and there is no denying its continuing influence on the way in which primary teachers view their task or that many of them continue to regard it as necessary to attempt to implement this philosophy in their teaching, even if they do not always have the conceptual clarity, or indeed the freedom from other pressures, to do this effectively. At secondary level too one can cite the Newsom Report (CACE, 1963) as having had an immediate impact not only on the organization of many secondary schools but also on their curricula.

A second major source of influence has been that of the theorists of education, whose views have been mediated most effectively through initial, and in some cases in-service, courses of teacher education. It is from this source that teachers have become familiar with the views of Plato, Locke, Rousseau, Froebel, Montessori, Dewey and other 'great educators'; and from this source, too, the influences of major figures in the field of psychology and child development have been brought to bear on thinking about education. Contemporary writers have also had their impact. Because of the work of Richard Peters (1965, 1966) the curriculum has long been influenced by the notion that there are certain 'intrinsically worthwhile activities' which must be at the heart of education and thus of the school curriculum; Paul Hirst's (1965) claim that knowledge and understanding have to be recognized as falling into several logically discrete categories has led to the continuing opposition to integrated approaches to the school curriculum; and the influence of Lawrence Stenhouse (1975) and Jerome Bruner's many publications has led to the recent emergence of that process-based approach to curriculum planning which we examined in Chapter 4.

Influences of this kind on the development of the curriculum may be regarded as being prompted by a genuine attempt to search after 'the truth' or at least to explore objectively issues raised by the planning of education and to seek rational and justifiable solutions to them. One can, however, also detect other, less objective and more partisan attempts to influence the school curriculum. The work of Ivor Goodson (1981, 1983, 1985a; Goodson and Ball, 1984), for example, has shown conclusively the extent of the influence of subject associations on the development and the establishment of their own subject interests within the curriculum. Age-group associations have exercised similar influences, as have teachers' unions, parents' associations and employers' groups. And there have been other influential bodies, with mixed membership, such as the Advisory Centre for Education (ACE), the Campaign for the Advancement of State Education (CASE), the Party for Reform in Secondary Education (PRISE) and, more recently, the

Gender and Mathematics Association (GAMMA) and Girls into Science and Technology (GIST). These are all pressure groups formed with the express purpose of influencing the development of education and the school curriculum in certain declared directions (Jenkins and Shipman, 1976).

Finally, we must not ignore the influence of the Church, or rather of various churches and religions, which has been a major and continuing factor in the development of education and the curriculum in the United Kingdom. The strength of that influence is best demonstrated by the fact that, until the recent institution of the National Curriculum, religious education was the only subject which the law required should be included in the curriculum of all maintained schools. And we must remember, as was mentioned earlier in this chapter, that the churches' interest in education and their preparedness to found and to finance educational institutions at all levels has been prompted not only by a wish to do charitable works but also, and more important, by a desire to exercise control over the content of children's education.

COMPETING IDEOLOGIES

Hence the curriculum can be seen as the battleground of many competing influences and ideologies. This, as we saw just now, has been a major theme of the 'new directions' in the sociology of education (Young, 1971) and of the 'politics of knowledge' to which it has given rise. Proponents of this view, as we have also seen, have not unnaturally gone on to claim that in such a battleground it is inevitable that the dominant ideology will exercise the greatest influence – even to the point of complete control. Some, therefore, like Illich (1971) and Freire (1972) have pressed for a 'deschooling' of society; others, such as Weingartner and Postman (1969) for an approach to education as a subversive activity, planned in such a way as to encourage pupils to challenge the values implicit in the curriculum which is imposed upon them by the dominant group or ideology.

More often, however, in practice, at least until recently, the actual curriculum in schools in the United Kingdom has not reflected one faction or ideology but an unhappy, and probably unsatisfactory, amalgam of many, as each source of influence or pressure has had a little, but not an exclusive, effect on its form and content. Thus a rather unsatisfactory compromise has usually emerged, in which, as was suggested earlier, one can see the conflicts and the tensions between these competing claims and influences, which might be broadly polarized as a conflict between the claims of society and those of the individual, the vocational and the liberal, the economic and the humanitarian, a national investment and the right of every child, the instrumental and the intrinsic, what education is *for* and what it *is*, élitism and egalitarianism, and perhaps, in general, between the possible and the desirable, between reality and idealism.

The history of the development of education in the United Kingdom reveals a constant swinging of these pendula; and the actualities of the curriculum as a result always represent some attempt at achieving a compromise view. It must be repeated that the degree to which idealism, concern with what might be, with the desirable, has predominated has depended to a very large extent on the degree of freedom or autonomy enjoyed by the teachers themselves, so that, as we shall see later, the political moves to press the school curriculum in the opposite direction, towards what is possible within the constraints imposed by the resources made available, towards the best economic return for the investment of those resources, have inevitably been accompanied by a major reduction in the extent and in the nature of teachers' control of curriculum planning. The rhetoric has been that of improved standards and quality; the reality has been that of increased political control. The dominant ideology has indeed begun to dominate.

OTHER CONSTRAINTS ON CURRICULUM DEVELOPMENT

Such direct political intervention has clearly been a major constraint on curriculum development and has now become direct control. This process and the nature and impact of those constraints and controls we will explore in some detail later in this chapter. We must note first, however, some of the other constraints within which teachers have always worked, lest it should be imagined that until recently respect for teacher autonomy has implied complete freedom and licence for them to do as they pleased with the school curriculum.

We must first note the influence of history or tradition. Curriculum development is essentially a matter of encouraging change in a curriculum that already exists, and the demands of any entity to be left substantially untouched are always strong. Curriculum change is one aspect of social change so that it shares that tendency of all institutions to resist any attempts to do more than chip away at it and introduce relatively minor modifications.

In the case of curriculum change the reasons for this are not hard to find. Teachers and headteachers have been trained in certain ways, to teach certain subjects or by certain methods, so that there is a strong temptation for them not to want these changed to a degree which will require them to start again from scratch, to learn new techniques or to lose the security of working within a subject or a set of techniques with which they are at home and in which they are confident of their knowledge and ability. The same is true of those who leave the classroom and the school to join the ranks of the inspectorate or other advisory bodies. Too much change in the curriculum or in approaches to teaching and they will know less about what is going on and have less relevant experience than those they are supposed to inspect or advise.

There are a number of different ways in which one can categorize the other influences and constraints to which curriculum development is subject.

To begin with it is worth distinguishing administrative from professional factors (Maclure, 1970). Both of these will be sources of influences and constraints on developments in schools and they are also likely to be in conflict with each other more often than not. In particular, financial restrictions will invariably constrain and inhibit professional ambitions for certain kinds of development, such as a reduction in the size of classes, improved in-service provision or any other contribution to curriculum development that involves increased financial support. Equally, however, decisions made about the organization of schooling, such as the introduction of comprehensive schools or the raising of the school leaving age, may conflict with, although they may also on occasion support, certain professional aspirations for curriculum development. It has been suggested that this very conflict of forces provides the right kind of basis for change, since it allows for the interaction of and the development of a balance between these two major influences acting on education and curriculum change (Maclure, 1970).

Such influences often take a more direct form through decisions taken concerning the allocation of resources, money, materials, equipment and staff to schools. We had progressed some way from the system of 'payment by results' but economic factors of a similar kind have continued to exercise this second form of influence on curriculum planning and development whenever resources are made available for developments in certain areas rather than in others. This factor clearly looms very much larger in a context, like that which applies at present, of great financial stringency. There is no doubting, for example, the effects that 'rate-capping' has had on the quality of educational provision in many areas and on the scope for curriculum development.

This is also a factor which has become prominent as a determinant of the nature and content of the school curriculum in recent years with the advent of schemes such as the Technical and Vocational Educational Initiative, which has been funded not by the local education authorities nor even by the

Department of Education and Science but by the Manpower Services Commission. This scheme has offered schools and teachers resources for the establishment of certain kinds of curriculum project, and the availability of the finance has depended closely, if not entirely, on the willingness of those schools and teachers to develop curricula and programmes acceptable to those responsible for the allocation of this finance. It is thus a scheme in which financial control has effectively meant academic control, and it is not so far removed from the 'payment by results' philosophy or practice as to render that approach obsolete. It is also clear that the latest legislation is taking us back to that era when the allocation of resources was conditional on achievement measured according to certain predetermined, and externally determined, criteria.

A further, not unrelated influence on the curriculum which teachers have always found difficult to resist and which, in fact, they have always recognized as perhaps the most obviously significant, is that exerted by the public examination system and, indeed, by all forms of external testing. Clearly, again, this is an influence which is likely to increase in significance with the advent of regular testing at seven-, eleven-, fourteen- and sixteen-plus, which is an essential part of the new policies for schooling in the United Kingdom.

This aspect of the public examination system has been recognized officially for many years. A good deal of evidence of this was offered to the Taunton Commission (Report of the Schools Inquiry Commission, 1868) and we find it reiterated in similar evidence included in the Beloe Report (Secondary Schools Examinations Council, 1960), which records that the committee was told by many people from many different areas of the education service that 'the examination dictates the curriculum and cannot do otherwise; it confines experiment, limits free choice of subject, hampers treatment of subjects, encourages wrong values in the classroom' (op. cit., p. 23, para. 77). It is clear too that this effect is as influential on the methods of teaching which teachers adopt as on the subject content of their work (Pudwell, 1980), and that it is 'an influence which extends to age ranges well below the fourth and fifth secondary years' (DES, 1981, p. 4). And of course, with the planned extension of the programme of testing, this influence will increase in strength and will extend well down into the primary school.

It should perhaps be made clear that what is needed is to find some way in which continuous curriculum development and the demands of the public examination can be reconciled. It is clearly not acceptable to abolish examination systems totally in order to free the curriculum from their pressures. What is needed is to devise an acceptable working relationship between the two, for a restricting influence on the curriculum is the *effect* rather than the *purpose* of the public examination system (Pudwell, 1980). Its purposes are quite different and we ought not to lose sight of these in the process of considering one of its side-effects, no matter how important that is.

What is needed is a close consideration of public examination systems to ensure that they provide those who need it with the right kind of accurate information about the achievements and perhaps also the potential of individual pupils, and that they do this without placing undue limitations on curriculum development. 'Examinations must be designed and used to serve the educational process' (DES, 1981, p. 4).

LOCAL INFLUENCES AND CONSTRAINTS

Public examinations and testing are another example, then, of national factors which act as constraints on the development of the curriculum. However, there are many local factors too.

When we turn to a consideration of these local influences on the curriculum, those that come most readily to mind are the influences on the schools exercised by those bodies and people responsible for running them. Where, as in the United Kingdom, ultimate responsibility for the financing and administration of schools has rested with local government, a good deal of power would seem to reside with local government officers, although we must not forget that most of the money they have to spend on education comes from the central government in the form of a rate support grant.

How far this power extends to direct influence on or control of the curriculum, however, is another matter. Certainly it is the task of the advisory staff to contribute to curriculum development. Equally certainly, as we continually mention, decisions made by those who hold the purse strings will often have important consequences for the curriculum. In practice the balance between professional and administrative interests is most obvious at this local level, the local politicians and education officers working in parallel with the advisers, and the teachers influencing organizational decisions either through their unions or by direct membership of certain advisory bodies.

A good example of the importance of achieving the right kind of balance is to be found in the effects on the curriculum of schools of the recent reduction in the numbers of their pupils. For the way in which a local authority responds to falling rolls will not merely influence but will in many cases determine the kind of curriculum a school can offer. Some authorities, for example, may encourage a concentration on the 'core' curriculum by giving priority to the staffing of subjects within this core (Davies, 1980), while others may wish to permit schools to continue to offer a range of choices, even where this may necessitate an improvement in the staff–pupil ratio. In the face of problems of this kind the nature of the balance between professional and administrative interests becomes crucial.

An attempt to achieve the same sort of balance can also be seen in the constitution of the governing bodies of individual educational institutions, where again political and professional interests meet. This has been especially true since the recent introduction to many governing bodies of teacher, parent and, sometimes, student members. Technically, these are the bodies responsible for the curriculum of the school. In practice, however, in the United Kingdom they have normally restricted their attentions to the general conduct of the school, leaving responsibility for the curriculum to the headteacher and thus to the school staff. Their power has been, therefore, somewhat limited in its effect but potentially it is great (Jenkins and Shipman, 1976), and the addition of more parent, teacher and student members is beginning to unleash this potential force. Certainly events, such as those at the William Tyndale School, which have led to attempts to tighten control over what the schools are doing, have resulted also in a wider exercise of their powers by governing bodies and a formal strengthening of those powers. It was with the intention of promoting this kind of wider sphere of influence that the Taylor Committee (DES, 1977a) made its recommendations on the membership of governing bodies. And, in suggesting that they should become more truly representative of the community as a whole, the Committee also recommended that such bodies should contribute more fully to policy-making within the school and exercise a more direct influence on its curriculum. These policies have been encapsulated in subsequent legislation.

A major feature of the changes proposed by the Taylor Committee was the increased involvement of parents in school government. In the United Kingdom parents have until recently had little scope for influencing what goes on in schools, in spite of their obvious concern for the standard and kind of education their offspring are receiving. Parent–teacher associations have tended to operate at the social level only, and even when committees of parents have been organized by local authorities their influence has not been very great (Jenkins and Shipman, 1976). In the USA, however, the influence of parents on the curriculum has been strong (Jenkins and Shipman, 1976); and now that they have direct access to, and increased representation on, the governing bodies of many schools in the United Kingdom their influence there has begun to increase. Certainly, if the potential power of the governing bodies is to be realized it is from this direction that the initial impetus is most likely to come.

It is this that gives interest to the proposals of the Taylor Committee, in the United Kingdom, to amend the constitution of governing bodies to make them more 'professional' by including a membership over half of which would be directly elected by parents and school staff, and by insisting that all governors, however elected, should be given a course of training which would include school administration, teaching methods, the curriculum and financial matters. Such a 'professional' governing body would then be given control of the school curriculum. Indeed, the new Education Act gives governing bodies, whether professional in this sense or not, the power to 'opt out' of local authority control and take charge of the affairs of the schools totally themselves, albeit within the confines of the prescribed and required National Curriculum and under the direct supervision of the Secretary of State. The Act also includes arrangements for the delegation of budgeting powers by local authorities to the 'local financial management' of governing bodies.

Developments such as these will not only have the effect of giving the parents more 'say' in the affairs of the school and especially in curriculum matters, they will also perhaps put the kind of teeth into the governing body that might enable it to become a more effective factor in curriculum change. It is essential, however, that teachers also be involved at this level, since, as we saw in Chapter 5, in the last analysis they will decide what actually happens in the classroom. The suggestion that if governors are given this kind of control over the curriculum teachers should retain their professional responsibility for methods would seem to acknowledge this fact, but to try to separate the curriculum from the methods used to implement it in this way is to misunderstand totally the nature of the educational process. Teachers must be involved with others in all aspects of planning.

CONSTRAINTS WITHIN THE SCHOOL

Whatever the relationship between teachers and their governing bodies, however, constraints on curriculum development and planning will also arise within the school itself. Most of these derive from those factors we considered in some depth in the last chapter when we were exploring some of the problems of promoting curriculum development within the individual school. Most of the factors which we saw identified there as barriers to change must also be seen as constraints on the activities of teachers wishing to change or develop their curricula. Such constraints were listed under three main headings by the Schools Council's study 'Purpose, Power and Constraint in the Primary School Curriculum' (Taylor *et al.*, 1974): 'Constraints imposed by the human element (personal)', 'Organizational and administrative constraints' and 'Physical constraints'. Most teachers will readily recognize the significance of all these factors in constraining any ambitions they may have for curriculum development.

Subsequent studies have reinforced this evidence of the effects of factors of this kind in any school on the nature of its curriculum. Increasingly, sociological studies have come to concern themselves with what has been called the 'micro-politics of the school' (Ball, 1987) and, although the emphasis there and elsewhere has too often been on management issues – grouping practices, styles of headship and other such organizational matters – it is slowly being realized that internal constraints and influences are not only a major determinant of curriculum content and style but also that these are likely to be idiosyncratic, a shifting and too uncertain basis for generalizations. For, first, what has to be recognized is 'the peculiar nature of schools as organizations' (Ball, 1987, p. 7), so that the application of organizational theory derived from other sources to the management of schools must be regarded with some suspicion. Secondly, because this has too often remained unappreciated, there has been little useful or productive research into the 'organizational aspects of school life' (ibid.). And, third, we must expect any such research not only to reveal a, perhaps unexpected, complexity of organization but also to demonstrate the individual, peculiar and continually changing nature of each unique school community.

In short, recent research would suggest that we generalize at our peril about internal influences and constraints on the curriculum, but that we run equal risks if we ignore the impact of internal organization, styles of headship or leadership and, in general, the complex interrelationships which exist in any individual school, when attempting to plan or develop that school's curriculum. All these factors clearly have important implications for the practice of school-based curriculum development which we discussed in Chapter 5 and, indeed, do much to explain why that approach to curriculum development has come to seem to some people as the only route to effective change. They thus also have important implications for the current policy of imposing a common national curriculum on all schools without regard for their individual characteristics as unique human communities.

THE SHIFT TO DIRECT INTERVENTION AND CONTROL

It was suggested earlier that, while there is a sense in which the whole social context of curriculum planning can be described as political, it is also possible, and indeed necessary, to identify more overt forms of political influence and pressure; in short, to note the point at which such pressure changes from being an influence on curriculum development to being a deliberate attempt to exert control over it. It was also noted that a change of this kind has occurred in the United Kingdom during the last few years.

We must now consider some of the ways in which those general influences which we have just discussed have become sharpened up by recent political developments to the point where their impact on education has become more clearly overt, direct and significant and where the degree of autonomy and of responsibility exercised by teachers has become correspondingly more limited. In short, we will be tracing the development of some of these influences into agencies of direct control.

For the present-day student of the curriculum must recognize that, although the other influences persist (and it is the conflicts that result from their persistence that brings complexity to his or her studies) and have a right to be recognized and acknowledged, the dominant influence at the present time is the political influence. And it is important to stress too that the political focus of current curriculum policies should not take the debate beyond either the concern or the reach of the teacher in the classroom, rather it renders his or her contribution to that debate especially important.

We must begin by noting that it is not unreasonable or unusual for those who hold the purse strings to have or to demand some kind of say in questions of how money shall be spent, as is clear not only from a review of education in other countries but also from the briefest examination of the history of education in Great Britain. For, from the earliest days of state aid, schools in receipt of such aid were required to meet certain conditions concerning the uses made of it, so that some schools were known to refuse badly needed financial assistance in order to retain their control (Davies, 1980). With the arrival of state-provided education too, responsibility for the curriculum was in the hands of the school boards, although usually exercised through curriculum committees or individual governing bodies. The same was true when, as a result of the 1902 Education Act, the counties and county boroughs took on responsibility for the schools, and that the ultimate authority for curriculum lay with the local education authorities was reaffirmed by the Education Act of 1944.

However, although this continued to be the legal position for many years, in practice a rather different system had developed. For the Hadow Reports of 1926 and 1931 emphasized the notion of the freedom and responsibility of the teacher in curriculum planning and thus provided a basis for the growth of the idea of teacher autonomy in this area.

It could be argued that the attempt to plan 'education for all' in the United Kingdom effectively began with the Hadow Reports, the main thrust of which was towards the creation of quite separate primary and secondary sectors within the school system. This was accompanied by much debate about and deliberate planning of the curriculum in the newly created primary sector. In the secondary sector, however, greater constraints on curriculum change existed, not least in the form of the syllabuses established by examination boards, so that little happened there beyond that process of 'unplanned drift' (Hoyle, 1969a) to which we drew attention in Chapter 1, what Maurice Kogan (1978, p. 53) has called the 'comfortable consensus in British education between 1945 and early "60s" '.

In this context there developed an acceptance of, although at no stage any official concession of, the notion of the autonomy of the teacher in the area of the curriculum. It was generally agreed that that was the sphere of his or her professional expertise and, although the freedom enjoyed there was relative, since, as we saw earlier, there are always and inevitably a good many indirect external constraints on curriculum planning, the teacher was conceded freedom from direct external control. The cynics might argue that teachers were allowed this only because they were doing nothing – certainly nothing radical – with it, but, whatever the reason, the fact remains that the official policy was one of *laissez-faire* and the teachers' autonomy in matters of curriculum continued largely unchallenged.

The challenge first came in the mid-1950s along with that felt need for deliberate curriculum planning to which we referred in Chapter 1. There was much concern that the West might be lagging behind in the race for technological advance and, not unreasonably, a prime area for the exploration of that thesis was the education system. It was also, of course, felt that, if the thesis proved to be true, changes in the curriculum would have to occur to correct the trend.

Thus, first in the USA and then in the United Kingdom money was made available for curriculum research and development, the emphasis of which was naturally on science and technology, although attention was not confined to these areas since there was a parallel stress on 'creativity' which considerably broadened the scope. In the USA this was accompanied by a good deal of encouragement to senior academics in the universities to interest themselves in the school curriculum and its development.

In the United Kingdom proposals of a similar kind were viewed by the teachers as a challenge to what they saw as their established autonomy on curriculum matters, so that the attempt by the government to set up in 1961 a curriculum study group, what the Minister of Education of the day, Sir David Eccles, described as 'a commando-type unit to enter the secret garden', a unit planned on similar lines to those earlier bodies of that name which had effectively controlled the curriculum in the schools of their day, led to conflict with the teachers' unions and the ultimate creation in 1964, under Sir Edward Boyle as minister, of the Schools Council for Curriculum and Examinations, a differently constituted, teacher-controlled and thus more politically independent body. It seems probable that Sir David Eccles's concern to open up the school curriculum to a wider audience and to increase the influence of central government on it was motivated 'by what he regarded as greater educational efficiency' (Lawton, 1980, p. 32), although one must note that this continues to be the rhetoric of political intervention. However, his attempt did not succeed, so that in 1969 he still had good reason to describe the curriculum as a secret garden, and those people, such as some intrepid governors of maintained schools, who attempted to trespass were very firmly warned off.

The subsequent two decades have seen considerable inroads made into that garden, and it is interesting to speculate on the reasons for this. One reason must be the evidence of that apparent ineffectiveness of the Schools Council in terms at least of real curriculum change, which we noted in Chapter 5.

A second factor has been the growth of public concern over the changes that were taking place in schools. The efforts of several generations of sociologists had combined with the pressures of the Labour party to ensure the spread, which after Circular 10/65 was to become almost total, of comprehensive secondary schools. In many of these, and in most primary schools, there were mixed-ability classes. Furthermore, some of the attempts of the teachers themselves at curriculum change were equally disturbing to some people. 'Modern' or informal methods in primary schools, schemes of integrated studies in secondary schools and other comparable developments were leading to a realization on the part of parents and others that the schools their children were attending were very different from those they had attended themselves. And, instead of recognizing that this was equally true of their homes, their cars, their places of work and their forms of entertainment, they began to get worried at the results of leaving the curriculum to teachers. As so often, autonomy was splendid, so long as no one used it.

These significant changes in the school curriculum can be seen as reflecting several aspects of what Lawrence Stenhouse (1980a) has called the 'curriculum development' or the 'curriculum research and development' era in British education. This was an era when attempts were being made to incorporate some of the things we were learning about curriculum development, especially through the work of the Schools Council, into the realities of curriculum practice in schools. In other words, this was a time when our knowledge of the complexities of education and of curriculum planning was being markedly extended by research of many different kinds and in many different contexts, and this was leading, quite properly, to the emergence of more sophisticated approaches to educational and curriculum planning. We were beginning to understand more clearly what it means to claim that education entails more than the mere acquisition of knowledge; we were questioning the sanctity of traditional divisions of this knowledge into subjects; we were becoming aware of the inadequacies of curriculum planning based on the achievement of simple behavioural objectives; we were learning more about the problems of educational equality, or rather educational inequality; and in particular we were coming to appreciate how far such inequality is a function not so much of the education system as of the curriculum itself.

A growing awareness of all of these factors, then, along with a concern to act on our increasing knowledge and understanding of them, was pushing the curriculum in directions other than those who are concerned primarily with the economic or political role of education in society wished it to go. For what underpins these factors is a concern with education as a process of individual development, which can be promoted only by curriculum provision tailored to the requirements of individual pupils rather than planned to force all through the same programme, by an educational diet designed to suit each person's unique intellectual metabolism rather than the offering of the same food to all, whether it helps them towards healthy educational development or makes them nauseous. In turn this leads to a move away from traditional forms of academicism; educational experiences can take many forms and are certainly not confined to what can be gained from studying traditional school subjects. And what seems most obviously to count as an educational experience is more likely to be found in areas which comprise what we call the humanities (the etymology of the word itself would seem to support this claim) or social studies than in the study of science and technology. This is the substance of that leaning towards 'idealist' approaches to schooling which, we noted earlier, is displayed by most teachers and is thus a significant effect of teacher autonomy in matters of curriculum.

In short, one can detect at least the beginnings of an ideological shift – from a prime concern with society's needs to a favouring of those of the individual, from the rhetoric of educational equality towards its realities, from the economic to the social function of schooling, from education as the transmission of knowledge to education as individual development, and from the notion of the teacher as instructor to a clearer view of the teacher as educator.

Two further factors can be seen as adding to the complexities of this movement. The first is the accelerating rate of technological advance and the consequent view that the educational system needs to be able to respond continuously to this. The second is the continuing economic recession, which has not only created a desire for schooling to be used to promote, above all else, economic productivity, but has equally and perhaps more significantly led to a reduction in the level of resourcing of education (as of all other social services) and thus to an ever increasing demand for 'value for money'. To put it rather simply, and perhaps crudely, there had been less concern with the resources and energies teachers were devoting to the promotion of educational equality, education as development, the 'social service' dimension of educational provision, when the state could afford this as well as the other, more economically useful, things that schools were doing and can do. But that 'golden age' (if it had ever really been such, except with hindsight and by comparison with the present) was about to end.

An increased rate of technological advance, along with a reduction in the resources made available to education (again a change paralleled in other social services), has resulted, therefore, in a move towards the increased external control of the school curriculum and of teachers, and a corresponding loss of teacher autonomy. That shift towards a more liberal view which we noted just now has had to be arrested. The movement has had to be reversed, away from the view of education as a social service, away from the Crowther Report's view of it as the right of every child regardless of return, towards the view of education as a national investment, towards an emphasis on its economic function, towards a curriculum framed solely in terms of subjects and with an emphasis on those subjects whose major contribution can be seen to be utilitarian. Lawrence Stenhouse's (1980a) era of 'curriculum research and development' has given way to an age of accountability, 'the fashion has swung from "curriculum reform" to "educational accountability" ' (op. cit., p. 259); and the period which Maurice Kogan (1978) describes as 'the onset of doubt', from 1964 to 1977, has become his 'struggle over curriculum and standards'.

This is a development whose major landmarks it will be interesting and enlightening for us to trace.

MAJOR LANDMARKS IN THE MOVE TOWARDS CENTRAL CONTROL

Denis Lawton (1980) argues with some conviction that the movement to establish greater central control over the school curriculum began immediately after the failure to establish the commando-style Curriculum Study Group in the early 1960s. That movement began to reveal itself in overt forms in the late 1960s and gathered increasing momentum throughout the 1970s and 1980s.

One of its first manifestations was the publication of a series of 'Black Papers' on education in 1969 (Cox and Dyson, 1969a and b). The contributors to these publications, in Jeremiah fashion, inveighed against all the forms of educational innovation we mentioned earlier as emerging in response to a growing concern within the profession for improvements in quality and the increased understanding of education and curriculum which was becoming available through various forms of research. These innovations, they claimed, were leading to a serious decline in educational standards, and, on their definition of educational standards, perhaps they were. In reality, it was the very concept of what might constitute educational standards which was changing. For them, however, since this was resulting in significant changes from traditional patterns of schooling, it had to be unacceptable. Like Plato in a former era they were concerned to reassert traditional views of knowledge and schooling in order to arrest change – not only educational change but its concomitant social change too – the assumption being, as it had been for Plato himself, that some kind of perfection had been reached so that any change from that must constitute degeneration and decline. It is an odd line of argument, perhaps odder in the twentieth century than it was in the fourth century BC, but nevertheless that was the line which was taken and promulgated. Individual contributors to the Black Papers attacked the comprehensivization of secondary schools with its concomitant 'destruction' of the grammar schools, the introduction of mixed-ability classes, the spread of informal approaches to teaching in primary schools with their emphasis on 'play' (a vastly misunderstood concept) and corresponding lack of attention to what they called 'the basic skills', but never clearly defined. In general, the claim was that all such developments were leading to a lowering of educational standards and this was asserted with no apparent recognition of the need for evidence to support such a claim, for some conceptual clarification of notions such as that of 'standards', or even for an acknowledgement of the research evidence which had led to the innovations in the first instance. In fact, the lack of any kind of respect for the basic principles of intellectual debate and argument has been a major feature of this movement from the beginning, and it continues to chime very oddly in the claims of those whose prime concern is stated to be the raising of academic standards.

Scaremongering, however, has never relied on evidence or logic or any aspect of rational argument. Its basic premise is that if you frighten people sufficiently they will begin to support your alternative, usually reactionary, policies. The first group formally to board this bandwagon was the Confederation of British Industry (CBI) which itself began to assert that schools were not doing enough to encourage high standards in what it also called, but never clearly defined, 'the basic skills', nor were they giving enough attention to *applied* forms of both the arts and the sciences. The cry now was not merely that educational standards were falling but that the economic function of schooling was being neglected.

This of course does represent a redefinition, albeit never made explicit, of what we might mean by educational standards; a redefinition, moreover, in terms of economic utility rather than of the intellectualism or academicism of the Black Paper writers. It thus represents perhaps the earliest evidence of what the purpose and the flavour of increased central control of the curriculum was to be. For the criteria by which schools and teachers are to be judged, evaluated and held accountable are clearly to be criteria derived not from their conceptions or definitions of their tasks as professional educators but criteria based on the expectations of those outside the schools and the teaching profession who see themselves as 'consumers' and/or as 'providers' and, in either role, as having the right to dictate policy. Developments since that time, up to the 1988 Education Act, can be properly understood only if viewed and recognized in those terms.

These critics were soon to have what they regarded as the most effective ammunition possible for their battle against curriculum development and innovation. In 1974 events at the ILEA's William Tyndale School were made much of by the press and were seized upon by the critics as overwhelming support for the criticisms they had been offering, the fears they had been expressing and the assertions they had been making about where teacher autonomy would take us. The same lack of concern for scholarship which had permitted them to make their earlier assertions without proper evidence now allowed them also to blow this piece of evidence up to something totally disproportionate to its significance. The events at William Tyndale School were in many respects highly unsatisfactory; they showed up many people, not least the ILEA inspectorate, in a very poor light; they did reveal what the abuse or misuse or injudicious use of teacher autonomy could lead to. What they did not do was offer evidence of a nationwide problem; they had no significance at all for the work of those tens of thousands of schools where teachers were exercising their professional autonomy to the best of their ability in what they saw as the best interests of their pupils. That, however, was the interpretation placed on them by those who wished to see things in that light.

At the very time when the William Tyndale affair was continuing, the nation suddenly found itself in the throes of the crisis created by the Oil Producing and Exporting Countries' (OPEC) decision to raise dramatically the price of oil. This event had an immediate impact on many aspects of the nation's economy. Its significance for education was not so readily apparent. The consequent economic recession, however, was bound to lead to major reductions in the resourcing of the education service and to those demands for 'value for money' referred to earlier. In fact, the education budget continued to expand in real terms until as late as 1977 (Kogan, 1978), but the problems of the economy soon caught up with it and, as we saw earlier, this became another element in the tale being unfolded here.

There followed a series of events which can be seen as leading remorselessly to the level of central control of education encapsulated in the 1988 Act.

In 1974 the Manpower Services Commission was created with a clear brief and the necessary resources to develop schemes to correct what was seen as a mismatch between the qualities and skills displayed by school leavers and the needs of employers. Its focus has been on the further education sector of schooling, a sector increasingly seen as embracing the age group from fourteen to eighteen, and successive schemes, such as its Youth Opportunities Programme (YOP), Youth Training Scheme (YTS) and Technical and Vocational Educational Initiative (TVEI) have led to a progressive separation of training from education which has resulted in 'the creation of a separate group of worker-pupils' (Ball, 1984a, p. 15), and thus in the emergence of a new form of tripartism in which 'a clear technical/vocational stream is being established alongside the academic stream within comprehensive schools' (Simon, 1985, p. 227) and in which 'it is likely that the intention is that this stream should bifurcate into a higher and a lower level, the majority focusing on more strictly vocational activities in the latter' (ibid.).

One can thus see the place of this development in the scheme of things we are describing here and, in particular, its significance for the redefinition of education and educational standards in instrumental, utilitarian and economic terms.

In the following year, 1975, the Assessment of Performance Unit was established. The role of this unit and its implications for curriculum development have been discussed in greater detail in Chapter 5. We must note here, however, that its creation was undoubtedly a further milestone on the road to greater centralized control of education and of the curriculum. For its main task was to monitor standards and to identify the incidence of underachievement in schools and, while there is no suggestion here that its concern was to be with any redefinition of standards in vocational or economic terms, it can be no coincidence that its initial attention was directed towards what were later to become the core subjects of the National

Curriculum (DES, 1987a) – mathematics, language and science – or that a major subsequent concern has been design and technology. There is no doubt that it was set up to act as a watchdog over the curriculum or that it has been viewed in that light, in spite of its many efforts to carve out for itself a more positive role in curriculum development. Its establishment thus represents another step towards centralized control.

At about this time, too, events were occurring in teachers education whose implications were to prove far-reaching. Miscalculations in the Department of Education and Science had led to a massive over-production of newly qualified teachers in the early to mid-1970s as school rolls fell dramatically. There was much unemployment among teachers, especially those just completing their initial courses, and clearly there was a need for tighter controls of entry to such courses. It was an opportunity to raise entry qualifications for the profession and it was used as such, first to create an all-graduate profession and later to make additional requirements for such qualifications as GCE 'O' level mathematics and English language passes for all new entrants.

It also offered, however, seemingly sound pretexts for intervention of a more direct kind in the work of institutions offering courses of teacher education. To reduce the number of students on such courses, colleges had to be 'diversified' (have their attentions switched to courses other than teacher education courses), merged with one another or with other institutions of higher education to make viable units, or even, in many cases, closed altogether. Decisions of this kind were to a large extent left to be decided at local level, but they ultimately depended on the allocation of student numbers by the Department of Education and Science. The Department thus gained effective control over the system through the distribution of these numbers and it is no great step, as subsequent events have shown and as we shall see in due course, from that kind of control to control over the nature and content of the curriculum of these courses. It is also the case that the teacher-education institutions, whether diversified, merged or closed, were the first sector of the education system to experience the problems of staff redundancies. Or, to put it differently, they offered employers the first experiences of how such redundancies could be handled. The need to reduce the number of teachers in training, therefore, was the thin edge of a wedge whose effects in prising open not only the colleges and departments of education but also the schools and, indeed, the universities and polytechnics were to prove very far-reaching indeed.

There followed a series of events which made overt and public the drive towards greater central control. For most people the first indication of this came in the autumn of 1976 with a famous speech by James Callaghan as

Prime Minister, at Ruskin College, Oxford, in which he mounted a direct attack on the teaching profession for failing to respond to the needs of society by permitting too many people to spend too much time studying subjects which he deemed to be not directly productive in commercial and economic terms. Too many sixth form pupils were studying humanities subjects and thus too few were studying science and technology. This perceived imbalance was leading to a similarly unsatisfactory pattern of study in universities and other institutions of higher education. This was seen as a result of allowing teachers at all levels too much 'say' in the planning of the curriculum, so that one obvious solution to the problem was to be found in a reduction of teacher autonomy and a corresponding increase in external control, particularly from the centre.

While this may have come as a surprise to many people, to some it was expected. All that was in that speech, and indeed much that has followed since, had been foreshadowed in 1976 in a supposedly confidential 'Yellow Book' which contained detailed plans for the achievement of greater central control of the curriculum. And, also in 1976, a report of the House of Commons Expenditure Committee had propounded the view that the Department of Education and Science did not have enough control over expenditure on education or, rather, that it contributed nothing to national planning of education beyond the allocation of resources. Policy-making was largely in the hands of local education authorities, which for a variety of reasons, some of them party political, did not always arrange the distribution of resources in accordance with policies of which central government would entirely approve. One of the recommendations of this report was for the establishment of a permanent group, with a significant lay membership, to offer an independent view on the planning of the education service at the national level.

Nothing that has happened in subsequent years can be understood as anything more than an attempt to put right these perceived deficiencies by this kind of device, by strengthening the control of central government over all aspects of educational policy and spending, and increasing the lay, and especially the industrial and commercial, involvement in educational planning.

The 1944 Education Act, by not laying down any requirements for the school curriculum (other than the necessary inclusion of religious education), had created, or perpetuated, a triangular form of control of both education and the curriculum, the three corners, or sides, of that triangle being central government, the local education authorities and the teachers themselves (Lawton, 1980). This was now being regarded in some quarters as a serious deficiency, so that calls began to be heard for a common, centrally determined curriculum – at least for secondary schools – for the reformation of and increased powers for governing bodies and for a corresponding reduction in the influence of the teachers in matters of curriculum. This, as we shall see, has subsequently been extended to include policies for reducing the powers of local authorities in all areas of educational provision, for the 1988 Education Act gives the Secretary of State unprecedented powers of control and, by reducing the roles not only of the teachers themselves but also of the local authorities, effectively replaces that triangular form of control with a set of mechanisms which are largely unidimensional.

The declaration of James Callaghan at Ruskin was followed by the so-called 'Great Debate' which was conducted through all the media and stage-managed by Shirley Williams, Secretary of State for Education and Science in that Labour government. Ostensibly, the point of this was to make education a matter of public concern and discussion. Its real purpose can be seen only as a step towards increased centralization of control.

This debate culminated in the publication in 1977 of a Green Paper (DES, 1977b), which set out an interventionist strategy based on several major proposals of a specific kind for, amongst other things, the establishment of a national curriculum, performance testing of pupils and the appraisal of teachers. In the same year, Circular 14/77 required local education authorities to produce detailed statements of their curricular policies, and this requirement was naturally and immediately passed on to schools, which suddenly found themselves faced with the task of preparing and producing curricular statements at a level of detail they had in most places never experienced before, for which, one must admit, few were prepared and of which fewer, sadly, were capable.

The year 1977 also saw the publication of the Taylor Report (DES, 1977a) on the government of schools, a report whose main recommendations, as we saw earlier, were that governing bodies of schools should be given increased powers, especially in relation to the school curriculum, and that there should be increased representation of parents on all such bodies.

Also at about this time began to appear that plethora of official documents on the school curriculum, emerging from Her Majesty's Inspectorate and from the Department of Education and Science, which we will examine in greater detail in a later section.

The first piece of the legislation which was to translate these discussions and proposals into official policy was the 1980 Education Act, which gave more power to local authorities in the matter of controlling the curricular provision of their schools, although at the same time requiring of them statements of their own general policies in this area, and also increased the powers of parents, not only by translating into statutory form some of the recommendations of the Taylor Report concerning membership of governing bodies, but also by giving them increased scope for the choice of schools for their children and, as a corollary to this, requiring schools to make public their curricula and their achievements, especially their results in public examinations.

Attention then turned to less prominent, although equally important, aspects of educational provision. The Schools Council was reconstituted in such a way as to remove that control by teachers over its finances which we have suggested elsewhere was so crucial to its work. This move effectively put an end to all open, teacher-controlled research in education. The money available through this channel for research (never, it must be said, a very large sum) was now to be spent according to policies generated by administering committees on which politicians and industrialists were to have effective control. It was no surprise, and not much more of a loss, therefore, when, with effect from 31 March 1984, all public funding of the Council was withdrawn and it was thus effectively killed off. It was immediately replaced by the Schools Curriculum Development Council (SCDC), which is essentially a political rather than professional agency, and which looks remarkably like that Curriculum Study Group which we saw Sir David Eccles had failed to establish in the early 1960s.

In the early 1980s the Council for Accreditation of Teacher Education (CATE) was also established, again a political agency with a very strict and detailed brief to review all courses of initial teacher education and to approve only those which conform to specifically laid down criteria. These are mainly quantitative, but they do reveal a clear underlying policy, since they include requirements such as that all four-year undergraduate courses leading to qualified teacher status must devote at least two of the four years to the study of a 'curriculum subject', even for students preparing to teach nursery age children – a clear example of the simple subject-based view of the school curriculum which pervades all current official policies. They require too the setting up of advisory committees to oversee the planning of courses in all institutions preparing teachers for entry into the profession, and these committees must include representatives from commerce and industry and from the employers of teachers as well as from the teachers and teacher-educators themselves. We noted earlier how, in response to the need to control entry to the profession, at least in numerical terms, the Department of Education and Science had taken to itself the power to allocate target numbers for admission to teacher-education courses in all institutions. We can see here how that power has been extended to encompass control over the content and the curricula of such courses since, if they are not accredited by CATE in terms of their content and curricula, they will be allocated no target figures and no resources, so that they must wither and die. We can see too how the imposition of this subject-based pattern on teacher-education courses must lead to, and indeed can now be seen to be a preliminary step towards, the imposition of a similar subject-based pattern on the school curriculum.

Not only then is there to be no more politically independent research in education, with the demise of the Schools Council, there is also to be no more politically independent initial teacher education. Teachers are not to be encouraged to ask the kinds of question about education and the school curriculum which our earlier chapters have tried to show are so important and which the work of the Schools Council and the courses provided in many colleges and departments of education have been prompting them to address. Their professional responsibilities are no longer to be regarded as extending that far. What they are to teach is now decided for them; how they are to teach it is to be their only professional concern.

This development was reinforced by the 1986 Education Act, which not only extended the work of the 1980 Act by further increasing the powers of governing bodies and the level of parental representation on them, but also introduced new arrangements for the funding of the in-service education of teachers (INSET). These arrangements effectively place control of the funding of all INSET work in the hands of the Department of Education and Science, to which all local education authorities must submit their proposals for approval for funding. In practice, this is resulting in most of the available money being devoted to short courses, often of a largely practical kind, mounted by the local authorities themselves or to school-based 'Baker days' – opportunities for the staffs of schools to explore together aspects of their curricula. And, while one does not wish to denigrate such provision, one must acknowledge that its corollary is that very little money is now being made available for teachers to attend courses of a more rigorous or more intellectually demanding kind in institutions of higher education, so that again it is that critical and analytical review of education and curriculum which such courses have come to provide which is being lost.

The slow disappearance of this element from INSET provision is reinforcing the loss of free, professionally controlled research and the reduction of opportunities in initial courses of teacher education for the development of properly critical professional attitudes, and it is taking the profession inexorably back to an era of much reduced professional responsibility and thus of greatly limited professional opportunities. That element of job satisfaction, which has attracted so many people to the teaching profession and which has been seen as compensating, at least to some extent, for low salaries and the total absence of any of those 'perks' that people of comparable abilities in almost any other walk of life enjoy, is disappearing very quickly indeed, so that one wonders what, if anything, will continue to attract young people into teaching and one is not surprised to learn of the increasing difficulties of recruitment being experienced by institutions.

The process which this section has endeavoured to describe has reached its culmination, at least for the present, in the Education Act of 1988. The pieces of the jigsaw have all finally been put together and, if the picture was in any way obscure before, it is now complete and clear. There is to be a subject-based centrally determined National Curriculum; its core subjects are to be mathematics, English and science, to which 30 to 40 per cent of curriculum time should be devoted, although at primary level 'the majority of curriculum time . . . should be devoted to the core subjects' (DES, 1987a, p. 6); in addition 'the foundation subjects should comprise a modern foreign language, technology, history, geography, art, music and physical education' (ibid.). There is to be a programme of national testing at four key stages during the period of compulsory education – seven-, eleven-, fourteen- and sixteen-plus. Local education authorities must prepare and submit to the Secretary of State for approval a formula by which they will allocate resources to the schools within their jurisdiction. These schemes must also show how responsibility for managing each school's budget is to be delegated to its governing body. Governing bodies are also to have greatly increased powers in respect of the appointment, suspension and dismissal of school staff. And they will have the right to apply to the Secretary of State for grant-maintained status, in short to 'opt out' of the supervisory control of their local authority and 'go it alone' with direct funding and supervision from the Department of Education and Science. There is also machinery for the establishment of city technology colleges, whose normal running costs will be met by central government but whose capital costs will be shared between the Secretary of State and whichever organization has offered to put up the money to establish each such college. It is assumed, therefore, that a significant number of schools will become independent of local authority funding and control.

Finally, although it is not our direct concern here, it is worth noting, since it reflects those general trends we have been identifying, that the Act also contains many clauses designed to ensure much greater centralized control over higher education. There will be new arrangements for the funding of universities, polytechnics and colleges through funding councils containing a significant non-professional element. Local authorities will lose any direct control they may have over polytechnics and other colleges of higher education currently within their jurisdiction, and here too, as in the case of the financing of schools, they will be required to obtain the approval of the Secretary of State for schemes for the delegation of budgetary responsibility to governing bodies of all but the smallest colleges. Furthermore, at least half the members of such governing bodies must in future be representatives of employment interests.

The trends, then, are virtually complete: direct central control, subject-based curricula, an emphasis on economically productive subjects, increased involvement of industry and commerce in the management of the educational institutions of all kinds, and a much reduced professional role for teachers at all levels from the nursery to postgraduate studies.

The slow build-up of this movement towards direct intervention at national level has also been accompanied by similar developments at local level and, although it will already be apparent that recent trends have been towards a reduction of local authority influence and control, it will be worth our while to spend a short time considering recent events at this level.

INTERVENTION AT LOCAL LEVEL

It will be clear from the last section that much of what has been done by central government has made direct demands on local government and has thus led to significant changes of policy at that level. Changes in the role, the composition and the responsibilities of governing bodies, demands for properly detailed accounts of curricular policies, responses to demands for teacher appraisal and accountability and new arrangements for the funding of INSET provision, along with the associated requirements for the approval of such provision, are just some of the measures taken by central government which have had their impact on local authority practices.

In addition to this, however, some local authorities and some individual governing bodies have seized upon the opportunities these changes have offered for direct intervention in the work and curricula of schools on their own initiative. And, while some of these interventions may well be seen as being in the spirit of what central government policy appears to be concerned to promote, equally there is no doubt that others have been distinctly embarrassing to the architects of that policy nor, therefore, that they have contributed significantly to the emergence of those measures which reduce local authority powers in relation to education and curriculum and place vastly enhanced powers in the hands of central government.

For many have seen this as an opportunity to influence schooling in general and the curriculum in particular in the direction of their own particular ideologies – especially in areas such as those of anti-racist and gender issues. Hitherto, government policy has seemed to point to intervention of a general kind, entailing the production of curriculum guidelines, policy statements, records of achievement and so on. In many areas this has been translated into interventions of a specific, individual and overtly ideological kind, sometimes in direct opposition to the ideology of the government's policy, so that schools, curricula, the careers of individual teachers and the education of significant groups of pupils have been damaged by becoming battlegrounds no longer merely for competing political influences but for competing political, even party political, interventions.

For the last several years therefore the media have been able to offer us story upon story of teachers and headteachers being suspended for allegedly racist remarks or behaviour; of groups which have used their authority to insist on the inclusion of homosexuality in the curricular provision of certain schools; of other groups which have insisted on the banning of material reflecting values of this kind; of the purging of libraries and collections of textbooks of all literature regarded as reflecting values of a racist or sexist kind; and of many other kinds of attempt to ensure not merely the deletion of anything reflecting values not shared by those exercising this power but also of the positive imposition of the values they do embrace and advocate. Nor is it only the 'loony left', as it has come to be called, that is responsible for this, although it is its behaviour that has attracted most attention from the media; the 'reactionary right' can also behave in precisely the same way, although of course from a different value perspective. Whatever the source, it is not difficult to argue that such behaviour leads to a form of schooling which is positively anti-educational, nor is it difficult to see and to deplore the kind of disruption it has brought into the school lives of too many children and, indeed, into the professional lives of too many teachers.

Nor is it confined to local authority policies. Quite often one finds that this is the way in which certain governing bodies have used their newly acquired powers of control over the curriculum. Having been given direct responsibility for the school curriculum, they have quite naturally begun to exercise a direct oversight of that curriculum, but, while many have done this in a very responsible way, there is no doubt that some have attempted to use these powers quite blatantly for the furtherance of their own ideological ends. Filibustering and other forms of disruptive behaviour have become far from unusual at meetings of some governing bodies; individual governors have been known to intervene physically in the work of schools – even on occasion to the point of having had to be excluded from the premises by recourse to the law; and this kind of behaviour has in turn resulted in the same kind of disruption of the work of these schools.

These developments were referred to by Kenneth Baker himself in a speech at the Conservative Party Conference in October 1986. He gave the example of an ILEA headteacher whom he claimed had been suspended for teaching children to strive for academic excellence and of the chairman of governors of a Haringey school who had declared that he would not offer a teaching post to a Christian, and he asserted of such behaviour: 'It is nothing to do with education, but is bigotry masquerading as equality and intolerance masquerading as freedom.' This is of course a good definition of direct political intervention in education from any ideological stance; it is thus a good definition of what we are describing here.

There are two aspects of this kind of development which must be commented on briefly here. The first is the point we have just made, that it represents an attempt to use the opportunities education offers not to open children's minds but to close them in ways dictated by individual groups or persons. The second is that it must create, as indeed it has created, a climate of mistrust and of lack of confidence in teachers and headteachers, who are increasingly feeling that they must look over their shoulders constantly not to people or bodies who might be concerned with the quality of their work (this no one can object to) but to those who may find fault with their work for quite different, less easily justifiable reasons of ideological intolerance, and who may, having found fault, take punitive action of a kind which may be equally unjustifiable. It is no surprise that so many teachers and head-teachers are opting for early retirement – no more so than that lack of recruitment of young persons to the profession which we noted above and which cannot be helped by this kind of evidence of the treatment one might be subjected to professionally for no good professional reasons.

Nor is it any surprise, therefore, that recent policies have been tending towards a reduction of local authority responsibility for education, reflected especially in that delegation of powers to governing bodies and that granting of the opportunity to 'opt out' which we saw earlier are important elements in the 1988 Education Act. No doubt the Secretary of State feels that, while it is impossible under present statutes to do very much from the centre about the policies of local authorities, much more can be done to keep individual governing bodies in line, not least through the centralized control of the allocation of their resources.

The last decade, then, has seen the secret garden of the curriculum invaded from all sides. It is now a park or even commonland. It may be helpful, now that we have traced the major elements in this process, to pick out briefly its main concerns and characteristics.

THE MAIN FEATURES OF THESE DEVELOPMENTS

The stated concern of these developments, which have led inexorably towards not only direct intervention in the school curriculum but also a very tight control over it, has been with educational 'standards'. In principle, such a concern is unexceptionable. However, as anyone who has given a moment's real thought to this issue will have quickly come to appreciate, 'standards' in education are very difficult to define, one person's view of 'standards' often being very different from another's not only in terms of their levels of expectation but also, and much more importantly, in terms of their definition. One person's concern may be with whether children have learned to read, to write, to perform mathematical computations or to understand technology; another may be far more concerned with whether they have learned to think, to explore all things critically or to appreciate art of all kinds.

It is necessary, therefore, for any discussion of 'standards', and consequently, and more crucially, any attempt to implement policies concerned to improve educational 'standards', to recognize the problematic nature of this concept and to begin from some attempted analysis or clearly stated definition of what these 'standards' might be or at least what they are taken to be in the context of the policy being pursued. It is intellectually dishonest, or at best inept, to fail to acknowledge this and to act as though it is not necessary to do any more than assume a consensus on such a contentious issue. It is even more unacceptable to adopt or assume that 'scientist' view of education, the inadequacies of which were explored in Chapter 1, and treat 'standards' as though they had some objective status which anyone of right mind can 'discover'. These kinds of approach must lead, as in this case they have done, to a view of educational 'standards' framed in highly simplistic terms.

In particular, they have led to a view of educational 'standards' in terms of traditional subjects and traditional subject-content, education as what the Hadow Report (Board of Education, 1931) criticized as 'knowledge to be acquired and facts to be stored'. We saw in Chapter 2 some of the problems associated with the notion of curriculum as content and, in particular, with the criteria for the selection of such content. Those problems are not recognized in current policies, which here again ignore several decades of debate, discussion and research in this area.

This unquestioning acceptance of a traditional, indeed outmoded, view of subjects and their role in education has further consequences which we must briefly note. It leads to the same kind of academicism which once underpinned the tripartite system of secondary education, a view of education as access to high-status knowledge – that taught in the grammar schools or, nowadays, in the city technology colleges. One consequence of that view must be, as it was in the days of tripartism, an élitist system – that new form of tripartism we referred to earlier – which clearly offers differentiated curricula, one version for those who have the ability, the motivation, the interest or the ethnic and social background to handle this form of academic curriculum, and another version for the rest, designed to prepare them for less demanding jobs and, since these continue to be few and far between, planned also with some notion of social control in mind, the 1980s form of 'gentling the masses'.

Hence there must be frequent testing and assessment. We must have a means of identifying which children will benefit from the academic curriculum and which must be offered something less. We must identify weakness from the earliest possible stage. It is no longer enough to apply selective procedures at eleven-plus; we must also apply them at seven-, at fourteen- and at sixteen-plus.

And all of this reflects a view of education with a quantitative rather than a qualitative emphasis, a concern with how much of the content-based offering children can absorb rather than with the quality of the experiences they can be offered by their years of compulsory schooling. It is very little different, therefore, from the approach to education which the Hadow Report (Board of Education, 1931) also criticized (and suggested was a thing of the past), an approach concerned solely 'to secure that children acquired a minimum standard of proficiency in reading, writing and arithmetic, subjects in which their attainments were annually assessed by quantitative standards' (op. cit., p. 16).

A further major feature of these developments is the emphasis on technology and on the resultant demands of the economy. The education system is now seen almost totally as a national investment and not as one of the welfare state's social services (or at least, in respect of this latter function, is being increasingly deprived of resources in the same way as the other social services). Thus the emphasis is on what schooling is *for* rather than on any notion of education having some kind of value for its own sake. This is most apparent in the vocational stress which is being placed on educational provision at all stages from the nursery to the university. But it is more important that we recognize the general instrumentalism which is its natural, if not inevitable, effect. It would be foolish to condemn out of hand the vocational aspects of schooling, or even of higher education, and to hanker after an educational system in which all was the pursuit of knowledge for its own sake. Clearly, all educational institutions have a duty to help their pupils or students towards the attainment of productive and satisfying careers. There must be a concern, however, at the extent to which the attempt to do that can lead to an instrumentalist philosophy being displayed in all aspects of schooling, so that nothing can be valued, or its inclusion in our curriculum justified, or, as is most often the case, the expenditure of resources on it approved or made possible, except by reference to what it will lead to. For, by that criterion, much that is valuable (some might argue most valuable) in our culture will be lost from our curricula, and thus ultimately from that culture. One does not study Shakespeare because it is economically useful to do so, so that such study must be put at risk if economic utility becomes the sole, or even the main, criterion of educational worth.

Another feature of the developments we are reviewing and one which also reflects that instrumentalism we have just noted is the prevalence of industrial models and imagery in much of the official pronouncements on the curriculum. We hear of the 'delivery' of the curriculum, of its 'products', of its 'consumers', of 'providers', and 'users' and of 'machinery'. We read about our 'competitor countries' (DES, 1987a, p. 3). We increasingly hear of teachers, and especially headteachers, as 'managers'. We are thus offered a factory, or even factory-farming, view of schools and schooling. Again, then, the analogy leads us to the instrumentalism of commerce. And it is worth remembering Elliot Eisner's comment that metaphors 'shape our conception of the problems we study' (1982, p. 6).

Nor does this remain at the level of analogy or metaphor. There are many aspects of current policies which not only use the imagery of commerce but move us positively towards the notion of schools and other educational institutions as commercial enterprises. The right now granted to schools to 'opt out' of local authority control is one such example; the invitation to industrial and commercial sponsors to subscribe financially to the establishment of city technology colleges, which can be created (or so we are told) only if such financial sponsorship is forthcoming, is another. Perhaps the most striking example, however, is the progressive reduction in the financing of universities and other institutions of higher education, which are now funded at such a level by the Department of Education and Science that they cannot maintain anything like an adequate level of resourcing for their teaching activities without engaging in extensive money-making activities, not only through raising research funding and academic endowments, but also through such things as subletting their buildings, including offering them as holiday accommodation, and the development of profit-making courses for students from abroad. Indeed, a recent report has suggested that all DES funding of universities should cease and that they should be required to become completely self-funding and thus commercially viable, most notably by the charging of full-cost fees to all students, whether from home or abroad.

We thus have here the early signs of what Thatcherism or the ideology of the 'New Right' means for the education service at all levels. The Thatcher-ite philosophy is that of paying one's own way, of no free 'hand-outs', of survival by one's own abilities, particularly the ability to pay for what one needs. It is manifested in the increased privatization of housing, in policies for a major shift in the National Health Service towards private provision and, in general, in a running-down of government funding of all social services. There is no reason to hope or expect that the education service should be any exception to this consistently applied policy. And the develop-ments we are tracing here reflect the application of this philosophy to the provision of education. It is well summed up in the advice given by Sir Keith Joseph, as Secretary of State for Education, that 'schools should preach the moral virtue of free enterprise and the pursuit of profit'.

This pattern of commercialization has been matched by an increased emphasis on the management of the system and of individual schools. Substantial sums of money have been made available to offer headteachers and other senior teachers opportunities for managerial training, through attendance on courses approved by the Development Centre for School Management Training. One can have no objection to such teachers being offered facilities for the improvement of their managerial skills. Indeed, one might claim that too often in the past teachers in senior positions have conspicuously lacked such skills. However, we must note again that the emphasis in such courses has been on industrial models of management and one might further argue that there has been a notable neglect of what might be seen as the specific and peculiar concern of educational management – management of the curriculum, its development and its implementation, in forms which reflect educational rather than commercial emphases.

This trend towards industrial forms of educational management has been matched by and reflected in the move towards the increased involvement of industry in the control of education. A major feature of the new structures for overseeing and planning educational provision is a significant increase in the number and proportion of representatives of industry on all major planning bodies – on national committees such as the Schools Curriculum Development Council (SCDC), the Task Group on Assessment and Testing (TGAT), the National Curriculum Council (NCC) and the School Examina-tions and Assessment Council (SEAC), on the new funding bodies for higher education, on local groups such as the advisory committees all teacher-education establishments must have to oversee their initial teacher-education courses, on the governing bodies of all educational institutions, schools and colleges, and on the top-level planning committees of institutions of higher education.

And there has been a corresponding weakening of professional influence and control. We have noted how the control exercised by the teachers themselves in curriculum matters has been progressively eroded. It is worth noting too that the developments, outlined in the last section, in the area of teacher education have considerably reduced the potential influence on curriculum development from that quarter. And the independent role that Her Majesty's Inspectorate was once said to play in education, offering advice to the makers of policy from an independent professional perspective, is now very little in evidence. Members of the national inspectorate are seldom heard to offer any comment on national policies, either publicly or to the politicians and civil servants themselves, and their role is now better understood in terms of the implementation of policies decided upon with little reference to them than in terms of the maintenance of any kind of independent professional stance.

We must note again the reduced influence of local authorities on the curriculum of the schools. The National Curriculum inevitably reduces that influence but, as we have seen, the powers now granted to individual schools to 'opt out' of local authority control weaken it even further. It is now at least technically possible for local authorities to disappear altogether; the Inner London Education Authority is to be the first so to disappear, as a result of a specific provision of the 1988 Education Act. If they do so, or where they do so, control of the schools for which they were once responsible will revert to the Secretary of State.

Effectively, therefore, it adds up to control from the centre.

A final feature of this scene which is worthy of mention is the control which has been achieved over all the official, publicly sponsored, documentation on curriculum issues made available to schools. It is to this that we turn in the next section.

OFFICIAL PUBLICATIONS ON THE SCHOOL CURRICULUM

A significant feature of the educational scene during the last decade or so has been the plethora of official documents on curriculum issues. These documents have fallen into three categories. Some have been surveys of the current practices of schools and other institutions, notable examples of which were the surveys by HMI of primary schools (DES, 1978) and secondary schools (DES, 1979). Some have been discussion documents such as *Curriculum 11–16* (DES, 1977c) and *A View of the Curriculum*

(DES, 1980a). Others have been sets of proposals for change such as *A Framework for the School Curriculum* (DES, 1980b). It is important when reading any of these documents to be quite clear what the document is setting out to do.

It is important too to note the source of these documents. Some are 'professional' statements, whether of 'facts' or of issues for debate which have been written by HMI. Others have been prepared by the administrators of the Civil Service and either do or do not reflect a professional input. It is for this reason that one can detect major differences in the earlier documents – especially those emerging in the late 1970s – not only in the views expressed but also in the quality of the arguments offered in support of them and of the discussion generally. *Curriculum 11–16* (DES, 1977c) is a substantial document raising many curriculum issues in a manner which invites free and open discussion and which also demands a properly rigorous approach to such discussion, while *A Framework for the School Curriculum* (DES, 1980b), which purports to translate many of the issues so raised into practical policy, would be unacceptable, in terms not only of its content but also of the quality of its argument, as a first essay from an education student on any level of course.

This evident mismatch of both opinions and quality, which is a notable feature of the early documentation, has become increasingly less evident during the 1980s. There is little evidence now in any official publication of disagreement between their authors, there is no real invitation to discussion, in spite of the claim of many of the publications to be 'discussion documents', except within the rather narrow parameters of the emerging official policy, reflecting that move we noted earlier away from professional or educational concerns towards those of an economic or political kind, and away from a concern with deeper issues of educational policy towards that concentration on methodology whose limitations we noted in Chapter 1. And there has been a consequent deterioration of the quality of argument offered in recent documents, as we have seen in earlier references to the HMI *Curriculum Matters* series, so that few, if any, now reveal the kind of intellectual quality one would expect from students. This loss in quality may well be the result of attempting to produce statements about education which are intelligible to the person in the street, and especially all those persons in the street in whose hands control of education is being placed, as we saw just now. Nevertheless, serious loss of quality there has been and this has led, like those other aspects of this policy we noted earlier, to a de-intellectualizing or a de-professionalizing of educational practice, a rejection of all that has been learnt about the complexities of the educational process from the research and development of the last two or three decades, a discouragement to any kind of political debate and a return to the simplistic notions of more primitive times.

What is perhaps even more serious, however, is that this is now the only public source of fuel for the curriculum debate. We noted earlier the loss of the free and independent research of the Schools Council. We must note here the resultant loss of the contributions which that body made to a continuing, open and wide-reaching debate on curriculum issues. Whereas all schools once received free copies of all the Schools Council's working papers, they now receive only the HMI/DES curriculum documents – which are published only if they have been given official, government approval.

The result of this has been the development of an official publications policy designed to reinforce the major tenets of the general policy we have been noting and the discouragement of discussions which might lead to a questioning of that policy or to an acknowledgement of its problematic aspects. There has thus been a serious loss in the intellectual quality of that debate and an equally serious narrowing of the scope and the range of the issues teachers are now encouraged to explore.

In this way official documentation has played its part in taking us away from a view of the wider and more individually focused potentialities of education provision towards that concentration on its economic and utilitarian aspects which we have seen as a major premise of the policies which have been developed. And it has made its own contribution towards the discouragement of that critical approach to curricular issues which this book is concerned to promote and which it claims is crucial to the professional development of teachers.

We must now turn to a consideration of some other, perhaps less apparent, premises or assumptions of direct intervention in the school curriculum.

THE PREMISES OF DIRECT INTERVENTION

There are a number of assumptions which underlie current educational policy and we must end our attempted analysis of this by briefly identifying them.

The first of these assumptions is that the education system is deficient and 'we must identify the deficiencies in the system and those who operate it, and devise ways of circumventing them' (Holt, 1987a, p. 7). We have noted that throughout the process of development which has been described, from the publication of the Black Papers through to the present day, a major element in the 'debate' has been criticism of standards and especially of the teachers responsible for those standards.

We must also note, however, that deficiency, like beauty, and like the notion of 'standards' itself, is in the eye of the beholder. And we have seen that the deficiencies identified have been deficiencies only in the context of the view of schooling and its purposes held by those identifying them – the failure to meet the needs of the economy, for example, or to maintain the traditional academicism. The deficiency, then, is more a failure on the part of teachers to meet the expectations of others than to attain the professional goals they have set for themselves.

A second assumption or premise of current policy, therefore, which arises from this is that it is not the role of teachers to make judgements of this kind. Teachers are, or should be, merely operators, passive agents, technicians rather than professionals, whose task it is to carry out the policies made for them elsewhere and by others, to instruct children in those things their political masters wish to have them instructed in; 'they become not people, but functionaries – "educational personnel" ' (Holt, 1987a, p. 7). Whether, in reality, teachers can be thus operated by remote control is another question, but it is certainly a premise and an assumption of current policy that they can and should be.

A third assumption, related to this, is that the curriculum can be planned, developed and implemented nationally by central agencies. The model is that which we saw in Chapter 5 has been called a centre–periphery model, and we also saw there how ineffective this approach has been when it has been tried elsewhere. This is yet another of those lessons we learned from the work of the Schools Council which is currently being ignored.

It might of course be argued that the attempts of the Schools Council at dissemination lacked the support of legislation, which the implementation of the National Curriculum does not, but what we know about the centre–periphery model's deficiencies and the problems of power-coercive strategies, allied to the point we have just made about the difficulty of operating teachers by remote control, suggests that this may make little difference, except perhaps by inhibiting development.

Certainly, there is a growing body of evidence from the attempts of other countries to conduct their education systems in this way that it is a model which is seriously deficient and which does not work. In a country which has led the world in some aspects of educational provision it is sad that we should only now be coming to a system which most other advanced societies are currently rejecting. The Japanese, for example, after many years of experience of this kind of subject-based national curriculum, have decided that it is too rigid and inflexible and are currently attempting to move towards more individual and personal forms of educational provision. It is worth noting, however, that one of the problems they are likely to face in this attempt is the lack of any tradition or research background of the kind such a development will undoubtedly require.

A fourth assumption or premise which lies behind attempts to move towards the centralized control of the curriculum is that educational planning is a scientific exercise, that education is an applied science and can thus be both studied and planned scientifically. Attempts to study society in this way and to produce scientifically based plans and prescriptions for social change were abandoned long ago, and for very good reasons. And we saw in Chapter 1 some of the fundamental flaws in this kind of approach to the study of education. The attempt to resurrect this as a model for educational research and planning is yet another example of the primitive nature of the underlying thinking of current policies – indeed of the lack of any depth of thinking.

These, then, are the underlying assumptions of the educational policy whose emergence over the last two decades we have been tracing. Inevitably, in our discussion of them we have been led to many criticisms. Some of these criticisms are clearly directed at the underlying ideology of these new policies which have developed and which are encapsulated in the provisions of the 1988 Education Act. As such, therefore, they might be written off as mere manifestations of the irritations and concerns of those who adopt a contrasting ideology. Others, however, are mounted not from the point of view of a different ideology but from a concern at the unsatisfactory nature of the thinking which underlies these policies and especially of the degree to which they ignore, in a manner which would be recognized as totally unacceptable in any other sphere, all the many advances in our understanding of the complexities of curriculum planning which this book is endeavouring to outline. It may be worthwhile to end this chapter, therefore, with a brief survey of the main features of this process of de-intellectualizing the educational debate and thus of effectively writing off any notion of curriculum studies as a productive undertaking of the kind we sought to define in Chapter 1.

THE DE-INTELLECTUALIZATION OF THE CURRICULUM DEBATE

Perhaps the most serious general problem with current policies is the limitations they are placing on debate about education, on independent research which might help us better to understand the educational process, in its own right and not merely as a means for instruction in economically useful skills. The development of a worthwhile system of education requires such a debate and it needs to be able to respond to whatever understandings such debate generates. Central control inhibits, indeed seeks entirely to stifle, the kind of debate that is needed, and certainly to prevent the translation of the understandings it may offer into policies or practice.

Several things follow from this. First, we have seen that it leads to a deterioration in the intellectual quality of much of what is said and published about education. In so many respects, the present policy represents a return to an earlier, more primitive era, when our understanding was far less than it is, or could be, now. Historians of education will tell us that the National Curriculum is to all intents and purposes the curriculum recommended by the Board of Education in 1902 and that we have gone back to the era of 'payment by results'. Curriculum theorists will draw our attention to all the lessons which current policies ignore – lessons about attempts at the scientific study of curriculum, about approaches to dissemination, about how the curriculum actually changes or can be changed and, perhaps above all, lessons about the very different approaches to education and curriculum which recent years have seen emerging – perhaps especially from the literature about primary education, a field whose distinctiveness current policies do not begin to appreciate. Philosophers will alert us to the simplistic, undefined, unanalysed and consequently too often muddled concepts with which the official literature abounds – not only concepts of education and curriculum but also more specific concepts such as 'standards', 'progression', 'continuity' and even 'subjects' – and the concomitant failure to acknowledge the problematic nature of such concepts. Logicians will point to the unquestioned assumptions with which these same publications, and even the legislation itself, abound. Sociologists will comment on the failure to appreciate the central role of the teacher in education and curriculum development and the lack of wisdom of attempts to deny his or her developed professionalism, to see him or her merely as 'a carrier of knowledge with transmission skills' (Goddard, 1985, p. 35) and to take the profession back to the days when teachers were mere instructors and education was something not many children were privileged to receive.

In general, then, the most serious effect of these policies has been to de-intellectualize the work of that profession which, above all others, should be concerned with the maintenance of intellectual standards. All the other difficulties which have emerged from our discussion stem from that basic weakness.

SUMMARY AND CONCLUSIONS

The purpose of this chapter has been, first, to establish the inevitability of the political context of educational or curricular planning and then to consider some of the more general and indirect controls, constraints, pressures and influences which constitute the context in which curriculum planning goes on, and which will affect, if they do not actually determine, the direction and form that it takes. The chapter considered next some ideological influences and suggested that these must be recognized as being often in conflict, that the curriculum had to be seen as a battleground for such competing ideologies and thus in many instances as an uneasy compromise between them. Then some specific influences and constraints were identified, the pressures on teachers and other curriculum planners which derive from established traditions, those which are generated by administrative decisions concerning such things as the organization of the school system or of individual schools and the allocation and distribution of resources, the pressures of public examinations and external testing, and those related pressures which are created by the 'consumers', especially by employers and parents. It also attempted to draw attention to some of the pressures which are produced by the school itself through its organizational structure, its facilities, its social climate and, especially, the attitudes and styles adopted by its teachers and headteacher.

The chapter then went on to show how some of these general influences have gathered strength and momentum and how, with the aid of appropriate legislation, they have created a climate in which the secret garden is no longer secret, in which their influence is no longer peripheral but has become central, in which influence has become intervention and direct control. It also suggested some of the difficulties which this process creates, practical difficulties of implementation as well as theoretical or philosophical difficulties of justification and intellectual difficulties centring on the quality of supporting argumentation.

It will have been clear throughout that, while the concern is to reduce the extent of teacher autonomy and influence, nevertheless the role of the teacher continues to be central. It will then be equally clear that, if teachers are no longer to be trusted with the essential decisions about the curriculum, there will have to be checks and balances to ensure that they do in practice implement the wishes of those who are so trusted. Evaluation, accountability and appraisal thus become key elements in the process which is now under way. It is naturally to these, then, that we turn in the chapter which follows.

7
EVALUATION, ASSESSMENT, ACCOUNTABILITY AND APPRAISAL

Most of that body of understanding which has come to be known as evaluation theory has been gleaned from attempts to evaluate existing curricular practices or, more often, innovatory curricula, so that it has been generated as a by-product, albeit an essential by-product, of attempts at curriculum development – as the fourth element of that simple curriculum planning model of Ralph Tyler (1949) which we noted in Chapter 1.

There has often of course been the additional concern for 'value for money', especially, for example, in the evaluation of the Schools Council's projects, and, while it is clear that that brings a political flavour into the brew, it has until relatively recently been a slight flavour only. In the last decade or so, however, in the United Kingdom, in the context of that political scenario which was painted in the last chapter, that flavour has been intensified and the focus of curriculum evaluation has begun to shift from curriculum development to teacher accountability and subsequently to schemes for teacher appraisal. It has begun to be seen as the measurement of teacher competence, especially through the assessment of pupil perform-ance; and this has become a major feature of the National Curriculum and its attendant assessment programme which have been introduced through the Education Act of 1988.

Thus, in addition, some important distinctions between evaluation and assessment have come to be blurred and we see yet again the kind of conceptual confusion, with all its unsatisfactory consequences for practice, which we have noted in several other contexts. For, as always, elements of all forms and features of evaluation and assessment can be seen attempting to coexist in many current practices and, again as always, it is the confusion of these, whether deliberate or merely as a result of a genuine lack of clarity over the important differences between them, which leads to many unsatisfactory aspects in much of what we can see currently being done in the name of evaluation.

No attempted overview of evaluation theory can, then, in the present climate, exclude some consideration of the related concepts and practices of pupil assessment, school and teacher accountability and teacher appraisal, and especially of the important distinctions between them. Nor can it ignore the political dimension of evaluation procedures. This is the major reason why, in this third edition of this book, this chapter on evaluation follows rather then precedes that which attempts to set out the political scene.

The chapter will first offer an outline of the major theories of evaluation, the important distinctions which have come to be made between different purposes, forms and styles of evaluation. This should then provide a backcloth against which to consider the implications, both for the theory and the practice of evaluation, of using these evaluation techniques primarily for political purposes, for teacher accountability and appraisal, and especially of viewing the assessment of pupil performance as a major, or even the only, source of data for educational evaluation. In short, again the concern will be to attempt to introduce, or to reintroduce, a measure of conceptual clarity into the curriculum debate as a basis for ensuring greater clarity of practice.

It is also worth noting at the outset that the development of our understanding of educational evaluation also has important implications for the evaluation of the work of individual teachers, since evaluation should be undertaken not only of major innovations but also of individual projects and even single lessons. Both the micro and the macro aspects of this issue must be borne in mind, then, as we turn to an outline of the major features of recent developments in evaluation theory.

THE DEVELOPMENT OF EVALUATION THEORY

It is certainly the case that many major curriculum innovations have not been accompanied by any attempt at evaluation. This was true of the many projects that were introduced both in Britain and in the USA in the late 1950s and early 1960s when public money was made available for curriculum development on a broader scale than had hitherto been possible. It seemed to be felt at that time that any curriculum change must be for the better. However, experience of later developments, particularly that which began to emerge as teachers in diverse school situations began to make many different uses of the projects and materials the developers presented them with, led to a gradual realization that evaluation had to be seen as an integral part of any curriculum *development*, so that in Britain arrangements for proper evaluation were made an essential requirement of all projects by such funding bodies as the Schools Council and every subsequent project had its own full-time evaluator (Hamilton, 1976).

Indeed, it is difficult to argue against the notion that particular innovations need to be evaluated and that we need to assess very carefully the results of any change that we introduce. In fact, it is to make a purely logical point to say that the recognition of a need for change implies an awareness of inadequacies in existent practices and thus of the need for some basis upon which both those practices and the innovations which may be introduced to replace them can be evaluated. We also need sophisticated techniques for evaluating all aspects of our own work as teachers.

However, the sheer rapidity with which we have reached this awareness has created several kinds of difficulty for both the theory and the practice of curriculum evaluation. For the recent rapid increase in the activities of evaluators in many different areas of the curriculum has led to the emergence of many new and different views of the nature and purposes of curriculum evaluation. Recent years have seen the appearance of a great diversity of curriculum projects and, therefore, a corresponding diversity of evaluation procedures (Schools Council, 1973; Tawney, 1975; Hamilton, 1976). The field we are about to enter, then, is a complex one.

What is curriculum evaluation?

Curriculum evaluation is clearly the process by which we attempt to gauge the value and effectiveness of any particular piece of educational activity – whether a national project or a piece of work undertaken with our own pupils. On such a definition, it might seem *prima facie* to be a relatively simple matter. However, the first complexity we must note is that which arises from an awareness of the variety of purposes that one can have in making an evaluation of anything, and the range of different conceptions one can have of such an activity, each of which may be perfectly suitable for some area of curriculum development. What might we be doing in evaluating a curriculum project or a particular activity? We might be doing no more than attempting to establish that the programme is in fact happening, since we have already commented several times on the gap that often exists between planning and practice. Or we might merely be attempting to ascertain if we have achieved what we set out to achieve. On the other hand, we might be endeavouring to compare a particular project or approach with other alternative methods, procedures or programmes in the same area. Is it really better than what it has replaced or than other new alternatives that are offered? Again, we might be concerned to do no more than to ascertain if it is acceptable to teachers and/or pupils (Schools Council, 1974a). Then again, we might be attempting to assess whether we have got our goals or our principles right.

In short, the purposes of any scheme of evaluation will vary according to the purposes, views, conceptions of the person or persons making the evaluation. We noted, when discussing the problems of dissemination in Chapter 5, that the conception of any curriculum project will vary according to the angle from which one views it, whether as planner, teacher, pupil, parent or whoever. Each will have his or her own conception or definition of the project (Shipman, 1972, 1973). For the same reason, each will have his or her own view of the purposes of evaluation and his or her own interpretation of the data which it produces. And so different people will make different uses of those data, some using them as a device for continuing course development, some for decisions concerning the allocation of resources, some for action of a more overtly political kind and so on.

Thus the selection of which information to collect, the range of purposes one may have in collecting it, the variety of uses to which it may be put and the range of the decisions it may lead to, make of evaluation 'a multi-faceted phenomenon encompassing a range of diverse properties' (Hamilton, 1976, p. 11).

Again, therefore, it will be helpful to avoid a tight definition of a kind that is likely to inhibit the further development of understanding in this area. The most sensible approach to adopt would seem to be to begin by considering some of the different dimensions of curriculum evaluation that people have identified.

First, a possible source of confusion may be avoided if we begin by noting that curriculum evaluation must be distinguished from the assessment of individual pupils. Although both may involve similar procedures, such as the gathering of evidence concerning changes of pupil behaviour or the extent of pupil learning that has resulted from any particular planned programme of experiences, the uses to which such data may be put and the purposes for which they are collected are quite different in the two cases. The crucial element in curriculum evaluation is that the data are gathered in order to provide a basis upon which decisions can be made about the curriculum and/or perhaps certain resultant and concomitant administrative changes, and not as diagnostic evidence for the making of decisions about any aspect of the work of individual pupils. If we make this distinction at the outset we may avoid one major kind of confusion into which several discussions of this issue have fallen, along with a good deal of practice.

Secondly, we must note that the questions to be asked in any process of evaluation are of at least two logically discrete kinds (White, 1971). Some of them are empirical questions which, like the investigations of a body such as the Consumers' Association, explore the relative merits of a project or approach in terms of its costs, its effectiveness and so on. For questions of this kind we are looking, therefore, for relevant empirical data. Other questions, however, are asked in the process of evaluating a curriculum which are not of this kind but raise those difficult issues of value that we can never get far from in any discussion of education. These are the questions about ends rather than means, which ask whether the purposes of the activity are the right purposes, whether the experience being offered to pupils is of educational value, whether the curriculum is good in itself rather than merely being 'delivered' effectively. Here the concern is to evaluate the goals or the underlying principles of the curriculum itself and not merely the effectiveness of its procedures.

Thirdly, it is useful to distinguish in-course and post-course evaluation, those procedures that are designed to assess the work of a project or activity as it proceeds and perhaps also to provide immediate feedback and those which are intended to be employed when the work is completed in order to assess its overall effectiveness.

Another related distinction is the contrast between 'formative' and 'summative' evaluation (Scriven, 1967). 'Summative' evaluation is concerned with appraisal of the work, it is a form of 'pay-off' evaluation (Scriven, 1967) and is concerned primarily to ascertain if the goals of the course have been achieved. 'Formative' evaluation, on the other hand, is concerned to provide feedback (Scriven, 1967; Stenhouse, 1975) and thus a base for course improvement, modification and future planning. As such, it may occur post-course, but it is more likely to take the form of continuous in-course monitoring of both goals or principles and procedures. It will, therefore, involve a number of dimensions, since it will be attempting to assess the extent of the achievement of the purposes of the project and to discover and analyse barriers to their achievement (Stenhouse, 1975), and it may also be concerned to contribute to a modification of those purposes themselves, in short, to ask the 'value' questions we mentioned earlier.

Thus we see that a number of distinctions have been made to reflect those different purposes that we identified earlier, and we can observe the emergence of several different models of, or approaches to, curriculum evaluation.

It is also important to recognize that the model of evaluation we adopt must match the model of curriculum planning we have adopted (Tawney,

1973). Otherwise there will be mismatch and distortion. In particular, the adoption of a model of evaluation which is based on the prespecification of curriculum objectives will have the effect of distorting an approach to the curriculum which is procedural or developmental, not least because its criteria of evaluation will not reflect the purposes of the planners or the teachers. It will be comparable to seeking to discover how many goals Donald Bradman scored in his last test match at the Oval.

However, too often the assumption has been, and continues to be, made that curriculum evaluation is possible only if curriculum objectives are prestated. And so it will be well worth our while to explore this issue in some detail.

Evaluation and the prespecification of objectives

Early discussion of curriculum evaluation certainly tended to be fixed well within the context of the simple behavioural objectives model of the curriculum. Ralph Tyler, for example, is quite explicit on this point. 'The process of evaluation is essentially the process of determining to what extent the educational objectives are actually being realized by the program of curriculum and instruction' (Tyler, 1949, pp. 105–6). And again:

> it is absolutely essential that they [the behavioural objectives] be defined in order to make an evaluation since unless there is some clear conception of the sort of behaviour implied by the objectives, one has no way of telling what kind of behaviour to look for in the students in order to see to what degree these objectives are being realized. This means that the process of evaluation may force persons who have not previously clarified their objectives to a further process of clarification. Definition of objectives, then, is an important step in evaluation.
> (Tyler, 1949, p. 111)

A good deal of more recent discussion has also followed a similar line. The prespecification of objectives is made an explicit precondition for all the four types of evaluation listed by Wynne Harlen (1971). The first activity that is involved in all of them, we are told, is 'clarifying objectives and analysing them to the point of expressing them in terms of behaviour changes' (op. cit., p. 129). Nor is this surprising since she is writing from her experience of evaluating the Schools Council's Science 5–13 Project, which attempted to remain very firmly rooted in a classical objectives model. The evaluator, as a member of the project team, helped the team to clarify its behavioural objectives (Harlen, 1971, 1973), which were published in detail for the use of the teachers who were to use the project materials and implement the programme in their schools. The actual task of evaluation was then restricted to determining how far the teachers' guides that were produced

enabled teachers to achieve these objectives and how they might be modified to increase their efficiency.

More topically, this same assumption is made by the authors of the HMI
Curriculum Matters series. Admittedly, they actually use the term 'assessment', but this approach is equally limiting in relation to the assessment of
pupils, since, as Robin Alexander (1984, pp. 36–7) has pointed out, 'assessment via *formal* testing or other publicly verified procedures can only deal
with very limited and specific areas of school work and is much less
important that the continuous *informal* (even unconscious) evaluation of the
pupil by the teacher'. Furthermore, it is clear that they sometimes mean by it
'evaluation' or, rather, that they do not distinguish these two concepts, and
that they regard the assessment of pupil performance as the only source of
data for measuring the value and the success of a teacher's work, since they
inform us, for example, that 'a second purpose [of assessment] is to enable
teachers to see how far their objectives are being met and to adjust them and
their teaching approaches accordingly' (DES, 1985a, p. 51). Thus the
booklet *Home Economics from 5 to 16* (DES, 1985d, p. 17) tells us 'unless
specific and clear objectives are set down for each lesson, each module of
study and ultimately for the conduct of home economics teaching in the
school, it is difficult to measure whether or not learning has taken place'.
Most teachers would not find this difficult at all. And *Geography from 5 to 16*
(DES, 1986b, p. 43) asserts that 'the clearer teachers are about their
objectives, the easier it is for them to identify criteria for assessment'. We
saw in Chapter 3 that HMI has revealed in this series (although it has never
explained) its commitment to an 'aims and objectives' approach to curriculum planning; we can now see that it regards this as the only basis for
evaluation or assessment.

A good deal of both the theory and the practice of curriculum evaluation,
therefore, has been set well within the context of an objectives-based
curriculum model, and for this reason evaluation has been seen as centrally
concerned to help with the framing and subsequent modification of objectives, the assessment of the suitability of the learning experiences to the
achievement of the objectives set and the measurement of the degree to
which the prestated objectives are being or have been attained. The demand
for accountability to which we have already referred also tends to encourage
the use of this kind of model.

On the other hand, it is equally easy to recognize the dangers that lie in
this kind of approach. For it is possible, and perhaps likely, that the kinds of
evaluative procedure available will tend to govern or determine the choice
of objectives, content or methods rather than merely to offer additional
information to those selecting them on other grounds. We are all familiar

with the teacher's everlasting complaint that the public examination syllabuses are the strongest determinants of the curriculum and the greatest
inhibitors of curriculum change. Furthermore, we have already discussed at
great length in Chapter 3 the difficulties and dangers that exist for curriculum planners in the view that all curriculum planning must start from a
prespecification of objectives.

Thus, although there may seem to be a *prima facie* case for the prespecification of objectives if adequate procedures of evaluation are to be found,
we must pause to ask whether evaluation becomes quite impossible if we are
not prepared to start with a statement of objectives and, if it does not, what
differences does this necessitate in our methods of evaluation?

It might perhaps be worth beginning by dispelling the illusion that may
have been created by what has been said so far that evaluation is an easy and
straightforward matter when we work from a clear statement of objectives.
For even here we face a number of difficulties, some of which derive from
the unsuitability of this approach to certain areas of curriculum planning,
which we have already examined extensively in Chapter 3.

We have already referred to the temptation this approach offers to settle
for those objectives whose achievement can easily be measured. The
converse of this is the inability of current techniques of evaluation and
assessment to measure the more sophisticated objectives teachers and
educators adopt, especially in the affective domain. As Schools Council
Working Paper 26 tells us in discussing 'education through the use of
materials', 'a problem arises in assessing teaching that seeks to attain such
objectives as "the development of desirable personality traits and attitudes" ' (Schools Council, 1969, p. 11). It is worth noting here too that this
was a major factor in the decisions of the Assessment of Performance Unit
not to attempt to monitor performance in the areas of aesthetic education,
physical education and social and moral education. In other words, there
exists a wide discrepancy between the scope of most sets of objectives and
the scope of evaluation (Taba, 1962) which will lead to inadequacies either
in evaluation or in our specification of the objectives themselves.

Inadequacy of the available techniques of evaluation leads to further
difficulties. At one level it can lead to conflict between the objectives made
explicit by the project and those implicit in the evaluative techniques used
(Taba, 1962). Thus, no matter how far, for example, a project stresses its
concern to develop pupils' understanding in a certain area of the curriculum,
teachers will emphasize the memorizing and regurgitation of factual material if the main thrust of the evaluation and/or assessment procedures is
towards this and better grades are obtained by those pupils who can
reproduce learnt, but not necessarily assimilated, material most readily and

in largest quantity. What is worse is that these procedures are often taken as indicators of the extent to which the real objectives of the programme have been attained so that a facility at reproducing scientific facts, for example, becomes confused with or is taken as evidence of the ability to think scientifically (Taba, 1962).

On the other hand, if we succeed in avoiding this situation and make the somewhat inadequate techniques we have do a reasonable job of helping us to evaluate the more sophisticated objectives we may set ourselves, a good deal of interpretation of the data our evaluation procedures produce is still needed (Taba, 1962). We need to measure against one another such things as memorizing and understanding, knowledge and interest, achievement and social or educational background, learning and psychological stages of intellectual and physical growth. The data our evaluation techniques produce, therefore, need to be interpreted against a broad backcloth and related to information from other sources and of other kinds, especially that coming from philosophical, psychological and sociological research. This is far from being a straightforward matter. Even when objectives are clearly prespecified, then, evaluation is not easy.

Furthermore, a proper evaluation requires a proper level of understanding of the process that is being evaluated (Stenhouse, 1975). A simple assessment of the attainment of objectives is concerned only with the success or failure of the programme; it is not concerned essentially with an understanding of it. It assesses without explaining (Stenhouse, 1975). Thus the value of such evaluation is limited, since it can offer little feedback, if indeed it offers any at all, upon which the objectives or the procedures can be modified, so that it may well fail to do the very job it is designed to do. Nor can it address those value issues, those questions concerning the worth of a particular project or activity, which we saw earlier are crucial to *educational* planning. It is seldom helpful to know in black-and-white terms whether a project or activity has succeeded or not. In fact, it will seldom be possible to make that kind of simple assessment. What is needed is a far greater complexity of data which can provide a basis for present and future curriculum development. This in turn implies the generation of evaluation procedures which do more than attempt to measure success or failure and which, in order to offer more, must be based upon a full understanding of the educational process itself.

Lastly, we must note that if we are dealing with an approach to education or a project for which the prespecification of objectives is deemed inappropriate, any evaluation based on such a model will be equally inappropriate, will add to the confusion and may have quite disastrous consequences (Weiss and Rein, 1969), not least in distorting the curriculum itself. We noted in Chapter 3 that many teachers, especially in primary schools, have felt that an objectives model is unsuited to their work. We saw too that some project teams have begun their planning from the belief that, at least for some areas of the curriculum such as the humanities or social education, an objectives model is not suitable. Any attempt, therefore, to evaluate the work of such teachers or such projects in terms of what are thought to be their objectives must fail either by providing inadequate, unsatisfactory and irrelevant data or by persuading teachers to alter their approach to the work in such a way as to change its whole conception and scope or by distorting the work itself through a mismatch of curriculum model and evaluation model. Perhaps the most common example of that is the demand teachers often face from inspectors evaluating their work for statements of their 'aims and objectives', with little concern for whether such statements are appropriate to that work – and undoubtedly from a lamentable ignorance of other approaches to planning.

On the other hand, to attempt no evaluation can be equally disastrous. This is well illustrated by the experience of those connected with the Goldsmiths' College development of Interdisciplinary Enquiry (IDE). Although a large number of schools were associated with this development and took it up with enthusiasm, no attempt was made to set up any formal scheme of evaluation. This was mainly due to the fact that no financial support was made available for what would have been an extremely expensive undertaking, although it was also in part a result of a conviction shared by most of the architects of the scheme that its value was self-evident. At all events, it was taken up or not taken up by schools and teachers according to their own private enthusiasms and convictions and it always lacked credibility in the eyes of its sternest critics, and especially those curriculum theorists who, quite rightly, felt it appropriate to ask for evidence of its effectiveness or value.

It must also be recognized that without evaluation there can be no proper base for course development or, at the individual level, for the development and improvement of our own work.

Hence others, who have been engaged in curriculum development or teaching activities for which they have felt the prespecification of objectives to be unsuited, have recognized the necessity to design procedures by which these could be evaluated and have thus faced squarely the problems presented by the evaluation of a programme whose objectives cannot be stated in advance and whose evaluation procedures, therefore, must be based on a different, more sophisticated view of what the whole process of curriculum evaluation is. Thus a more sophisticated, developed view has begun to emerge from the work they have done.

Evaluation without prespecified objectives

The Schools Council's Integrated Studies Project which was set up at Keele University in 1968 had a brief which required it to consider a new way of organizing the curriculum rather than to measure the outcomes of pupils' learning in particular subjects, since its task was 'to examine the problems and possibilities of an integrated approach to humanities teaching in secondary schools' (Jenkins, 1973, p. 70). Thus its concern was not to assess the extent to which certain purposes had been achieved but rather to evaluate the aims and purposes themselves of such an approach to the organization of the curriculum. To specify objectives at the beginning and to work on the production of materials designed to achieve those objectives was quite inappropriate.

The team, therefore, adopted a 'horizontal' curriculum model 'in which aims, learning experiences and material were developed concurrently' (Tawney, 1973, p. 9). As a consequence of this, evaluation was seen not as a process for measuring the results of an experiment but as a device for continuously monitoring the project as it developed and constantly reviewing its aims, the packs of material that were produced and the practical problems that arose when it was introduced into schools. A major technique that was used was that of participant observation (Tawney, 1973) and what emerged was not so much objective scientific data as a growing collection of experience and understanding of the issues and problems involved, which offered teachers, therefore, not a curriculum package as such, but a set of principles and a body of experience to which they could refer and from which they might profit in developing their own schemes.

The most interesting project from the point of view of evaluation procedures, however, is the Humanities Curriculum Project, to which we have already referred on several occasions. We saw in Chapter 3 that this project eschewed the idea of the prespecification of objectives more vigorously and more completely than any other. Being concerned to encourage pupils of secondary age to explore issues within the humanities and through discussion of all kinds to reach their own conclusions, the project team saw from the outset that to prespecify learning outcomes would be to contradict their own first principle and to pre-empt the very questions they wanted to raise.

However, 'in an approach which is not based on objectives, there is no ready-made niche for the evaluator' (MacDonald, 1973, p. 82). Furthermore, the team also felt it inappropriate to evaluate a curriculum project during its trial period so that, although Barry MacDonald, the project's evaluator, was appointed during the developmental stage of the project, his job was to prepare evaluation procedures for use after the project was firmly established in schools.

Both of these factors combined to present a particularly difficult set of problems in evaluation (Stenhouse, 1975), difficulties which were acknowledged but which nevertheless were regarded as being there to be overcome. 'The evaluation then had to cope with an attempt at creative curriculum development with variable components, obvious disturbance potential and a novel approach' (MacDonald, 1973, p. 83).

To meet these difficulties, Barry MacDonald adopted a 'holistic' approach. 'The aim of that stage [i.e. during the trial period] was simply to describe the work of the project in a form that would make it accessible to public and professional judgement' (MacDonald, 1973, p. 83). It was not possible to define in advance what data would be significant, so that all data had initially to be accepted. 'In view of the potential significance of so many aspects of the project, a complete description of its experience was needed initially, as was awareness of a full range of relevant phenomena' (ibid.). Selection within and between such data could be made only later when the criteria of such selection began to emerge from the continuing experience. 'Evaluation design, strategies and methods would evolve in response to the project's impact on the educational system and the types of evaluation problems which that impact would throw up' (ibid.).

In this spirit the work of the thirty-six schools which experimented with the project was monitored, all possible techniques being used to collect a wide variety of data. Then attention was narrowed to eight schools which became the subjects of detailed case studies. The procedure appears to have been entirely justified since this method resulted in the acquisition of data and a recognition of phenomena that would never have been expected or envisaged in advance of the project's arrival in the classroom (MacDonald, 1973).

Furthermore, there also emerged from this holistic approach a number of principles of significance for curriculum planning as a whole rather than merely for the evaluation of this particular project, principles which reflect in an interesting way some of the general points that have recently been made about curriculum development.

For example, it emerged very clearly that, as we saw in Chapter 5, what actually happens when a project is put into practice varies considerably according to the local conditions prevailing in each school, whereas more simple evaluation procedures tend to assume that there is or should be very little variation between schools. Furthermore, the variations in the reaction of different schools led to the conclusion that the judgements of the teachers in them are crucially important, every bit as important as those of the project designers, in making decisions concerning the curriculum of any individual school. It also became obvious that a gap often yawned between the conception of a project held by its developers and that held by those implementing it in the school.

It also became apparent that, as we have just seen, curriculum innovations and, indeed, all educational activities have many unexpected but clearly valuable results, many 'unintended learning outcomes', and that again these are not, and cannot be, allowed for in simple evaluation procedures or, as we saw in Chapter 3, in simple objectives-based planning models.

What was learnt from these processes of evaluation was seen, then, not so much as contributing to some statement of the project's effectiveness but as providing information for 'consumers', those who have the responsibility of making the decisions concerning the curriculum. Four main groups of these were identified – sponsors, local authorities, schools and examining boards – and the task of evaluation was seen as to provide them with the kind of understanding of the problems of curriculum development that will help them to make their decisions (MacDonald, 1973).

The same general approach has been adopted by those who have proposed the notions of evaluation as 'portrayal' (Stake, 1972), as 'illuminative' (Parlett and Hamilton, 1975) and as 'responsive' (Hamilton, 1976). Portrayal evaluation is seen as an attempt not to analyse the results of a project in terms of its prespecified goals but to offer a comprehensive portrayal of the programme which will view it as a whole and endeavour to reveal its total substance.

Similarly, the primary concern of illuminative evaluation is 'with description and interpretation rather than measurement and prediction' (Parlett and Hamilton, 1975, p. 88). Such an approach to evaluation has three stages: 'investigators observe, inquire further and then seek to explain' (op. cit., p. 92). As a result of this threefold procedure an 'information profile' is put together which is then available for those who need to make decisions about the project.

> Illuminative evaluation thus concentrates on the information-gathering rather than the decision-making component of evaluation. The task is to provide a comprehensive understanding of the complex reality (or realities) surrounding the project: in short, to 'illuminate'. In his report, therefore, the evaluator aims to sharpen discussion, disentangle complexities, isolate the significant from the trivial, and raise the level of sophistication of debate.
>
> (op. cit., p. 99)

'Responsive' evaluation too seeks to respond 'to the wide range of questions asked about an innovation and is not trapped inside the intentions of the programme-builders' (Hamilton, 1976, p. 39).

In similar style, the purposes of the evaluation unit of the Humanities Curriculum Project were defined as:

> a) to ascertain the effects of the project, document the circumstances in which they occurred, and present this information in a form which would help educational decision-makers to evaluate the likely consequences of adopting the programme;
> b) to describe the existing situation and operations of the schools being studied so that decision-makers could understand more fully what it was they were trying to change;
> c) to describe the work of the project team in terms which would help the sponsors and planners of such ventures to weigh the value of this form of investment, and to determine more precisely the framework of support, guidance and control which were appropriate;
> d) to make a contribution to evaluation theory by articulating problems clearly, recording experiences and, perhaps most important, publicising errors;
> e) to contribute to the understanding of the problems of curriculum innovation generally.
>
> (MacDonald, 1973, p. 88)

It is perhaps these last two points, and especially the last one of all, that are most interesting and draw our attention to the full significance of the developments in evaluation procedures consequent on the adoption of a non-objectives curriculum model. For what has emerged as a result of the work of projects of this kind is a new and more sophisticated model of curriculum evaluation – a process model – which does not content itself with measuring the results of one project in simple and often consequentially unhelpful terms but sets out to provide continuous feedback to all of those concerned with the planning and implementation of this particular project and of curriculum development generally. Its concern is to disclose the meaning of the curriculum as much as to assess its worth (Stenhouse, 1975), and, in order to do this, it attempts to document 'a broad spectrum of phenomena, judgements and responses' (Hamilton, 1976, p. 38). In some situations this will be done to help the planners to modify their objectives and other features of the project in the light of developing experience; in other circumstances it will be concerned to guide the continuing development of a non-objectives curriculum. Furthermore, the aim will be to do this not only in relation to one particular project but to offer illumination for curriculum development as a whole. The holistic approach to curriculum evaluation implies that we do not restrict ourselves to a narrow canvas, in any sense.

Thus curriculum evaluation becomes part of curriculum research, as, for example, in the recent work of the Assessment of Performance Unit. As Lawrence Stenhouse (1975, p. 122) said, 'Evaluation should, as it were, lead development and be integrated with it. Then the conceptual distinction between development and evaluation is destroyed and the two merge as research.' In general, all evaluation procedures see all curriculum planning and approaches as hypotheses to be tested (Taba, 1962), but the holistic view sees evaluation as part of a continuous programme of research and development, and recognizes that the curriculum is a dynamic and continuously evolving entity. It thus encourages the adoption of a more sophisticated model not only of curriculum evaluation but also of curriculum planning and one which may be more suited to the notion of education as a process whose ends cannot be seen beyond itself.

Not only is it possible, then, to make an evaluation of a non-objectives curriculum; it also seems to lead to a more fully developed view of the role of evaluation in curriculum development. The procedural principles which we suggested in Chapter 4 provided a better basis for an educational activity than prespecified objectives can and should be monitored, and this monitoring will give us continuous feedback in our efforts constantly to modify and improve our practices. Again, as we also saw in Chapter 4, such a model reflects much more accurately than a simple means–end model what happens in practice when we make an evaluation of any educational activity. For we are seldom content merely to measure outcomes and, when we do, we experience uneasy feelings that we have somehow missed the educational point of the activity. And indeed we have, since we have failed to evaluate the goals of the activity and have obtained no data upon which to make judgements concerning its educational worth.

One final point needs to be made about this approach to curriculum evaluation. We have seen that its concern is not to make decisions but rather to provide information for decision-makers. It is thus a highly suitable form of evaluation for school-based curriculum development and equally for the evaluation, and self-evaluation, of the work of individual teachers. In fact, the emergence of these more sophisticated techniques of evaluation has itself contributed much to that shift towards school-based development which we noted in Chapter 5. However, as we also noted there, this is a trend which raises important political questions concerning the control of the curriculum and its decision-making processes. The major thrust of 'process' forms of evaluation is identical with that of school-based forms of curriculum development, since its direction is away from forms of external control and evaluation towards the view that the teachers themselves must have a central involvement in both processes. It thus raises important questions about who should conduct the evaluation procedures and, in particular, about whether their prime concern should be political or educational, and, indeed, whether these concerns are compatible with each other.

CURRICULUM EVALUATION AND THE INDIVIDUAL TEACHER AND THE INDIVIDUAL SCHOOL

The questions we have just seen posed must lead us first to a consideration of the role of the individual teacher in curriculum evaluation. And we must first recognize the force of that point we made at the beginning of this chapter that evaluation theory is as important to the individual teacher for the making of those day-by-day, minute-by-minute evaluations of his or her own work as it is to project directors or others concerned with monitoring or developing the curriculum on a national scale. Thus the teacher must be involved in evaluating his or her own work, since, without that, it is difficult to know how that work could ever improve; and there is much in what has been learnt about evaluation from the work of large-scale projects which can add to his or her understanding, offer insights into the complexities of educational evaluation at any level and provide techniques which can be used in each individual school or classroom.

Robin Alexander (1984, p. 128) makes the point that 'until recently "curriculum development" meant not something teachers do but the activities of teams based on universities and colleges'. It is hoped that enough has been said already in this book to stress that every teacher is a curriculum developer and that the lessons which have been learnt from the activities of those 'teams in universities and colleges' are of value not only to other such teams but to every individual engaged in the practice of education. This is perhaps especially true in the field of evaluation, where teachers have the need to learn from the kinds of research and development activities which we have just reviewed and, in particular, from those offering more sophisticated techniques of evaluation which go beyond the simplistic notion that all education must be objectives-based and are thus more suited to the subtleties of most teachers' classrooms. For, if teachers evaluate their work merely in terms of how far they have achieved what they set out to do, much that is of great value to pupils will be lost, as every teacher is well aware.

It must be noted, however, that, while the developments in evaluation theory we have considered offer the beginnings of a highly sophisticated approach to evaluation and especially one which enables us to make judgements about all aspects of an educational activity – its value or worth as well as the most effective methods of implementing it – in the context of the 1988 Education Act and especially of the National Curriculum which that Act imposes, there is little scope for action by teachers at anything other than the methodological level. For the scope of teacher autonomy is now restricted to decisions about methods of 'delivery' and no longer embraces decisions about the content of pupils' learning and still less about its processes – at least as we have defined them. Subjects are fixed by law; attainment targets are set and will be the subject of regular assessments; there is discretion only in the area of the methods by which children will be taught those subjects and led towards those attainment targets.

It is for this reason, as we shall see later, that the establishment of this simplistic form of curriculum is about to be matched by a return to simplistic, objectives-based forms of evaluation. And so it may seem a waste of time to explore here the role of the teacher in curriculum evaluation and development when that role is in process of being much reduced. However, it is important that understandings once acquired should not be lost through neglect. It is also important that we be fully aware of what is being lost. Furthermore, it is the case that individual teachers have in recent times become increasingly involved in self-evaluation and in school self-evaluation schemes, and the question still remains as to how far teachers will or should be included in whatever evaluation of the curriculum is planned which goes beyond their own work in their own schools and classrooms.

It is thus, for several reasons, worth considering both the role teachers might play in the evaluation of work prompted by initiatives of whatever kind from outside the school and the task they must undertake of evaluating their own work, both as individuals and as members of a school's staff.

The first problem that faces us is that of achieving some kind of objectivity in evaluation, something which is likely to be especially difficult in relation to any form of self-evaluation.

Particular, and perhaps unnecessary, difficulties will arise, however, if we see evaluation as some kind of pseudo-scientific activity and thus the search for objectivity as the pursuit of absolute certain knowledge of a God-given kind. Such knowledge we have already proposed is impossible in any sphere. We have suggested that a more realistic view of knowledge is that which sees it as a system of interrelated hypotheses, each of which fits the evidence we have but is also subject to amendment or rejection in the face of new evidence. The essential ingredients of objectivity are that we recognize the need for evidence, that this evidence should be public and that it should be considered with as much impartiality as is possible.

In short, it may be better to think not so much in terms of achieving objectivity in some absolute sense as of avoiding the most extreme forms of subjectivity and dogmatism that derive from views that are totally idiosyncratic or blindly prejudiced (Hamlyn, 1972). This we can best do by recognizing the need to communicate our views, values and interpretations to others, to produce evidence in support of our claims and to be prepared to discuss them with others who may perceive or interpret things differently in as impartial and open a manner as we can achieve. Objectivity comes from recognizing the need to give reasons for our judgements and thus to open them up to rational discussion and debate.

Who should evaluate a curriculum project in order to achieve this kind of objectivity? Again *prima facie* it would seem that we might get closest to it by arranging for external evaluation. This is certainly the feeling of those who advocate the monitoring of standards of achievement in schools by such people as local or government inspectors, and it is also the principle that underlies systems of public examinations.

The main difficulty with such an approach to evaluation would seem to stem from the fact we have referred to on several occasions that all curriculum projects, at whatever level, are highly complex entities with an intricate interlinking of theoretical and practical elements of a kind that it is unlikely anyone could understand from the outside. External evaluation of this kind therefore would almost certainly lead to an over-simplification which would do violence to the work.

To avoid this over-simplification and to achieve the breadth of under-standing necessary to make a useful evaluation of the wider aspects of the curriculum, such an outside person would need to get inside the project, to become a specialist evaluator. It was for this reason that in most of the projects of the Schools Council, evaluators were appointed as members of project teams. This practice recognized the need for the evaluator to become involved in the overall planning in order that he or she should be able to achieve an understanding of the complexities of the project, whether his or her job is merely to assess its outcomes or to contribute through his or her skills as an evaluator to the ongoing development of the scheme. In other words, whatever view is taken of the purposes of evaluation and whatever model is adopted, it is recognized that it is desirable and necessary for the evaluator to join the project team at some stage in order to become in a full sense a part of the project.

The message here, especially in the context of current policies, is that any evaluator needs to understand the complexities of what he or she is evaluating and that kind of understanding can seldom be satisfactorily achieved from outside the activity; some attempt must be made to get on the inside and to evaluate what is to be evaluated on its own terms. Again, experience of recent HMI inspections suggests that these do not always attempt this but are often content to make their evaluations not in the terms of the curricular offerings themselves but according to their own predilec-tions or the political criteria they are increasingly required to apply. This must, therefore, cast doubt on the *educational* value of those exercises.

However, although this kind of practice will ensure that the evaluator has a view of the project that is as close as possible to that of the project team, he or she will remain, like the other members of that team, external to the schools in which it is being implemented. Furthermore we saw, when we considered the problems of the dissemination of innovation in Chapter 5, that there is always a large and important gap between the conceptions of the planners and the realities of the teacher's work. The teacher's perspective is also, therefore, important and we must examine his or her role in curriculum evaluation.

There is a further reason why it is important to consider the part that the teacher himself or herself must play in evaluation and that is that much of his or her work is based on his or her own planning and not on that of a project team, so that, as we suggested earlier in this chapter, discussions of evaluation must concern themselves with the problems of evaluating the work of the individual teacher and not just of attempts at innovation of a large-scale kind.

First of all, then, attention must be drawn to the fact that the teacher is the person who possesses a good deal of the data the evaluator needs so that he or she must be seen as having an important contribution to make to evaluation at that level. However, many have seen the role of the teacher in evaluation as going beyond being a mere provider of data. Wynne Harlen (1971, p. 133) has summed this up in saying that 'teachers should be as thoroughly and genuinely involved in the evaluation as they are, or should be, with the development of the material'. They should not merely be asked to provide data, especially where this is mainly a form-filling exercise, but should be involved in continuous discussion of the questions being asked. The effects of this are two-way. For in the first place the teachers develop the kind of understanding of the problems of evaluation that will make them better at providing appropriate data and, second, the evaluators can gain insights that will lead to a better framing of questions. Teachers can and should also be involved in the testing and marking of children where this is included in the evaluation process. Full involvement of teachers in all aspects of the development of a curriculum project is crucial to maximizing its success. 'Improved attitudes of teachers towards evaluation will certainly follow from improved attitudes of evaluators towards teachers' (ibid.).

Although this point was made in the context of the evaluation of a national project, it perhaps has even more force in relation to the engagement of teachers in evaluations of their own day-to-day work.

Serious barriers do exist, however, to the achievement by teachers of anything approaching an objective appraisal of what after all they are responsible for at the coal-face, as some of the work of the Ford Teaching Project has revealed. A key concern of this project was to get teachers to evaluate their own work, to engage in a kind of self-monitoring or self-evaluation process, and it was assumed that this implied the adoption by the teacher of an objective stance. However the whole idea of self-criticism and self-evaluation is threatening to many teachers; the organizational set-up in most schools does not help teachers to engage in this kind of self-appraisal; and many teachers find it difficult to discuss their problems with their colleagues (Elliott and Adelman, 1974).

The experience of those engaged in the Ford Teaching Project, however, led them to be 'optimistic about the capacity of the majority of teachers for self-criticism' (Elliott and Adelman, 1974, p. 23) and to assume that the barriers to objectivity in such cases are no more than practical difficulties which can be overcome. They also realized that subjectivity of evaluation can in any case be avoided by checking the accounts teachers give of their work by reference to other sources. Thus they developed a procedure they called 'multiple interview' or 'triangulation' in which accounts are obtained not only from the teacher but also from the pupils and an independent observer. This is another dimension of the holistic approach to evaluation that we have already discussed. Not only are all kinds of data grist to the evaluator's mill, but also all those involved in the process are to be seen as evaluators.

We saw earlier that a holistic approach sees evaluation as an integral part of curriculum development; it represents a form of continuous action research and feedback. If this is so, it becomes a question not of *whether* but rather of *how* teachers are to evaluate their work. For, as we also noted earlier, self-evaluation is a vital part of the teacher's armoury of professional techniques. Indeed, it might be claimed that in all spheres of human activity improvement can come only from a full and personal awareness of one's own previous inadequacies. Such an awareness, however, does not always come from within and there is little doubt that it can and should be augmented and assisted by the observations of those who are in a position to view one's work from different perspectives.

Self-evaluation by teachers, then, is important for the continued development of their work, and the recent attempts by some local authorities in the United Kingdom to encourage teachers to try this kind of self-assessment is to be welcomed. It must be seen, however, as one of several approaches to the evaluation of the work of the school or the teacher, as a necessary but by no means a sufficient condition of effective evaluation. Comment and criticism from all relevant perspectives are needed and must be accepted if we are to ensure a proper coverage and even that limited form of objectivity we suggested earlier was all that is possible.

The difficulty created by the inevitable tension between self-evaluation and that of external bodies or individuals may be eased, or at least lose some of its force, if we consider the possibilities of peer-evaluation, the use of fellow professionals for the external evaluation of one's work. This is a system which has worked effectively for many years in higher education, where every course has its external examiner or examiners whose task it is not merely to check on the standards of the students' performances but to offer comments on the curriculum of the course in order to help in the continuing process of course improvement. Again, it is a device which some local authorities in the United Kingdom are currently exploring, by encouraging the exchange of teachers between schools and inviting the comments of each upon the work of the other. Clearly, this kind of scheme itself presents difficulties. For, just as many teachers find it difficult to take anything other than the most favourable view possible of their own work, so they often find it correspondingly easy to take the most unfavourable view of that of their colleagues, especially those in what might be regarded as 'rival' institutions. It is important, however, that the possibilities of this kind of device are fully explored, since the attainment of a proper level of professional evaluation is vital if evaluation is to promote curriculum development rather than inhibit it.

In this connection it is worth adding a brief comment on some of the schemes which have recently emerged for school self-evaluation (Elliott, G., 1981; Elliott, J., 1981; Rodger and Richardson, 1985). Such a development is certainly highly desirable, although, as we saw earlier, it will now have a much more limited effect on the curriculum and, indeed, the quality of individual schools than it might have had, and it certainly represents a major step forward from the time when most evaluation of schools was conducted from the outside, by such agencies as Her Majesty's Inspectorate and local education authority advisers/inspectors. It can also be taken as reflecting, at least in some local authorities, a move away from the grosser, more simplistic forms of evaluation to something more sophisticated, to formative approaches, to evaluation with a qualitative rather than a largely quantitative emphasis, to process evaluation and especially to a proper involvement of the teachers themselves in the activity.

It has been suggested, however, that it raises a further important distinction, that between what Maurice Holt (1981) has called 'process' and 'procedural' evaluation. By process evaluation he means that holistic, illuminative approach to evaluation which was described earlier; and he stresses that in such an approach there is no doubt that the prime focus is on curriculum development. Procedural evaluation, however, falls short of this kind of evaluation, not least in that it is concerned to provide evidence for some form of external accountability and, as a result, is essentially objectives-based. Thus some schools and teachers have been asked to engage in a process of self-evaluation but required to do so through producing curriculum guidelines, writing reports, completing checklists and, in general, providing evidence, usually of a largely quantitative kind, for outside agencies. If there is any resultant curriculum development, or qualitative improvement, from this kind of activity, it is as a spin-off and not as a central purpose of the exercise. Furthermore, it may even be counter-productive to the development and the improvement of the school curriculum, not least because of that tendency, noted before, of such external evaluation to be prescriptive of what schools and teachers are to do rather than supportive of them in their own professional judgements.

School self-evaluation requires a good deal more than merely ticking checklists and answering questions posed from outside. For although 'to the outside world, checklists appear to offer an interesting compromise between external guidance and authority and internal choice and responsibility' (Becher, Eraut and Knight, 1981, p. 89), in reality 'within the school itself their strong management orientation can seem to belie their declared purpose of guiding self-evaluation' (ibid.). Thus external support for school self-evaluation needs to go beyond what Robin Alexander (1984, pp. 200–1), after quoting the above comment, calls 'the more familiar LEA approach of merely sending the school a list of questions to be answered'. It must be a more sophisticated process than that, and must include what Alexander describes as 'the strength of the Schools Council/Bristol University "GRIDS" approach (Bristol University, 1983)', namely 'that it provides detailed guidance on school self-review strategy as a cyclic process and specifies the various steps and tasks to be undertaken' (op. cit., p. 200).

For the more simple kind of approach does not do justice to the complex knowledge teachers have about their pupils, their school and its curriculum (Holt, 1981) nor to the complexity of educational experience generally, since it reduces these to a checklist of skills, objectives, attainment targets or whatever. Nor does it offer any clear strategy for the use of the data thus collected (Simons, 1980), since, while it makes curriculum development a stated and ostensible aim, its real purpose is the collection of data for purposes of accountability. In fact, it again represents that unhappy confusion of purpose and conceptual muddle we have noted on more than one occasion. Thus again, one cannot merely assume that schemes for school self-evaluation *per se* will solve many, or even any, of the problems we have identified in other approaches; everything depends on the form and nature of particular schemes. And it will be plain that some of these are schemes of school self-evaluation in name only.

The message of this discussion of the roles of the individual teacher and the individual school in the evaluation process is that, if we are to attain a form of evaluation which will genuinely support and advance curriculum development in the full sense, and thus lead to an improvement in the *educational* quality of what schools have to offer, what is needed is the inclusion of as many perspectives as we can obtain, including vitally that of the teacher himself or herself.

This clearly leads us to a consideration of the political dimension of evaluation. For it suggests a particular stance on the issue of the control of the curriculum and points us towards the notion of 'democratic' as opposed to 'autocratic' or 'bureaucratic' evaluation (MacDonald, 1975).

These distinctions are offered by Barry MacDonald from a recognition that evaluation is a political activity and the styles he describes represent several different ways in which that activity can be carried out. 'Bureaucratic evaluation is an unconditional service to those government agencies which have major control over the allocation of educational resources. The evaluator accepts the values of those who hold office, and offers information which will help to accomplish their policy objectives' (op. cit., p. 133). 'Autocratic evaluation is a conditional service to those government agencies which have major control over the allocation of educational resources. It offers external validation of policy in exchange for compliance with its recommendations' (ibid.).

'Democratic' evaluation, on the other hand, is defined as

an information service to the community about the characteristics of an educational programme. It recognises value pluralism and seeks to represent a range of interests in its issue formulation. The basic value is an informed citizenry, and the evaluator acts as a broker in exchanges of information between differing groups . . . the evaluator has no concept of information misuse . . . The key concepts of democratic evaluation are 'confidentiality', 'negotiation' and 'accessibility'. The key justificatory concept is 'the right to know'.

(op. cit., p. 134)

It will be clear that this is the only form of evaluation that will facilitate that kind of continuous adaptation at the level of the individual school and the individual teacher which this book is concerned to argue is the only route to the proper development of the curriculum. It will also be clear that it is a form of evaluation which requires the fullest participation of the teachers themselves.

It will be equally plain, however, that in the United Kingdom we are now facing a significant shift in the style of educational evaluation and in its main forms and purposes. It is to a consideration of this shift that we now turn.

THE IMPACT OF CURRENT POLICIES

What has been said so far reveals the major strides which have been made in our understanding of curriculum evaluation, along with its relation to curriculum planning, development and, indeed, implementation, over a considerable period of time and through a process of painstaking research, both empirical and conceptual. It will also be clear that this research has taken place in a context in which the main concern has been with educational advance and improvement. It is important now to consider what is currently proposed in today's rather different context, not only because this will reveal perhaps the best evidence we have of the fact that those current policies choose to ignore the lessons of such research and the understandings and insights it has led to, but also to identify the implications of these policies in respect of curriculum evaluation and their consequent impact on the experiences children will have in schools.

Let us first pick out some of the chief, and most relevant, aspects of what we have seen so far.

It is clear, first, that we need to begin any act of evaluation from a clear idea of what it is we are doing, which of the many possible purposes of such an act we are attempting to attain. Are we setting out to measure how far certain prestated objectives have been attained? Are we wishing merely to describe what has occurred in as neutral a manner as possible in order to provide information which different agencies may use as they think proper? Are we seeking data as a basis for making evaluative judgements? If so, what kinds of evaluative judgements are we wishing to make: judgements about the value of what is being offered? or about the effectiveness of its 'delivery'? or about the competence of the teachers? or about the levels of attainment of the pupils? In short, we need to be clear, open and honest about the purposes of our evaluative exercises and especially about whether the main focus is administrative, political or educational.

A main weakness of many current practices and many aspects of current policies is that their purposes are not clearly stated, except in the form of some political rhetoric, so that too often – as, for example, in the HMI *Curriculum Matters* booklets – different and sometimes incompatible purposes are run together in such a way as to blur the issues and render any results invalid. We must also note that, as was suggested earlier, this leads to a confusion between the purposes of the curriculum and those of the evaluation procedures and, perhaps more importantly, as we also saw earlier, to the imposition of the purposes and values of the evaluation procedures on the curriculum itself, so that evaluation comes to lead curriculum planning rather than vice versa, and to do so in a confused, confusing and often distorting manner. It is essential that the evaluation model should match the curriculum model, since, if we look at things wrongly, we produce wrong, inadequate and misleading data (Holt, 1981).

This leads us naturally to our second major point. If our concern is with the making of evaluative judgements, not only do we need to be clear about the kinds of judgement we are seeking to make, we also need to be clear about the criteria against which we plan to make them. For, as the etymology of the term 'evaluation' indicates, its concern is with the making of value judgements; it is not, as we saw earlier, a scientific exercise leading to the production of objective data. As Maurice Holt (1981, p. 80) has said, 'the tester's search for objective certainty is a quest for an unattainable goal'. Given, then, that evaluation is a judgemental act, we must acknowledge that, for it to be academically, rationally and even morally acceptable and respectable, our criteria of judgement must be made explicit.

Again, a major weakness of many current policies and practices is that such criteria are seldom clearly stated. One has only to consider again the practice of Her Majesty's Inspectorate in undertaking evaluative inspections of institutions of all kinds to appreciate both the lack of respect for this first principle of judgemental evaluation and its unsatisfactory consequences, not to mention the fact that the continuing policy of making such judgements 'on the hoof' is evidence of a disturbing ignorance of all those understandings of educational evaluation this chapter has attempted to set out. 'Our criteria of evaluation are based on inspection' was the incredible reply I recently received from an inspector to a request that such criteria be made explicit. A major consequence of this is that it is never clear whether a course or a particular curricular activity is being evaluated in its own terms or according to some externally imposed criteria, or, if the latter is the case, the justification for making an evaluation by reference to criteria which may be completely different from, and incompatible with, those of the course planners. One can think of no other area of human endeavour where such practice would not be immediately recognized as being not only irrational but of doubtful morality too.

A prime example of this in the current scene is the pattern of HMI inspections of teacher-education courses, in which the particular style and ethos of a course, the principles and values of those who planned it, are given little or no weight in the evaluation exercise, and external criteria, largely political, are used as the basis for the evaluation; for obvious reasons these are not only unacknowledged but even vehemently denied, so that no clear and justified base for the exercise is established and consequently the judgements made lack not only validity but credibility too. If there are no grounds for laying claims to an objective, scientific status for the findings of curriculum evaluation (and if anyone *is* making such claims they need at the very least to be substantiated), the value positions from which the evaluation is being made must, if it is to have any force or worth, be clearly stated. Many current policies and practices neither attempt to offer arguments for such a scientific base nor state their value positions. They are thus fundamentally flawed.

A notable exception to this is some of the recent work of the Assessment of Performance Unit, perhaps especially in its newest project, that in the field of design and technological activity. For, aware of the significantly different value positions implicit in the several different approaches to work in this area of the curriculum, and conscious as a result that any attempt to evaluate them all as if they did not represent such differences of position would lack all validity and would thus be of little or no value, the team responsible for monitoring this area of the curriculum has insisted on declaring its own value stances before undertaking the monitoring exercise, on making clear the criteria against which its evaluations are to be made, and, indeed, inviting comment on them (Kelly *et al.*, 1987). It has thus made these criteria themselves a part of the evaluation exercise. In short, it has recognized that the concept of the subject or area of activity must itself be open to critical evaluation, as well as the effectiveness of its 'delivery'.

This leads us to the third general point which emerges from what has been said so far about our understanding of evaluation theory, and one which is particularly relevant to the current political scene: the importance of distinguishing what we saw earlier John White (1971) once described as the empirical and the conceptual questions which need to be asked about any curriculum activity or innovation. If we are to make a genuinely *educational* evaluation, we need to ask questions, which again are value questions, about the worth (or value) of the activity or the innovation, not merely those methodological questions which relate to the effectiveness with which teachers 'get it across'. We need to explore not only whether the curriculum is being 'delivered' effectively but also – and more crucially – whether it is *worth* 'delivering'.

Again, this important distinction is being blurred, and perhaps lost altogether, in what is currently planned and in many current practices. We have already seen that recent work of the Assessment of Performance Unit has attempted to embrace both these aspects of curriculum evaluation. We must note, however, that current plans are for the APU to wither away over the next few years, largely because, it is claimed, its role will be taken over by the newly created School Examinations and Assessment Council and the National Curriculum Council. These bodies will indeed in the not too distant future be in possession of or have access to a great deal of data but, to a very large extent, these data will be gleaned not from attempts at curriculum evaluation but from the programmes for the assessment of individual pupil performance and attainment. There are several aspects of this which are worthy of note.

To begin with, as was suggested earlier, although the assessment of individual pupils may well provide *some* data of value in the evaluation of the curriculum, it cannot provide *all* the data we need. And so, if those are all the data we have, the scope of any evaluation process will be severely limited. There are two major, and related, ways in which this limitation will manifest itself. In the first place, we will have been taken back to those simplistic forms of objectives-based evaluation whose inadequacies, especially in relation to exploring all aspects of the curriculum or the curricular experiences of pupils, we noted earlier. For the assessment of pupils will be carried out according to certain predetermined 'attainment targets', statements of the levels of attainment certain wise bodies believe children should have reached at various points pronounced to be crucial in the age-related assessment programme and in the major areas identified as 'core' in the National Curriculum – English (*sic*), mathematics, science and possibly also technology. And, while one may welcome this attempt to make clear the assessment criteria, one must note again the limitations of converting these into a series of attainment objectives. For the inadequacies of this approach both to curriculum planning and curriculum evaluation have been thoroughly explored and explicated in this book, not least in our consideration of the 'checklist' approach to evaluation, so that a return to such simple practices deserves at least some kind of explanation and even justification. It is very important to note, however, that such explanation or justification could be framed and offered only on political grounds. And it is the political thrust of current policies, not their educational merits, which is taking us in this direction.

A second source of limitation in this policy takes us back to the central point under consideration here. For data gleaned from assessments of pupil performance can tell us nothing about the worth or value of the kinds of performance we make our central concern or thus of the curriculum which pupils are being offered (although they might, as a by-product, tell us much about the reaction and the response of many pupils to that curriculum). Thus, an approach to evaluation which restricts itself, as the *Curriculum Matters* booklets recommend and as the brief of the two new councils seems to suggest, to a concern with the assessment of pupil performance, while it may tell us much about the effectiveness of schools and teachers in 'delivering' the National Curriculum, will offer no evidence at all which might have a bearing on whether that curriculum is worth 'delivering' or, indeed, about whether the attainment targets set for the assessment programme are reasonable, let alone valuable. Again, therefore, we must note that what we have here is a return to those simplistic forms of evaluation whose inadequacies have been fully exposed and which, as we have seen, because of those inadequacies had been supplanted by more sophisticated techniques of a kind to support the continuing development of the curriculum. And again we note that the thrust is political rather than educational, and that the prime concern is with teacher appraisal and accountability rather than with curriculum development or improvement.

In fact, it suggests that the evaluation procedures are to be used more for the control of the curriculum than for its development, more for manipulating the education system than for raising its quality or its standards. And it reflects a major shift from what, as we saw earlier, has been described as a 'democratic' style of evaluation to that which has been called 'bureaucratic' or even 'autocratic' (MacDonald, 1975).

Let us turn finally in our discussion of curriculum evaluation to an exploration of the notion of teacher accountability and the practice of teacher appraisal. For it will by now be plain that, although most of evaluation theory has been developed with the purpose of improving the curriculum, evaluation has increasingly come to be regarded as a device for appraising the work of teachers and the institutions in which they carry out that work, and for ensuring that both can be held politically accountable.

APPRAISAL AND ACCOUNTABILITY

The first point that needs to be made about teacher accountability is that it must be accepted rather than opposed. It is of the essence of life in a democratic society that no one should be unaccountable for his or her public actions; that is a privilege enjoyed only by those who hold power in totalitarian states.

Indeed, the need for accountability was recognized by the architects of democratic government, the Athenians of the fifth century BC, as being as crucial, if not more so, than free elections through the ballot box and other forms of participation by the citizenry in the government of the state. The most important element in Athenian democracy was not the free election of government members and officials; in fact, many of these were chosen by lot rather than by election, since the Athenians felt – with some justification one feels – that the gods would make better choices than they would themselves, or that anybody could make as good a job of governing as those who thrust themselves forward as self-styled experts, or that selection by lot would discourage the attempts of self-seeking individuals to achieve positions of power. Nor did they regard the opportunities for frequent votes on major issues of policy as in themselves adequate to secure completely democratic government, since they well realized that often decisions have to be taken quickly and that a consistent policy cannot always be attained by constant reference to the people as a whole. The most important element in their system was the frequently used arrangement for the accountability of all government members and officials. This is a feature of their democratic procedures which has been too readily overlooked by commentators and by political theorists. For the Athenians believed that true democracy could be attained only if procedures existed, and were used, for calling politicians to account on the completion of their periods of office. Thus quite frequently trials were held, before citizen juries, of politicians whose behaviour had given cause for concern, and, if these juries decided against the defendant, a fine, banishment and even, on some occasions, execution would follow. It is a system whose attractions are enhanced by the actions and policies of many present-day politicians.

A second important point that emerges from this brief excursion into ancient history is that, in addition to being perhaps the most essential ingredient of democracy, accountability is also essentially *post eventum* (Downey and Kelly, 1979). It makes neither practical nor logical sense to endeavour to make someone accountable for his or her actions before he or she has performed them. A fundamental feature of the concept of accountability is that it comes into play after someone has had the freedom to exercise professional judgement and take whatever action he or she has deemed appropriate. In the context of teaching, therefore, accountability cannot be interpreted as entailing giving in advance an account of what one intends to do, although it has been interpreted by many people in this way and has thus been seen as adding its weight to those demands for the prespecification of teaching objectives.

Indeed, this has been a major feature of those schemes of accountability which have been introduced in many areas of the USA (Hamilton, 1976; Atkin, 1979) and which have been taken as the model for similar schemes which have recently been advocated in the United Kingdom. By 1974 nearly forty states in the USA were attempting to establish a legal base for demanding the accountability of teachers (Hamilton, 1976) and a major characteristic of their projected schemes was a concern with outcomes or outputs (Atkin, 1979), their focus being on 'management by objectives', 'programme budgeting' and even 'performance contracting', a system by which outside agencies are paid to work with teachers to raise the achievement levels of pupils (Atkin, 1979). In short, the emphasis has been on achieving increased external control over education by intervention at the beginning, rather than by permitting teachers to exercise their professional judgement and calling them to account when they have done so. Given that these demands for increased control, as we have seen, have resulted from a dissatisfaction with what teachers have been doing, this approach is, of course, understandable. But it must be seen as another aspect of that attempt to provide education in a more business-like way, to make it more 'scientific', particularly through detailed formal planning, the inadequacies of which we discussed fully in Chapter 3.

It is clear, then, that demands for teacher accountability can be interpreted and implemented in a number of quite different ways, so that the crucial question becomes not whether teachers should be accountable for their work but how this is to be achieved. In other words, we must seek for the most suitable model of teacher accountability. Furthermore, a crucial aspect of such a model will be the answer we give to the question of to whom should teachers be accountable, and that question also deserves our careful attention. It is equally important also to consider what teachers can reasonably be held accountable for, since there are aspects of the development of pupils which are clearly beyond the scope of their influence. And we need too to ask who else should be held accountable for educational achievement, rather than taking it for granted that the teacher is the only person who can be expected to contribute to this. All these issues we must consider in a little more detail.

In broad terms, two major models of teacher accountability can be identified as a result of recent practices and debate on this issue. One of these is that instrumental, utilitarian, hierarchical, bureaucratic model that we have just suggested has been widely adopted in the USA. This is the model which Lawrence Stenhouse (1975, p. 185) described as the 'systematic efficiency model'. The second might be described as the intrinsic, democratic or professional model.

The main feature of the first of these models is that it holds the teacher accountable to the public as taxpaying providers of the resources he or she is expending (Sockett, 1976b). It is a crude model, whose major focus is on the economic issues of resource allocation and value for money, and whose central concern is thus with the results obtained for the money spent. It is for this reason that it views the teacher as accountable to those who decide on the allocation of resources, that is, the government at local or national level, rather than to parents, pupils, employers or professional peers. It is also for this reason that it stresses the achievement of prespecified performances and thus adds its support to the adoption of the objectives model of curriculum planning (Atkin, 1979). The main means it adopts to assess teacher competence is setting tests which are administered but not designed by the teachers concerned (Sockett, 1976b), and the future provision of resources is decided by reference to the results of these tests, a system of 'payment by results'. Its main characteristics then are that it is instrumental, economic and political.

The basic assumptions of this model are also worth noting (Elliott, 1976). For it assumes, firstly, that teachers are concerned to bring about only a limited range of outcomes; secondly, 'that achievement scores can be used to assess the causal effectiveness of what teachers do in classrooms' (op. cit., p. 49); thirdly, that teachers can be praised or blamed, rewarded or punished, especially through the allocation of resources, on the basis of these causal evaluations; fourthly, that the teachers themselves have no rights of participation in such evaluations. Lastly, it also adopts a model fo the teacher as a technician responsible for, and thus accountable for, no more than the 'delivery' of a curriculum whose objectives or attainment targets have been determined by others.

In the light of earlier discussions in this book, it is not difficult to identify the inadequacies of this model. To begin with, it trails with it all those difficulties associated with the objectives model of planning which we discussed in Chapter 3. In particular, it encourages the acceptance of simplistic educational goals by suggesting that what cannot be measured cannot be taught (Sockett, 1976b), for the model cannot be used to assess educational goals which cannot be defined in behavioural terms or clearly prespecified. It thus threatens to 'destroy schools as places where *education* goes on' (Elliott, 1976, p. 51). Secondly, it substitutes teacher accountability for teacher responsibility or, to express this differently, it gives teachers responsibility without freedom (Stenhouse, 1975). This in turn has serious effects on teacher morale, as is evidenced by the increasing militancy of teachers' unions (Sockett, 1976b). Thirdly, the kind of data that this form of accountability produces does not help in any way with decisions as to how the performance of individual schools or teachers can be improved (Sockett, 1976b). In other words, it does not reveal why children have scored badly on the tests, merely that they have. The reasons why they have done badly are quite crucial, since it may be that these would justify the allocation of additional resources to the school, as was once felt to be the case with those schools in the United Kingdom decreed to be in Educational Priority Areas. It is for this reason that it has been claimed that one effect of this model of accountability may be to 'benefit the dominant middle class sectors of society to the disadvantage of minority communities' (Elliott, 1976, p. 50), since if a school performs badly, even where this is directly attributable to the social class background of its pupils, this kind of scheme is likely to lead to a reduction in its resources, whereas social justice might be felt to require the opposite. In fact, it might be argued that its real purpose is to cut the costs of education rather than to improve its quality.

In contrast, a major characteristic of the intrinsic, democratic, professional model of accountability is that it is 'for adherence to principles of practice rather than for results embodied in pupil performance' (Sockett, 1976b, p. 42). It thus eschews all links with curriculum planning by prespecified objectives, and suggests rather, or at least makes possible, the adoption of a 'process' model of planning. For it is a model which is based on a recognition that educational value resides in the teaching–learning process itself rather than in its outcomes (Elliott, 1976), so that, whereas the hierarchical model assumes that decisions concerning what is valuable in education are to be taken outside the school, this model recognizes that such decisions must be made within it, as part of the process of education itself. It also acknowledges that teachers have rights as a profession (Elliott, 1976) and that they must be regarded as autonomous professional people. Thus it accepts that teachers have a 'right of reply' or of direct involvement themselves in the accountability process, and that any action consequent on the evidence gleaned in that process must be reached after consultation with fellow professionals and not in total independence of their expert opinion. It concedes, therefore, that teachers should be accountable not only to the agencies of government but 'to a variety of "audiences" in society' (Elliott, 1976, p. 51), 'to diverse constituencies rather than to the agglomerate constituency of the public alone' (Sockett, 1976b, p. 42), and that among this diversity of audiences, or constituencies, must be included the teaching profession itself. The form of evaluation it recommends, then, is not the simple summative form of measuring pupil performance associated with the instrumental model, but rather an illuminative form designed to provide information for this diversity of agencies.

The major difficulties with this model clearly stem from its complexity. It has the merit of recognizing that education is a far more sophisticated activity than the advocates of the other, cruder model appear to think, but along with this must be accepted the difficulties of devising suitable and workable schemes for its translation into practice. These difficulties are virtually identical with those associated with the more sophisticated forms of curriculum evaluation which we fully explored earlier, and focus particularly on the problems of evaluating activities which are concerned with adherence to principles rather than the attainment of outcomes and those concerning the competence of teachers to evaluate one another's work. We must reiterate here what was said there, namely that the solution to these difficulties is to recognize the complexities of education and work towards similarly sophisticated techniques of evaluation and accountability rather than to reduce the work of teachers to the simplistic levels that existing techniques can measure. Schemes of accountability, like all forms of evaluation and assessment, must follow and support the process of education rather than governing and controlling it.

Our discussion of the two major models of accountability has taken us some way towards an answer to the other questions we suggested need to be faced on this issue. For it will be clear that teachers should be regarded quite properly as accountable to a plurality and a diversity of interests in a democratic society, and it should also be indisputable that prominent among those agencies should be the teaching profession itself, possibly in the form of a general teaching council. A major reason for that is that no one knows better than the professional what lies within the scope of his or her professionalism, and it will be plain that teachers can in justice be held accountable only for those things which it lies within their powers to affect. Their work will be constrained by many factors beyond their control – not only the out-of-school experiences of their pupils, their social background, their exposure to the influences of the media and so on, but also the allocation of public resources and all those other constraints we noted in Chapter 6. It will also be apparent that those who are responsible for these factors – parents, local authority officials, politicians and, indeed, society as a whole, including, not least, those responsible for the media and the uses to which these are put – must take their share of accountability for pupils' attitudes and thus for their educational performance.

What will also be plain, however, is that current political policies for education are reflecting the same kind of shift in relation to teacher accountability that we noted earlier in the context of evaluation. Evaluation is now primarily concerned with the accountability of teachers, and accountability itself is directed centrally at the performance of teachers and is focused increasingly on teacher appraisal. In both cases too, this is accompanied by a change of model, a return to simplistic forms, an emphasis on the objectives-based, instrumental approaches to both education and accountability, whose concern is with political control rather than with educational development or improvement, and with checking teacher competence rather than supporting teacher development.

It is possible to find systems of teacher appraisal which have as their central concern teacher development, but there is now no area of the education system, from first schools to higher education, which is free of the need to appraise teachers against externally imposed criteria of appraisal. 'Performance indicators' have been established for the evaluation of the work of university institutions, for example, and these are to provide a basis for deciding on appropriate levels of funding and resourcing; and these, like those checklists for the 'self-evaluation' of schools which we noted earlier, are procedural rather than process-oriented, instrumental rather than 'intrinsic', quantitative for the most part rather than qualitative, and are thus more likely to impose criteria of evaluation and accountability on institutions than to help them to develop their own. The attainment targets of the National Curriculum assessment programme can be seen in much the same light.

It is thus difficult, if not impossible, to see any system of teacher appraisal, in any kind of institution and whatever its stated philosophy, as anything other than a political act whose aim is to increase external control rather than to raise internal quality. And, just as we saw that this is accompanied by a shift from a 'democratic' to a 'bureaucratic' or 'autocratic' style of evaluation, we must note here the strong tendency for it to be associated also with a move from a 'democratic' to a 'utilitarian' or 'bureaucratic' form of accountability. Indeed, there can be no place for the former in what, as a consequence of the 1988 Education Act, has become a completely bureaucratic education system in which all decisions of any consequence or significance are made by the politicians and their aides.

The rhetoric of current policies has made much of 'teaching quality' (this was in fact the title of a White Paper issued in 1983); there have even been arguments for increased external control of education institutions on that ground; the reality is that evaluation, accountability and teacher appraisal are no longer to be conducted in a manner which will facilitate the advancement of education in the full sense, even though they might raise 'quality' in a utilitarian, 'value for money' sense and maintain or even improve standards in the limited meaning given to that term by those outside the teaching profession and in the official documentation which has accompanied the introduction of these new policies.

IMPLICATIONS FOR EDUCATIONAL RESEARCH

These changes must also have far-reaching implications for educational research – its extent, scope and, indeed, nature. And it would be remiss to conclude this chapter without some reference to these implications.

The link between evaluation and research in education, as in any other sphere, is a close one. Both are concerned to discover more about the activity and, certainly in the case of those forms of evaluation which are aimed at curriculum development, both are directed at the improvement of practice. Thus we noted earlier Lawrence Stenhouse's vision of a time or phase when 'the conceptual distinction between development and evaluation is destroyed and the two merge as research' (1975, p. 122).

We saw too in Chapter 5 that this view is also reflected in Stenhouse's notion of 'the teacher as researcher'. For what this essentially requires is that teachers should develop appropriate skills in the art of self-evaluation and that they should use these skills to make continuous appraisals of their own work as a basis for its continuing development. We also noted there how the idea of 'action research' had grown from similar assumptions about the teacher's task and the most effective ways to promote teacher development. We saw that this view of educational research had arisen at least in part from a dissatisfaction with traditional approaches and especially with their failure to explore educational practice from the inside. We noted Elliot Eisner's criticism of these approaches on the grounds 'that we have distanced ourselves from the phenomena that should be central to our studies, that we employ models that have been designed to deal with other than educational phenomena, and that we reduce what is a rich source of data into a pale reflection of the reality we seek to study' (1985, p. 262). The central purpose of action research has been to bring the researcher from the outside to the inside of the activity, in order to ensure both that he or she understands that activity with all its many nuances and that his or her research efforts make a worthwhile contribution to improving the practice of those directly engaged in the activity (Ebbutt, 1983), rather than, as has too often been the case, actually inhibiting that practice (Kelly, 1981). It is not difficult to see how the notion of 'action research' merges with that of 'teacher as researcher' into a concept of educational research as a process which requires the continuous monitoring of any educational activity by the teacher, supported by what-ever contributions can be made by a 'sympathetic third party', with the prime intention of improving performance and developing teaching skills.

If we now draw together the issues explored in our consideration of strategies for curriculum change and development in Chapter 5 with our re-view of evaluation theory in this chapter, we can see that what emerges from both is the view that real curriculum development must rest in the hands of the individual teacher; that it is not a general but a particular matter; that, if it is to be influenced for the better by anyone else, that other person must first get on the inside of the particular situation; that evaluation, if it is to be effective in improving the quality of any teacher's work, must, in a fun-damental sense, be self-evaluation, perhaps supported from outside through some form of action research, but not directed from outside by the imposi-tion of guidelines and checklists; that every evaluative activity, if it is to promote development and improvement, must be formative rather than summative, descriptive rather than prescriptive, illuminative rather than directive, 'democratic' rather than 'bureaucratic'; and finally, that account-ability and appraisal must take forms which match this concept of research and evaluation, they too must be 'democratic' and must support educational development rather than inhibit it.

None of this should be taken as implying that other forms of research in education have no value whatever. There is no doubt that much of the work of agencies such as the Schools Council and the Assessment of Performance Unit has illuminated areas of educational activity to the benefit of education in general and individual teachers in particular. It is to say, however, that such research has no value unless individual teachers take ownership of it by recognizing its relevance to their practice. To impose 'findings' on them whether they see their relevance or not will be to inhibit rather than to promote their professional development.

We can now see, therefore, that if, as was suggested above, current policies are taking us back to more simplistic notions of educational evalua-tion and to more politically grounded forms of accountability, they must lead to more limited views of educational research. Certainly, the shift to greater centralized control of the curriculum must have the effect of reducing, if not eliminating altogether, the scope for action research as we have seen it has been defined and developed and for any notion of the teacher as researcher, since it effectively reduces teachers' freedom to make any really significant changes in their curricular offerings whatever their own research or evaluation of these tells them. Again, therefore, we can see that it is not only in relation to evaluation and accountability that the focus has shifted from educational advance to political control; it is in the associated area of educational research too.

Finally, we must note that, for the same reasons, future research on a national scale is also likely to reflect this same shift of focus. We have already on several occasions suggested that it is probable that future research will not direct its attention to the worth or the value of the National Curriculum but will content itself with a monitoring of the effectiveness of its 'delivery'. We have noted too, especially in our discussion of the work of the Schools Council, that there is now very little opportunity for funded research in education which is not politically directed and thus controlled. The Depart-ment of Education and Science is now the only major source of funding for educational research and the use of its funds is, probably quite properly, carefully controlled by its political masters. Again, therefore, one is forced to the conclusion that, whatever the political rhetoric, the reality is that the immediate future will see little improvement in the quality of education and no advance, in fact possibly even a regression, in the levels of our under-standing of educational theory and practice, whatever might be the effects of current policies on vocational training and economic productivity.

Like all things human, educational evaluation, accountability and research can be used for good or ill, to promote educational improvement or to inhibit it. There is every sign that the pendulum has now swung towards the latter end of this scale.

SUMMARY AND CONCLUSIONS

This chapter has traced the development of evaluation theory from its rather primitive beginnings to the point where it had begun to offer teachers the opportunity for securing important insights into their curricula, both as individuals and as a profession, as a basis for their continued development and improvement. It then drew attention to the fact that those political pressures which were explored in Chapter 6 and the new policies they have led to are taking us back to more simplistic forms of evaluation, sometimes to forms which cannot, or do not, distinguish it from pupil assessment, and are stressing the political purposes of evaluation rather than its educational advantages.

This took us naturally on to an exploration of teacher accountability and schemes for teacher appraisal. We noted first that these are, or should be, natural concomitants of any public role in a democratic society, and accepted that the crucial question is the forms that these activities take and the nature of the schemes devised to achieve them. Here again we saw that they can be used either to facilitate continuing curriculum development or as mechanisms for curriculum control, and that current policies are emphasizing the second of these functions to the detriment of the first.

Finally, we considered some of the implications of these policies for educational research, and concluded that here too the recent advances made in our understanding of the kinds of research which might promote educational advance and improve the quality of teachers' practice are being set at naught by the desire to encourage only those kinds of change which have official sanction or which are likely to lead to improved efficiency in 'delivering' the National Curriculum.

It is to a consideration of that National Curriculum, an examination of the theoretical issues it raises and an exploration of how far it reflects the kinds of understanding and the advances in our thinking about the curriculum which previous chapters have attempted to explicate that we turn in the final chapter, a chapter which, from this focus, will set out to draw together many of the perspectives which have so far been offered.

8
THE NATIONAL CURRICULUM

Perhaps nothing sums up the dramatic changes that we have seen in attitudes to the school curriculum in the United Kingdom during the last ten years so well as the fact that the concluding chapter of the first edition of this book, published in 1977, was called 'A Common Curriculum', that of the second edition in 1982 'The Whole Curriculum' and, now, the third edition concludes with 'The National Curriculum', reflecting a somewhat sorry progression from an open discussion of the issues, towards exploration of a deeper educational issue which that discussion raised, leading to one kind of solution framed in educational terms, a solution that has subsequently been overtaken and indeed overturned by policies whose thrust is essentially political, utilitarian and economic.

A major topic of discussion throughout the 1970s was the notion that there should be a centrally determined common curriculum in all schools, as there is in most other countries. The main aspects of that theoretical debate we shall look at shortly. Towards the end of that decade, especially as a result of the survey of secondary schools carried out by Her Majesty's Inspectorate (DES, 1979), which revealed, among other things, programmes of study for many pupils in the upper reaches of those schools which seemed to lack overall coherence, there emerged a growing awareness of the need to view and plan the curriculum as a whole and a concern with the notion of curriculum balance. All that theorizing about curricular issues has now been overtaken by those accelerating political policies whose main features have been the subject of our last two chapters, so that we now have a centrally determined core of 70 per cent of the school curriculum – in primary as well as in secondary schools, in spite of the fact that a comparable HMI report on that sector (DES, 1978) produced nothing like the same critical evidence. And it does appear, as we shall see later, that both the National Curriculum itself and the translation of it into the realities of school subjects and testing programmes owe more to those political pressures than to the theoretical debate which they have largely ousted.

This chapter, then, will attempt several things. Firstly, it will explore that theoretical debate, considering the case for and against the idea of a common curriculum and examining the associated concept of curriculum balance. It will do this partly to provide a theoretical base from which to evaluate the actualities of the National Curriculum now in place, but also because the arguments offered continue to provide the same kind of culmination of the theoretical discussions of the early parts of this book as they did in 1977 and 1982. Secondly, the chapter will explore the political case for a common curriculum and show how it reflects a quite different approach to schooling and one that owes nothing to that theoretical study of the curriculum of which this book has attempted to provide an overview. Indeed, we shall see that in some fundamental ways it represents a rejection of that study. And, finally, it will be argued that that study must continue if we are not to lose our hard-won appreciation of the potential and the possibilities of the kind of education which becomes attainable through curricula which are properly framed by people who understand the complexities of curriculum planning.

The chapter will, therefore, highlight that tension and conflict which have been present throughout our earlier discussions, and will thus offer a summary as well as a culmination of those discussions.

It is perhaps worth reminding ourselves from the outset that the United Kingdom has been an exception in allowing its teachers and headteachers the degree of freedom over the curriculum of their schools that they have hitherto enjoyed. We have already noted the hidden constraints and influences that they are subject to in this respect and it is worth noting that, as a result of these, the most interesting features of the curricula of most schools in the United Kingdom are their similarities rather than their differences. Nevertheless, the fact remains that legally there was no binding requirement on any school to include any particular subject or activity in its curriculum other than a weekly period of religious instruction.

This freedom contrasted most markedly with the procedures in other countries, most of which lay down, in varying degrees of detail, essential requirements for the curriculum of all schools. Thus there is a core curriculum established for the ten-year school in the USSR which sets out the range of subjects to be included for each year group and also lists the number of hours that are to be devoted to each every week. Nor does this requirement leave much scope for the addition of other subjects at the discretion of the individual school, since very little of the working week is left to provide any such latitude. This scheme has provided the basic model for the curriculum of all eastern bloc countries.

A similar approach to curriculum control can be seen also in most countries. There are, of course, variations in the degree of control. Not all countries, for example, specify the number of hours to be devoted to each area; some leave rather more time for optional areas of study; there is some variation in the extent of the control that is exercised in relation to different age groups of children; and sometimes, as in West Germany for example, more than one common curriculum is established to cater for children declared to be of different intellectual abilities. However, the principle of central control over what are seen as the most important areas of the curriculum is well established and almost unquestioned outside the United Kingdom.

However, in the United Kingdom the tradition has been very different. The idea that there should be a common curriculum for all pupils is a comparatively recent one, and the realities of this as expressed in the new National Curriculum date only from the 1988 Education Act.

THE CASE FOR A COMMON CORE TO THE CURRICULUM

Broadly speaking, three kinds of argument are produced in favour of the idea of a common curriculum, all of which we have touched upon in earlier sections of this book. First of all, we have those philosophical or epistemological arguments which base their recommendations for both the idea and the content of a common curriculum on those rationalist views about the nature of knowledge and of culture which we noted in Chapter 2. Second, we have certain social or sociological arguments which develop their case from the idea of equality of educational opportunity and the consequent need for all pupils to have access to the same educational diet. Finally, we have those very different political or economic arguments which claim that the school curriculum should be planned in such a way as to ensure that all pupils have the opportunity to develop to a certain standard the skills and knowledge which will enable them to meet the demands and to contribute to the continued growth of a technological and industrial society. This last line of argument we will return to later.

The argument from the nature of knowledge

The first kind of argument, then, claims that, since certain kinds of knowledge have a status and value superior to others they have a prior claim for inclusion in any curriculum that is to be regarded as educational in the full sense. We have already noted the claim of Richard Peters that education is concerned only with those activities which have an intrinsic value (Peters, 1965, 1966). To this we might add the theory of Paul Hirst, that knowledge is to be divided into seven or eight discrete forms of rationality, each distinguishable from the other through its unique logical structure, and of education as the initiation of pupils into all of these forms (Hirst, 1965). If this is the view that one takes of education, it will follow that the curriculum for all pupils must consist of these intrinsically worthwhile activities and of all these forms of knowledge or understanding (Hirst, 1969; Hirst and Peters, 1970). On this kind of argument any pupil whose curriculum excludes him or her from any of these areas of human knowledge and understanding is being offered an educational provision that is by definition inferior or is not receiving an education in the full sense at all.

The sociological version of this same argument is the one we also noted in Chapter 2 that is based on the idea that it is the task of the school to transmit the culture of the society and that the curriculum must be designed to convey what is worthwhile in that culture to all pupils – what Matthew Arnold once called 'the best that has been thought and said'.

This kind of consideration has formed the basis of the cases that have been made out hitherto for a common core to the curriculum. These, for example, are John White's major reasons for suggesting that the essential elements of the compulsory curriculum at secondary level should be communication, mathematics, the physical sciences, art appreciation and philosophical thought (White, 1973). The same kinds of consideration too underlie Denis Lawton's recommendation that the curriculum should contain six core areas – five disciplines and one interdisciplinary unit. The six areas he suggests are mathematics, the physical and biological sciences, the humanities and social sciences (including history, geography, classical studies, social studies, literature, film and TV and religious studies), the expressive and creative arts, moral education and interdisciplinary work (Lawton, 1969, 1973, 1975).

This kind of argument for a common curriculum, then, is based on those particular views of knowledge and of society that we considered earlier in this book and on the belief that it is possible to establish some kind of value system that will enable us to choose what is worthwhile in knowledge and in the culture of the society.

The argument from equality of opportunity

The social or sociological arguments for a common curriculum start, as it were, from the opposite end of things. For they begin by considering some of the implications of *not* offering a common form of education to everyone. They have been prompted by recent attempts to base education on the interests of children, to try to make school work meaningful and relevant to them by planning it in relation to their experience of their own immediate environment. The suggestion made by the Schools Council's Working Paper No. 11, for example, that we might base the education of pupils in part on the experience to be gained from a study of 'the 97 bus' (Schools Council, 1967) was particularly effective in sparking off this kind of reaction. For it is claimed that an approach such as this can lead to a form of social control every bit as sinister as the imposition of one culture or one set of values on all (White, 1968, 1973). If a child's experience is to be limited to his or her own culture, his or her own environment, what he or she is already familiar with before he or she enters school, then there is a real risk that he or she will be trapped in that cultural environment and given little opportunity of gaining experience outside it.

Furthermore, if we once concede that two or three curricula might be generated to meet two or three broadly different kinds of need, we are almost certainly accepting implicitly the idea that Plato made quite explicit, that education in the full sense is capable of being achieved only by some gifted people and that the rest must be offered something inferior, which can only be some form of indoctrination or 'education in obedience' (White, 1968). We thus have, it has been claimed, a 'curriculum for inequality' (Shipman, 1971).

This is an idea that has followed in the wake of the wider notion of education for all. There is no logical connection between the idea of education for all and that of a common curriculum, nor do demands for educational equality imply that all must have the same educational diet, since, as the Plowden Report (CACE, 1967) asserted, there is no incompatibility between the idea of equality of educational opportunity and variety of educational provision. Originally, therefore, the ideal of education for all, as it was expressed in the 1944 Education Act, was interpreted as requiring not that all should have the same educational provision but that the content of education should vary according to such considerations as age, aptitude and ability.

This was a natural development of what can be discerned throughout the history of the educational system of the United Kingdom, since this has been characterized from the beginning by the development of two or more separate curricula, those of the grammar and of the elementary schools and later of the grammar, technical (where they existed) and the secondary modern schools. Again we note the dead hand of Plato manipulating us still in the twentieth century and encouraging us to see education as having at least two forms, one for the able and another for the less able.

As a result we find many actually criticizing the work of the secondary modern schools in the 1940s and 1950s on the grounds that they were 'aping the grammar schools' by setting up a curriculum that appeared to be for the most part no more than a watered-down version of the grammar school curriculum. Equally, however, it is not surprising to find them doing this, since the inadequacies and inaccuracies of the selection procedures employed, well documented in many research studies of the time, make it clear that even if the generation of two or more curricula is in itself justified, the practical implementation of these, and especially the matching of pupils to them, is far from clear cut and easy.

Problems of selection, then, are the focus of the criticisms that have been levelled at the tripartite selective system of secondary education, but these have also been accompanied by charges of unfairness and inequality which have resulted in the ending of selection and the replacement of that system by a pattern of comprehensive secondary education, a movement which would seem to imply a need for some commonality of educational provision. Thus we find the claim now being made that, if justice and fairness are to be attained and the ideal of education for all achieved, all pupils should have access to the same areas or bodies of knowledge and learning.

SOME PROBLEMS AND DIFFICULTIES

Let us now consider some of the problems and difficulties raised by these arguments for the idea of a common curriculum, problems and difficulties which, as we shall see, are both theoretical and practical.

First, in so far as many of the arguments offered in support of the idea of a common curriculum derive from certain views about the nature of knowledge and of values, we need do no more than remind ourselves of the difficulties of this kind of argument which we examined in some detail in Chapter 2, when discussing this same question of the basis upon which we can decide upon the content of the curriculum. For we noted then that there is a variety of positions one can take on this issue of the nature of knowledge and that among the least convincing of these is that which claims some kind of objective status for knowledge. Even less convincing, we claimed, are those arguments which attempt to demonstrate the superiority of certain kinds of knowledge and human activity over others. If we were right to argue there that there is no firm foundation upon which we can establish the prior claims of some areas of human knowledge and activity to be included in the curriculum, then that same argument has even more force in the context of proposals to establish a common curriculum for all pupils on this basis.

This becomes immediately apparent when we ask what is to be the content of such a common curriculum. For even if we agree in principle that some of the arguments for a commonality of basic educational provision are strong, such agreement immediately breaks down when we come to decide what such basic provision should consist of. What is it that all pupils should be introduced to as part of their education? Those proposals that have been put forward for the content of such a curriculum are far from indisputable. For they are derived, as we have seen, either from a particular view of the nature of knowledge or from some idea of what is valuable in the culture of society or some attempt at combining both of these considerations (White, 1973; Thompson and White, 1975; Lawton, 1969, 1973, 1975). John White's suggestion, for example, which we noted earlier, that the compulsory curriculum at secondary level should consist primarily of communication, mathematics, the physical sciences, art appreciation and philosophical thought would hardly have universal acceptance. There is probably no single activity that will have universal support in its claims for inclusion in a common core of the curriculum. Even the teaching of reading has been described and criticized as a subversive activity that schools should not promote (Postman, 1970).

The converse of this is also true. For just as there will be minority views opposed to the inclusion even of those things that have almost universal acceptance, there will also be minority interests that will be vociferously demanding the inclusion of those things that they themselves happen for personal reasons to be committed to. A good example of this is the demand made at the political level for the inclusion of religious instruction of some kind in the common core. Once the principle of a common core curriculum is accepted, such idiosyncratic demands will proliferate and thus render its implementation almost impossible.

Thus the establishment of a common curriculum must founder on the practical issues of what should be included in it and who shall decide on this.

To these problems that derive from the difficulty, even the impossibility, of establishing any universally accepted criteria for judging the relative worth of different kinds of knowledge, we must add the further difficulties that are raised by the criticisms of the content of the curriculum which have been made by many sociologists (Young, 1971; Whitty and Young, 1976). For, as we have seen, their claims that all knowledge must be recognized as being socially constructed lead not only to an awareness of the lack of such objective criteria; they also raise further issues of a more sinister kind concerning the likely results of imposing a common system of knowledge on all pupils.

For, as we saw in Chapter 2, it is argued the knowledge is socially constructed, that culture is impossible to define and that many cultures can be identified in a modern pluralist society. It is also argued that to impose one culture, one set of values on all pupils regardless of their origins, their social class, race or creed is to risk at best offering them a curriculum that is irrelevant, meaningless and alienating and at worst using the educational system as a means of effecting an inhibiting form of social control.

For it is claimed that such a process results in the attempt to introduce children to areas of knowledge that they find irrelevant to their own lives and meaningless in relation to their own experience and thus encourages them to reject what they are offered, so that it leads not to education but to disaffection and even alienation from both the content of education and society itself. Further, as an attempt to impose a particular value system on pupils, it is difficult to defend such practice even from the charge of indoctrination, so that such a system is not only inefficient and counter-productive, it is also open to criticism on moral grounds.

Further support for such a view has come from the activities of those who have been attempting in practice to develop programmes of work that would be relevant and meaningful to pupils and would as a result encourage in them a fuller and therefore more educationally productive involvement in their work. Thus, as we have already noted, recent years have seen an accelerating movement at all levels of education towards 'progressive', 'pupil-centred' methods, heuristic approaches of all kinds, learning by experience, learning by discovery, learning through interests and so on. The general trend of this movement, as we have seen, has been towards a greater individualization of education. And it is again an example of how a different theory of knowledge will lead to a different view of education and to quite different proposals for educational provision.

Thus we have the strange situation that the idea of a common educational provision which is argued for on grounds of equality, justice and fairness is opposed most vigorously for precisely the same reasons by those who see the imposition of knowledge as a form of social control and those who even go so far as to advocate total deschooling.

We are, therefore, presented with yet another dilemma, or rather with evidence that we are faced by a debate about means rather than ends. For on both sides we have a commitment to the ideal of educational equality but we are faced with a headlong clash on the question of how such an ideal is to be achieved, whether by insisting that all pupils have access to the same knowledge or by tailoring educational provision to suit their individual needs. This is a point we must return to later.

First, however, it will be helpful if we spend a little time considering the associated concept of a 'balanced' curriculum, since a major feature of the arguments of both the factions we have just referred to is a concern that all pupils should be given a 'balanced' set of educational experiences.

A 'BALANCED' CURRICULUM

Without closer consideration, the use of the term 'balance' appears to bring with it those connotations of scientific exactitude which we have seen on other occasions and in other contexts to be spurious and misleading in any debate about education. The notion of balance in physics is precise and can be expressed as a mathematical formula, for it is a function of the weight of the objects in balance in relation to the distance of the forces they exert from the fulcrum around which they exert them. It would clearly be a mistake to look for this kind of precision in any educational context and we must recognize that the use of such terms in education is figurative and that any promise of exactitude they seem to offer is spurious. Like all other such notions, that of balance in education must be recognized as relative, taking its meaning almost entirely from the value system of the person using it. In short, we will all have our own view of what constitutes a balanced curriculum and what that view is will in turn depend on what we see as the fundamental principles of education. We must begin, therefore, by recognizing this and noting once again, as we did in Chapter 2, the essential and problematic value element in all educational debate.

This notion does bring several elements into the debate, however, which take us a good way beyond the idea of a common curriculum. For, in the first place, the demand that the curriculum be balanced requires that we view it and plan it as a totality and not in the piecemeal fashion hitherto adopted. The dangers of the piecemeal approach to curriculum planning within subjects emerged clearly and disturbingly from the survey of secondary education in England conducted ten years ago by Her Majesty's Inspectorate (DES, 1979). It became apparent from that survey that the 'options' system employed by most secondary schools for their fourth- and fifth-year pupils has resulted often in a curriculum for some individual pupils which few would or could describe as balanced, whatever their notion of education. And so the survey went on to argue that 'teachers need a view of the school curriculum as a whole . . . if they are to coordinate their pupils' learning and provide them with some sense of coherence in their programmes' (op. cit., p. 42).

One important element, then, which the notion of curriculum balance introduces into the curriculum debate is the need to plan the curriculum as a totality if we are to ensure a balanced educational diet for all pupils.

A second element, which also emerged from this survey, is that the need for balance must be recognized not only within education but also between education and the other demands that the schools must respond to. For the criticism offered of some of the work reviewed was not only based on the fact that it represented an imbalance in educational terms, by losing opportunities, for example, 'to enlarge experience and understanding', but also that it failed to achieve a balance between educational and vocational considerations. This suggests, therefore, a further dimension to the notion of curriculum balance, that in planning the curriculum we should be looking not only for a balance of educational experiences for each individual, but that we must also be aiming for a balanced response to the conflicting claims of the interests of the individual and those of society, of the needs of the individual for both personal and vocational preparation. It suggests too that we must strive for balance between demands for the development of the pupil's capacities and those for the learning of certain necessary bodies of knowledge, and between the need for specialization and that for breadth of study and experience. The balance we are looking for, then, is that of the juggler rather than that of the scientist, the engineer or the architect.

In fact, it is a more delicate notion than that, since the juggler, although needing to keep many balls in the air at one time, must achieve this by adherence to certain scientific and mathematical principles. These are not the principles that apply to calculations of educational balance. For here 'balance should not . . . be thought of in terms of equal quantities; the balance referred to here is a judicial balance rather than a mathematical one' (Schools Council, 1975c, p. 27).

Again, therefore, we must remind ourselves that the notion of balance in education must be loose, flexible and relative. If we do so, we can recognize that it not only introduces into the debate an acceptance of the existence of competing interests whose demands have to be accommodated to one another. It also introduces the idea of the need for individual interpretation and reveals precisely why we should concede a good deal of freedom in curriculum matters to local authorities, to schools, to teachers and even to individual pupils. For it makes clear that successful educational planning must always be of an *à la carte* rather than a *table d'hôte* kind, and that a balanced education, like a balanced diet, must be suited to the needs of the individual organism.

It suggests too the need to be tentative rather than dogmatic in educational planning, and thus illustrates what is the root inadequacy of the plan to establish a common core to the curriculum. For, in a somewhat paradoxical manner, the introduction of the apparently precise term 'balance' into the educational debate brings connotations of inexactitude, imprecision and the need for individual interpretation. For a common curriculum would in practice result in a very unbalanced curriculum for a majority of pupils, as we suggested earlier.

COMMON PROCESSES AND PRINCIPLES

External guidance, then, should take the form not of directives or specific statements of subjects or subject content, but rather of broad principles or guidelines. And it is this that points us towards the desirability of adopting that 'process' approach to curriculum planning which we discussed in Chapter 4. For it suggests that the basis of educational planning should be certain broad principles which are susceptible to individual interpretation and which provide a basis for the selection of appropriate content, rather than lists of subjects or lists of goals or aims to be translated into step-by-step hierarchies of objectives or attainment targets. 'The true balancing agent lies not in the subject content but in the methods and approaches of the teacher and his [or her] inter-reaction with the pupils' (Petter, 1970, p. 43; Schools Council, 1975a, p. 18).

For the major error committed by the advocates of a common core curriculum is one that can be detected also in the work of most educational theorists. For almost all of them, from Plato onwards, having set out their educational principles, have immediately translated these into prescriptions for subject content, and have thus failed to recognize that education consists of learning *through* subjects rather than the learning *of* subjects. A number of problems follow from this kind of misconception, some of which we noted in earlier chapters, but the major difficulty it presents is that it denies the possibility of interpretation and adaptation to individual needs and circumstances.

If we are to make this possible, and thus to resolve the problem we noted earlier of the conflict between pressures for external control and the requirements of internal development, we have to recognize that what is or should be common to everyone's education, what is essential to it, what constitutes a balanced educational diet cannot be defined by listing subjects but only by listing broad procedural principles. In the same way, and for the same reasons, what constitutes a proper nutritional diet cannot be defined merely by listing foodstuffs but only by establishing broad dietary principles to be translated into individual prescriptions to suit the requirements of each separate and unique physical constitution. We would rightly look with some suspicion on a doctor who prescribed the same diet or medicines for all his or her patients. We must begin to view educational prescriptions in a similar light, and to recognize that variations in methods of delivery do not reflect the necessary degree of differentiation. It is not how you take your pills that matters; it is what pills you take.

Broad procedural principles, then, are the only basis for curriculum planning and for planning a common curriculum, as some exponents of the primary school curriculum suggested a long time ago (Board of Education, 1931). For it is by reference to these that choice of subjects and of content is made; that objectives are chosen when they are chosen; that those objectives are modified and changed; that the value of 'unintended learning outcomes' is gauged; and it is by reference to these that the content of education can be varied to meet the needs of individual schools, teachers and pupils, with no loss of educational value or validity.

We are likely to find too that agreement is easier to attain at this level than at that of subjects or subject content. For the question to be asked is what it means to be educated, and few would wish to argue against the propositions that it means, for example, to have learned to value some activities for their own sake, to have learned to think for oneself, to have developed the ability to view the world critically, to have acquired understanding, to have achieved this in a number of fields, to have gained insight into several areas of human experience, to have been assisted to develop emotionally, aesthetically and physically as well as intellectually and, in general, to have developed capacities and competences of a number of kinds. Few would want to argue too against the proposition that education must prepare the individual to take his or her place in society with all that that entails. For these reasons, few have raised serious objections to the eight adjectives which Her Majesty's Inspectorate offered to 'identify 8 broad areas of experience that are considered to be important for all pupils' – aesthetic/ creative, ethical, linguistic, mathematical, physical, scientific, social/ political and spiritual (DES, 1977c).

Two things are worth noting here in relation to this important suggestion. The first is that it reflects a view of education and an approach to curriculum planning very much in line with that process or developmental approach we explored in Chapter 4, and that, for that reason and because, as we saw there, such an approach requires more rather than less teacher autonomy and less rather than more external control and direction, it has now largely disappeared from DES/HMI publications on the curriculum, all of which have now returned to a combined content/objectives model, as we have seen. The term 'areas of experience' is used in *Curriculum Matters 2*, but it is offered there not as an alternative form of curriculum, which if it is to have any real significance, it must be, but as 'only one perspective' (DES, 1985a, p. 15) which must be 'complemented' by 'the second perspective . . . the knowledge, concepts, skills and attitudes which all schools should seek to develop in their pupils' (op. cit., p. 36).

The second point which we must note is highly germane to our discussion here, for these proposals for a curriculum framed in terms of eight 'areas of experience' became the basis for the 'entitlement' curriculum, which was the subject both of a subsequent HMI publication (DES, 1984b) and of an attempt to translate it into practice in six local authority areas. In short, thinking – even at the official level – was moving towards the view that a common curriculum was needed to provide genuine equality of educational opportunity for all pupils, but that the best way to avoid those problems of alienation and disaffection which we saw earlier do, and must, arise when this is interpreted in terms of common subjects or a common body of curriculum content to be imposed on all, is to define that common curriculum in terms of common 'areas of experience' or processes, to produce a set of curriculum guidelines rather than what is in effect not so much a common curriculum as a common syllabus, thus ensuring equality without uniformity, a genuine equality in difference.

It is at this level, then, that we can hope to achieve some kind of agreement about what should be common to the curriculum of all pupils. We must, however, resist the temptation to translate these immediately into subjects or bodies of knowledge-content, since it is this that creates not only controversy but also some of the confusions and resultant inadequacies, as we noted earlier. The pressures to do so are, of course, strong. The organizational structure of universities and secondary schools, the related system of public examinations, the traditional view of schooling adopted by parents and pupils, the basis of the Inspectorate at both local and national levels, the shape of courses of training for teachers, the constitution of the Schools Council and its early approach to curriculum development, the structure of the new National Curriculum, along with many other factors, which we have noted in earlier chapters, all combine to press us into this direction. But, for all the reasons given throughout this book, they must be recognized as unsatisfactory.

The solution to that theoretical dilemma we noted earlier would seem to lie in a move from the notion of education as transmission and curriculum as content, the problems of which we saw in Chapter 2, to that view of curriculum as process and education as development we explored in Chapter 4. Agreement on broad common principles should be the aim. The interpretation of those principles and decisions as to how they apply to individual schools and individual pupils must be left to the individuals concerned.

We must also resist the temptation to see these principles as aims and to translate them into hierarchies of curriculum objectives. For we must remember that, as was stressed in Chapter 4, the distinction between principles and aims in curriculum planning is very much more than a semantic one; it is quite fundamental. And we must bear in mind that, as we also saw there, to translate aims into objectives is to be committed to an approach to curriculum planning which is diametrically opposed to and incompatible with that which translates them into procedural principles. The failure to recognize this bedevils attempts, such as that of the Schools Council's Working Paper 70, *The Practical Curriculum* (Schools Council, 1981), to solve the problem we have been discussing. For, although it begins with statements of the underlying principles of the curriculum and recognizes that the 'most important of the practical arguments for agreeing underlying principles, and basing action on them, is that this may be the only way of guaranteeing an effective curriculum for every child' (op. cit., p. 13), it quickly reverts to calling these 'aims' and, in no time at all, is deducing from these 'more specific aims' and thus leading us back into the whole hierarchy of linear, objectives-based approaches to learning, the problems of which were elucidated at some length in Chapter 3.

It is important, then, to treat principles as principles, to recognize that they are fundamental to planning that is to be educational in the full sense, to acknowledge that, while permitting a degree of centralized control, they also invite that complementary degree of local interpretation which we have seen is essential not only for the satisfactory education of every pupil but also for the continuing evolution of the curriculum itself.

The failure to appreciate the force of this case for the planning of education in terms of broad common principles which are then open to individual interpretation is the most salient feature of current political policies as they have been codified in the 1988 Education Act, and especially in its National Curriculum. We must now briefly consider, therefore, the arguments used in support of the new National Curriculum, or rather we must attempt to pick out the main elements in the policy for education and the view of the school curriculum which underpin it.

THE POLITICAL CASE FOR A NATIONAL CURRICULUM

We should perhaps note very firmly at the outset that none of those theoretical arguments we considered earlier plays any part in the case for the new National Curriculum. In fact, it is worthy of comment that the implementation of the legislation setting up this National Curriculum has not only reflected a disregard for all research evidence, whether empirical or conceptual, but also a very positive and deliberate rejection of this, and displays what can be described only as an anti-intellectual stance towards curriculum theory and planning. 'Political energy from the centre has focused educational debate upon economic questions . . . New initiatives depend on a ruthless slander of previous efforts rather than research and evaluation; argument proceeds by political assertion, not the accumulation of evidence' (Barker, 1987, pp. 8–9).

And so, there has been no suggestion anywhere that its content has been selected on the basis of a rationalist view of the intrinsic value of certain bodies of human knowledge (Peters, 1965, 1966; White, 1973), or a concept of rationality as divisible into several forms of understanding (Hirst, 1965) or 'realms of meaning' (Phenix, 1964), or a carefully thought-through policy for the achievement of equality of educational opportunity, or even a theory, whether carefully thought out or not, of what might constitute a balanced curriculum. The case for the inclusion of the core subjects of mathematics, English and science is clearly derived from considerations of social and economic utility. These are of course to be supplemented by other 'foundation' subjects. And the 1988 Education Act speaks of 'a balanced and broadly based curriculum' which in addition to preparing pupils 'for the opportunities, responsibilities and experiences of adult life' also 'promotes the spiritual, moral, cultural, mental and physical developments of pupils at school and of society'. However, the subsequent definition of the curriculum in terms of 'knowledge, skills and understanding' and 'matters, skills and processes' makes it plain that a developmental curriculum, such as we explored in Chapter 4, which might make possible the promotion of those many varied aspects of development, is not what is envisaged, but rather the emphasis is on the acquisition of knowledge-content. The realities must be seen through the rhetoric.

Fundamentally, therefore, the case is an instrumental one, concerned primarily with what education is *for* rather than with what it *is*. And schooling is seen as largely, if not entirely, concerned to ensure vocational success for the individual pupil (or for some individual pupils) and economic and commercial success for the nation. This instrumental, vocational, commercial flavour comes through very clearly in the 'consultative document' which was offered as the only real attempt to explain and justify the National Curriculum (DES, 1987a). For, as we saw in Chapter 6, the imagery of that document is that of the market-place, of commerce and industry. It is a factory farming view of schooling.

The Crowther Report (CACE, 1959), in an attempt to explicate the egalitarian philosophy of the 1944 Education Act, spoke of the 'burdens and benefits' of the education system, and in doing so it identified 'the two purposes that education serves' (p. 54) – as 'a national investment' (ibid.) and as 'one of the social services of the welfare state' (ibid.), as 'the right of every boy and girl' (ibid.), a right which 'exists regardless of whether, in each individual case, there will be any return' (ibid.). It went on to say (p. 55), 'We have made no attempt to disentangle these two purposes of education.' The 'philosophy' behind the present legislation, although never made explicit, is located very firmly at the national investment end of this spectrum.

We must not appear to be claiming that the economic health of society should be of no concern to those planning the school curriculum or that they should totally ignore the vocational interests of pupils. We have, or should have, left behind those simplistic polarities of the individual and society or liberal and vocational education. What is apparent, and disturbing, in these current policies is that there is no awareness that different educational purposes require different forms of planning and, in particular, that while the instrumental, economic and vocational aspects of schooling may well be properly served by the adoption of a content and/or objectives model of planning, other kinds of educational purpose necessitate other kinds of approach. The fact that the whole of the National Curriculum is framed in terms of its content and explicated in the form of curriculum objectives means that in its entirety it becomes instrumental and must inevitably fail to achieve, except perhaps by accident, those more subtle developmental goals we saw just now it also sets itself; for these require more subtle developmental approaches to the curriculum of a kind that the Act does not allow or, indeed, acknowledge.

We must also note that, as a corollary of this basic instrumentalism, this kind of curriculum must also be élitist in its effects, even if it is not élitist in its intentions. We noted earlier that any curriculum framed in terms of a common content to be offered to all pupils whether they regard it as congenial or not, whether it reflects their own cultural background or not, must inevitably lead to the alienation and disaffection of some pupils, and to different levels of response to the content offered – differences which in no sense are a result of differences in 'ability', however that is defined. We suggested, therefore, that such an approach cannot offer a route to equality of educational opportunity. The case for this form of National Curriculum, then, must be seen as including, if not a positive commitment to an élitist system – although the Secretary of State has in a televised interview publicly justified it on the grounds that 'people are naturally competitive' (they are naturally aggressive and lustful too) – then certainly an acceptance of such a system as an inevitable outcome of policies framed in this way.

This point links closely with our former one in another way too. For élitism is a *sine qua non* of competitive commercialism, to which there is little point if all are to end up with equal shares. Both the instrumentalism and the content base of the National Curriculum, then, must take the education system away from that egalitarian road the 1944 Education Act, with its declared aim of achieving 'education for all according to age, aptitude and ability', set it on.

It is also worth reminding ourselves of the point we also noted in Chapter 6 when considering the increasingly vocational aspects of current policies and especially those initiatives prompted and funded through the Manpower Services Commission, namely that these, along with the establishment of city technology colleges which is a further provision of the 1988 Act, must lead to a new form of tripartism and inequality, reflecting not only a grammar/technical division but also a division within the technical 'stream' between technologists and technicians, higher and lower levels of vocational training and preparation. For, as Dan Finn has said:

> The pattern emerging has similarities with the tripartite system . . . an academic elite will be separated from a middle tier doing something like TVEI and the bottom 40% will be suitably differentiated and offered a curriculum which no doubt will more adequately prepare them for employment, or more realistically for places in the two year YTS.
>
> (Finn, 1987, p. 171)

The most important conclusion from this, however, is that the National Curriculum reflects an educational policy and a view of the school curriculum which is at odds with most of those developments in curriculum theory which the earlier chapters of this book have attempted to explicate. And, if we have been right in arguing that curriculum development is possible only if full account is taken of the understandings and insights which we have in recent years acquired through studies of the curriculum of both an empirical and a conceptual kind, the implications of such a National Curriculum for curriculum development are serious and profound. It is to an exploration of some of these, then, that we must now turn.

THE IMPLICATIONS OF THE NATIONAL CURRICULUM FOR CURRICULUM DEVELOPMENT

There would seem to be four important general developments in our understanding of the theory and the practice of curriculum planning, change and development which studies during the last two or three decades have led to, and which have been thoroughly explored in the earlier chapters of this book. These all imply an enhanced rather than a reduced role for the individual teacher in both the planning and the implementation of curricula suited to the educational needs of pupils.

First, there is that increase in our knowledge and understanding of how children's minds develop which, as we saw in Chapter 4, has come from the work of Jean Piaget, Jerome Bruner and those many others who have taken on the approach to the study of child psychology which they initiated. The important point about this work, as we saw there, is not that it compels us to adopt an approach to schooling which is based on it – no one could validly argue for that – but that it has revealed to us the potential and the possibilities of a form of education based on that kind of understanding. It has thus both extended our range of choice in curriculum planning and made it necessary to explain and justify the choices we make. Thus it is more than reasonable to ask for an explanation and a justification of the choice made by the architects of the National Curriculum not to take advantage of these insights and to go for a different (let us not at this point say outmoded) kind of approach to the planning of the school curriculum.

Secondly, we have seen that, allied to this increase in our understanding of how children develop, there has emerged a curriculum model which is a reaction to the perceived limitations of those models whose prime concern has been with either the content of the curriculum or its objectives, a model whose emphasis and starting point are the processes of education and their translation into procedural principles, a model which in more recent times has been developed to reveal how those insights of the developmental psychologists might be adapted to the realities of curriculum planning and practice (Blenkin, 1988; Blenkin and Kelly, 1988a). We explored all the many dimensions of this debate about curriculum planning models in Chapters 2, 3 and 4. The conclusion reached there was that planning by statements of content or by lists of 'aims and objectives' is severely limiting in terms of what it enables us to do in education, while taking clearly declared procedural principles as the base opens up far greater possibilities and also reflects more accurately the realities of any educational situation.

What is important here, however, is not the conclusion we reached but rather the fact that again this development opens up the range of choices available to curriculum planners, and thus, again, makes it necessary for anyone planning a curriculum at any level, but especially a nationally imposed curriculum, to explain and justify his or her choice of curriculum model. It is important too to note that the adoption of a process model places far more dependence on the autonomous, professional judgement of the individual teacher.

The third major advance in our understanding of the curriculum is that which emerged from our discussion of strategies for curriculum change and development in Chapter 5. For we saw there how the experience of twenty years of planned dissemination by the Schools Council had produced extensive evidence of the difficulties of bringing about change from outside the school, of some of the explanations of this, and of the need for any kind of curriculum change or development to be approached and tackled from the inside, and for any research intended to be supportive of such development to be a genuine form of action research. In short, we saw that the only genuine changes in the school curriculum, changes in the 'actual' rather than the 'official' curriculum, in the 'received' rather than the 'planned' curriculum, are those which result from developments which are school-based.

Again, the important point to note is the emphasis this places on the role of the individual school and on the individual teacher, on the concept of 'the teacher as researcher', along with the doubts it raises about the effectiveness, in real terms, of any kind of attempt to manipulate the actualities of the school curriculum from outside. Syllabuses can be laid down centrally; tests can be conducted regularly to see how effectively those syllabuses are being taught; but how far this will influence children's education, as opposed to their acquisition of knowledge, is less easy to predict. Education is an interactive process, and the quality of that interaction must always depend on the professional capability of the individual teacher. It cannot be brought about by remote control, even when that control has the backing of the law of the land. In this connection, it is worth noting that the declared aim of the 1944 Education Act to bring about educational equality for all pupils was never matched by the realities of the system. That is the lesson of those attempts at changing and developing the curriculum which we considered in Chapter 5. Again, therefore, it is legitimate to ask for explanations and justification of the decision by the architects of the National Curriculum to ignore that lesson.

Fourthly and finally, a further major development in our understanding of the complexities of the curriculum and its planning is that which has emerged from those advances in evaluation theory which were outlined and examined in Chapter 7. There are several things of note there. First, we noted the sophisticated techniques of evaluation which have been developed to match those more sophisticated approaches to education to which we have just made reference. Secondly, we saw that these have included a concern with evaluating all aspects of the curriculum, and especially with attempting to make judgements of its worth and not merely of the effectiveness of its 'delivery'. Thirdly, it was emphasized too that this kind of evaluation necessitates our collecting data which go well beyond the mere assessment of pupil performance. And lastly, we concluded again that the teacher himself or herself had to be seen as central to this process, since in this context too we recognized the importance of action research and of the notion of 'the teacher as researcher'.

Again, therefore, we note that these developments are ignored in the new policies for education; indeed, we saw in the last chapter a shift in the style both of evaluation and of accountability towards a more bureaucratic or autocratic style as part of that general move towards more centralized control whose other aspects we traced in Chapter 6. Again too, however, we must acknowledge that the development of more sophisticated techniques and, indeed, different forms of evaluation and accountability have opened up the range of choices available to educational planners and thus here too have made some kind of explanation and justification of the forms adopted obligatory.

Two general points emerge, therefore. The first is the increased range of choice which has been made available to curriculum planners by all these developments, and the consequent need to explain and justify choices made. The second is the centrality of the teacher to that form of education which stresses development, which is based on processes, which requires school-based curriculum development and leads to, and indeed necessitates, democratic forms of evaluation and accountability. And it is of course this second factor which explains, even if it does not justify, the choice of approach made by the architects of the National Curriculum, whose prime concern is with centralizing control of the curriculum rather than with its continued development as an instrument for promoting an individually tailored, 'bespoke' rather than an 'off-the-peg' education for all pupils. Indeed, it will be clear that all the evidence points to the fact that the former kind of educational provision is incompatible in every respect with centralized control.

There is no doubting the need for improvement in the education system, so that criticisms of the new policies should not be interpreted as implying that one thinks that all is well. Indeed, it would go against everything that has been said in earlier chapters not to acknowledge and, indeed, proclaim the necessity for continuous development. What is highly depressing about current policies is that they are designed in such a way as to arrest that process of development, and that they do not capitalize on the possibilities for improvement which can be found in that extended understanding which this book has attempted to outline. For there is a base there for developments of a kind which might not only enhance the life experiences of a majority of pupils, nor only ensure greater equality of educational experience; they might also contribute more to the needs of the economy than that narrowly conceived utilitarianism and vocationalism which we have seen to be the core of current policies.

These are developments, however, to which the teachers themselves are central and of which increased scope for the exercise of professional judgement is a *sine qua non*.

The central theme of this book, then, has been that the task of the teacher, at least of the teacher *qua* educator, cannot, and indeed should not, be defined in the kind of mechanistic terms that current policies imply, that education in the full sense can proceed only if teachers are able to make professional judgements on a much larger scale, and that any attempt to inhibit them in the exercise of this kind of judgement is likely to rebound to the disadvantage both of education and of their pupils.

Furthermore, it has also been argued that it is only through the exercise of this kind of judgement that curriculum development of any meaningful kind can proceed. If this is true, it reinforces what was said earlier in the book about the variations in interpretation that there will be of any curriculum imposed from outside; it suggests too that such an approach will bring out the saboteurs; it raises the question whether, as a result, the imposition of a common curriculum is not likely to lead to less efficient rather than more efficient teaching; it also must cause us to reflect that if the central factor in curriculum development is thus rendered largely ineffective, the overall effect will be the ossification of the curriculum.

It is also likely to lead to the ossification of curriculum theory and curriculum research. Indeed, one has wondered constantly throughout the exercise of revising this book what the purpose of that exercise might be in the context of a National Curriculum which discourages debate of any depth about curricular issues and, as we have seen, denies and negates all the recent advances in curriculum theory and research, a policy which I have suggested elsewhere (Kelly, 1989) is comparable to denying doctors the advantages of transplant surgery. It will be worth our while, therefore, finally to consider some of the implications of current policies for curriculum theory.

IMPLICATIONS FOR CURRICULUM THEORY

We looked at some of the difficulties facing curriculum research at the end of the last chapter when we were concluding our review of evaluation theory. In particular, we noted the unavoidable limitations to the scope of that research if, at the national level, it is to be confined to the collection of data about pupil performance, and if individual teachers evaluating their own work in their own classrooms are at liberty to adjust only their methods and are not permitted to modify either the content or the goals of their teaching, whatever their own evaluative activities indicate to them. We might remind ourselves here that, as we saw in Chapter 6, the training of teachers, directly at the initial level and indirectly at the in-service level, is currently being controlled in such a way as to ensure that teachers will not be encouraged to ask questions of the latter kind about their work in any evaluation exercises they undertake.

For the focus now is on content and method, on the *what* and the *how* of schooling and not on the *why*; indeed, it is likely that they soon will not be required to pursue any kind of course of teacher *education*, but will be expected merely to take a degree in a relevant subject in order to acquire the knowledge-content for their teaching and then serve an apprenticeship in a school to learn on the job the most effective methods of 'delivering' it or 'getting it across'. Perhaps soon, therefore, most teachers will not even know that there are more fundamental questions to be asked about educational theory and practice or that a proper professionalism demands that they be equipped to ask them.

The implications of these moves for the continued development of curriculum theory are serious and far-reaching. It will be clear that those understandings we have explored in the earlier chapters of this book are placed at risk by current policies, which, as we have seen, ignore, reject without explanation or even vilify them. Curriculum theory is one of the chief targets of the anti-intellectual, even de-intellectualizing, process we referred to earlier as a salient feature of current policies for the schooling system.

It will also be apparent, however, that most, perhaps all, of these insights into the complexities of education and the many facets of curriculum planning are the results of research, both empirical and conceptual, which has been conducted in a context free of the constraints of direct political controls, and especially of controls based on a limited view of education and an unwillingness to permit it to become anything other than a national economic investment and/or training system. We have referred constantly throughout this book to the work of the Schools Council; and it would not be difficult to demonstrate that most of those major advances we listed earlier received a great boost from its work – if not those advances in cognitive psychology we referred to, then certainly, and massively, the emergence of a process model of curriculum planning (mainly through the work of the Humanities Curriculum Project), the move towards school-based curriculum development and the progress made in evaluation theory. The freedom of the Schools Council to conduct, always of course with the full approval of all concerned, experiments in curriculum design and, above all, to encourage free and open debate of all forms of curriculum issue by teachers and others in the full knowledge that ideas which seemed, or even proved, successful and worthwhile might be put into practice, had an inevitable influence on the growth of our understanding of all aspects of that multi-faceted phenomenon we saw in Chapter 1 the educational curriculum to be.

In this respect it is worth noting that there is little in the educational literature of other countries, i.e. those where a national curriculum is long established, which reflects this quality of debate or research. There is some of a largely speculative nature, but little that has empirical substance to back it. Some is interesting, as we have seen, but is derived from fields other than education, such as some of those theories of dissemination we looked at in Chapter 5, and is thus of limited value and validity in relation to education itself. It is interesting too to note that, as we saw in Chapter 6, some countries, such as Japan, which have had this kind of national curriculum for some time, are now endeavouring to get away from the rigidity and the inflexibility of the system, which they have come to see is not even the best route to economic success, yet they are encountering major difficulties in planning and implementing more individual forms of education because they lack the kind of theoretical and research base for this approach to educational planning which we have acquired from those developments in curriculum theory we have been exploring in earlier chapters.

Nor is it only national agencies like the Schools Council which have used the freedom schools and teachers have hitherto enjoyed to develop new approaches to the school curriculum. The schools themselves and individual teachers within them, especially in the primary sector and even more specifically in the infant/first schools, where they have been less constrained even by those indirect pressures we explored in Chapter 6, have used that freedom to develop work of a most interesting and imaginative kind. It is not long since people travelled from far and wide to see the English primary school. For in some schools in this sector was to be seen an approach to education and the curriculum of a kind unmatched elsewhere. From this source too, then, many understandings have been generated and much theoretical speculation promoted (Blenkin and Kelly, 1981, 1987).

Opportunities for this kind of free experimentation and for the more speculative theorizing to which it gave rise no longer exist. Major national research projects, as we saw in Chapter 7, are politically vetted and have important limitations placed on their scope. The 1988 Education Act does permit certain schools to experiment with their curricula outside the National Curriculum, but only after the Secretary of State has given his or her approval and on condition that regular reports are made to him or her. There is little or no scope, therefore, for anything that goes beyond the officially approved orthodoxy. And, while one might argue that it was precisely that transgression of the accepted orthodoxy which gave rise to the events and problems of the William Tyndale School, which we noted in Chapter 6, one has also to acknowledge that it has led to many advances and developments of which it would be difficult for anyone to disapprove. Freedom will always lead to some abuse; but this must always be measured against the advances it makes possible. Freedom to succeed must imply freedom to fail. However, as John Stuart Mill pointed out in his essay, 'On Liberty', without the clash of contrary opinions there can be no advance towards truth of any kind, and even the true opinion is held with greater conviction if it has been measured against contrary views.

This clash of contrary opinions, except in relation to teaching methods, is not now to be permitted, at least at the practical level, in matters of the school curriculum.

What does this imply, then, for curriculum theory? First of all, it must be stressed that we must strive to maintain the understandings we have achieved. No one who has read this book can have failed to recognize and acknowledge the complexities of the educational process and of the activity of curriculum planning which it reveals. And it would be difficult for anyone having appreciated those complexities to argue that it is legitimate, rational or even moral to ignore them in planning the curriculum. It is important that knowledge and understandings gained in any field should not be lost.

Secondly, it is important that knowledge and understanding gained should not be lost merely because it has been decided by those at any one time in a position to enforce their decision that they will not be used at that particular point in the development of the human race. This is important not least in order to ensure that they continue to be available both to make clear to those who come after that there is a wider range of available options than that currently on display, and to provide a theoretical base for any planners who might subsequently decide they wish to do things differently. It would be a great pity if, after all the progress that has been made in our understanding of the ramifications, both theoretical and practical, of more democratic, egalitarian and individual approaches to educational provision, we were to find ourselves, like the Japanese, starting from scratch if and when a future decision were made to move in this direction or to return to this kind of educational philosophy.

Maintaining these understandings, then, is important. It will not be easy in a context in which teachers will increasingly find them irrelevant to their practice, but every attempt must be made to maintain their presence in the consciousness of as many teachers as possible, not in order to press a particular view of education but to ensure continued awareness of the wider range of possibilities which exists for schooling.

Continued advance and development will be even more difficult to ensure, however. The present system places no bar, nor could it, on our thinking about education, however much it may seek to control our practice and even our research. At the conceptual level, therefore, there is no barrier to the continuation of those exercises in conceptual research, in clarification of concepts, in explication of the implications of different ideologies and practices, which have, as we have seen, made important contributions to the development of our knowledge and understanding of curriculum planning.

There is little scope now, however, to back these up with empirical research, study or experimentation. And it is impossible to tell how far theorizing about education can go without the backing of practical experience. Theory unrelated to practice has long been a target for criticism both within and outside the teaching profession; indeed, the disregard of theory by most teachers has done as much as any other factor to make it easy for the politicians and their aides to dismiss the findings of educational research and thus to de-intellectualize educational practice. It is difficult, therefore, to predict that theorizing about education and in particular the curriculum, of the kind this book has attempted to explicate, can advance very far in the absence of all real practical reference. If there is one general lesson to be learned from the experiences of recent years, it is that in education, and probably in all other spheres too, theory and practice must go hand in hand and side by side if either is to benefit in any significant way. The lack of any kind of theoretical underpinning to the new National Curriculum is its major weakness – one can think of no other field in which such sweeping prescriptions could, or would, be made with no research base of any kind – and its rejection of the need for such constitutes the main threat to both the maintenance and the continued advance of curriculum theory.

SUMMARY AND CONCLUSIONS

This chapter has attempted to round off the book's exploratory overview of the main developments both in the theory and the practice of curriculum planning of recent years by relating those perspectives offered in the first four or five chapters to the new context created by the policies which have now emerged from those accelerating political pressures which were outlined in Chapter 6 and picked up again in the context of evaluation theory in Chapter 7. In particular, it has been concerned to establish the links, if links there be, between the insights and understandings achieved through the research and experience of two or three decades of study of the curriculum with the practicalities of the new National Curriculum, or rather, since such links are difficult to identify, to assess critically that National Curriculum in the light of those understandings and to consider its implications for their maintenance and continued development.

The chapter began by looking at those theoretical arguments for a common curriculum which have been an accepted part of the curriculum debate for some time. We saw that they are based on a particular, and problematic, view of knowledge and of culture. We also considered in detail the associated argument from the notion of curriculum balance and saw that too to be equally problematic. And we noted that the realities of offering a common curricular diet to all pupils can be seen from experience to be, in many cases, alienation, disaffection and thus inequality of achievement. We saw also, however, that one of the strongest theoretical arguments for such a common curriculum was the need to ensure equality of access to educational opportunity for all pupils. It was then suggested that this dilemma might be, could only be, resolved by looking again at what we mean by 'curriculum' in this context, and especially by recognizing the merits of planning a curriculum for all, whose commonality was to be found in its processes, its underlying principles, and not in its content or its 'aims and objectives'.

We then turned to the actualities of the new National Curriculum. And we noted here that the introduction of this has not been accompanied by any supporting arguments of a curricular kind, and especially not by arguments based on the notions of worthwhile knowledge or cultural values, or on any concern for equality of opportunity. On any kind of analysis, its motivation can be seen to be starkly instrumental, its concerns to be economic productivity, its view of education to be that it is a national investment, and its concept of curriculum, therefore, to be no more than a list of mainly useful subjects and a series of syllabuses of attainment targets within those useful subjects.

This approach, therefore, puts the National Curriculum outside the curriculum debate we have been overviewing throughout this book, since it neither accepts the value positions which are basic to that (i.e. a concept of *education* and a commitment to translating that into curricular realities) nor, as a result, pays any heed to the insights and understandings generated by the activities of those who are committed to those value positions and who thus have come to recognize some of the many complexities (and indeed possibilities) of planning a curriculum for education in the full sense.

This led us to two major conclusions. The first was that, since these insights and understandings now exist, and since a wider range of educational choices is consequently available to curriculum planners, there is an obligation on anyone, including the architects of the National Curriculum, to give reasons, explanations, justifications for the choice they have made, since giving a full account of one's policies and actions is a *sine qua non* of democratic living.

The second conclusion we reached was that the rejection within current policies of those perspectives this book has outlined, and their consequent absence from the realities of teachers' experience, are likely to put the continued development of our understanding at risk and even to jeopardize the maintenance of those insights we have already attained. We concluded, rather lamely perhaps, that every effort must be made by those who are aware both of these advances and of their educational significance and value to ensure that the ground which has been hard won is not lost, to the ultimate disadvantage of future generations.

The central message of all we have come to learn and understand about the complexities of the school curriculum is that its educational value for any child will depend entirely on the quality of the interaction which his or her teachers make possible, that the 'real' curriculum is thus in the hands of the teacher, that, to quote what has long been an educational cliché, all curriculum development is teacher development. If this is so, then in educational terms all attempts to manipulate the curriculum by remote control will prove valueless. Only if one takes the view that education is merely teaching, the transmission of knowledge, can it be planned in this way from outside. But then, if that is all society wants from schooling, it must quickly realize that it can be done better by computers, so that teachers will become superfluous. The message of this book, however, has been that if one takes the teacher out of the educational equation, or turns him or her into a mere cypher carrying out the dictates of others, one has removed what is the real essence of education and reduced what is offered to the nation's children to something of far less value than we have seen education can be for them. We risk not only throwing out the baby with the bath water, but losing the bath as well.

Much will depend of course on how the new policy is implemented, on how the requirements of the 1988 Act are met in practice. There are signs in the work already done by various working groups charged with aspects of its interpretation that the over-simplifications of the Act itself are quickly coming to be realized and that the actualities of implementation may be somewhat more sophisticated.

These groups are working very hard to flesh out the provisions of the Act, to set levels of attainment and assessment targets and to create and standard-ize assessment tasks by which children's achievements can be measured. However, most of this work, especially in relation to assessment at seven-plus, is having to be done without a proper research base and with no time to acquire one. For such research data and experience as are available, again especially in relation to the early years curriculum, relate, as we saw earlier, to other approaches to education and the curriculum and to other styles.

Furthermore, the over-simplifications of current policies as encapsulated in the Act remain a barrier to be overcome; and the basic concern with subjects, with knowledge-content and with learning skills must continue to stand between those planning the implementation of the National Curriculum and the use of other approaches to curriculum planning. They may see education, even within subject areas, as concerned with processes of development, but the task they face is the implementation of a curriculum whose central concern is with the transmission of 'knowledge, skills and processes' (of a very different kind), whose underlying rationale is instrumental and whose view of human learning is that it is essentially a simple linear matter.

The understandings of which this book has attempted to offer an overview demand that, if we wish to raise *educational* standards, the curriculum must be carefully planned and developed as a discrete entity and that, if assessment techniques are required, they be devised to support rather than to control that process. In short, assessment should be curriculum-led. If the curriculum comes to be assessment-led, as seems more than possible – indeed seems inevitable if the assessment procedures are designed primarily as mechanisms of quality control – curriculum planning as we have defined and explored it will be a thing of the past, the anti-educational impact of the public assessment system which has long been recognized in the final years of secondary schooling will extend to all years, including those of the infant phase, and books such as this, along with their authors, will have joined the dinosaurs.

It may well be that good will come of the National Curriculum, that those schools and teachers whose standards are said to be low will be improved when it is implemented, to the advantage of their pupils. One suspects, however, that this may be in spite of rather than because of the legislation. And one will forever wonder what progress might have been made if the same money, time and energy had been devoted to supporting the development of the curriculum and the raising of teacher quality by means other than the mere tightening of external controls. It is far from self-evident that negative measures are the best devices for securing positive ends. And there can be no more positive end than that of devising the most effective curriculum possible for developing the capacities and the potential of all the nation's children.

BIBLIOGRAPHY

Alexander, R. J. (1984) *Primary Teaching*, Holt, Rinehart & Winston, London and New York.

Archambault, R. D. (ed.) (1965) *Philosophical Analysis and Education*, Routledge & Kegan Paul, London.

Ashton, P., Kneen, P. and Davies, F. (1975) *Aims into Practice in the Primary School*, University of London Press.

Atkin, J. Myron (1979) Educational accountability in the United States, in Stenhouse (1979).

Ayer, A. J. (1936; 2nd edn 1946) *Language, Truth and Logic*, Gollancz, London.

Baldwin, J. and Wells, H. (1980) *Active Tutorial Work – Book 3*, Blackwell, Oxford.

Ball, Elaine (1981) *School Focused Curriculum Development: Constraints and Possibilities*, unpublished MA thesis, University of London.

Ball, Elaine (1983a) An approach to school based curriculum development, in Blenkin and Kelly (1983).

Ball, Elaine (1983b) Supporting curriculum development: case study of a school-focused support scheme, in Blenkin and Kelly (1983)

Ball, S. J. (1984a) Facing up to falling rolls; becoming a comprehensive school, in Ball (1984b).

Ball, S. J. (ed.) (1984b) *Comprehensive Schooling; A Reader*, Falmer, Lewes.

Ball, S. J. (1987) *The Micro-Politics of the School*, Methuen, London.

Bantock, G. H. (1968) *Culture, Industrialisation and Education*, Routledge & Kegan Paul, London.

Bantock, G. H. (1971) Towards a theory of popular education, in Hooper (1971).

Barker, B. (1987), Prevocationalism and schooling, in Holt (1987b).

Barnes, D. (1976) *From Communication to Curriculum*, Penguin, Harmondsworth.

Becher, A. and Maclure, S. (1978) *The Politics of Curriculum Change*, Hutchinson, London.

Becher, A., Eraut, M. R. and Knight, J. (1981) *Policies for Educational Accountability*, Heinemann, London.

Bell, R., Fouler, G. and Little, K. (eds.) (1973) *Education in Great Britain and Ireland*, Routledge & Kegan Paul, London and Boston with the Open University Press, Milton Keynes.

Bennett, N. (1976) *Teaching Styles and Pupil Progress*, Open Books, London.

Bennett, N., Desforges, C., Cockburn, A. and Wilkinson, E. (1984) *The Quality of Pupil Learning Experiences*, Erlbaum, London.

Bennis, W. G., Benne, K. D. and Chin, R. (1969) *The Planning of Change*, 2nd edn, Holt, Rinehart & Winston, New York and London.

Bernstein, B. (1967) Open schools, open society?, *New Society*, 14 Sept.

Blenkin, G. M. (1980) The influence of initial styles of curriculum development, in Kelly (1980b).

Blenkin, G. M. (1988) Education and development: some implications for the curriculum in the early years, in Blyth (1988).

Blenkin, G. M. and Kelly, A. V. (1981; 2nd edn 1987) *The Primary Curriculum*, Harper & Row, London.

Blenkin, G. M. and Kelly, A. V. (eds.) (1983) *The Primary Curriculum in Action*, Harper & Row, London.

Blenkin, G. M. and Kelly, A. V. (1988a) Education as development, in Blenkin and Kelly (1988b).

Blenkin, G. M. and Kelly, A. V. (eds.) (1988b) *Early Childhood Education: A Developmental Curriculum*, Paul Chapman, London.

Bloom, B. S. *et al.* (1956) *Taxonomy of Educational Objectives. I: Cognitive Domain*, Longman, London.

Blum, A. F. (1971) The corpus of knowledge as a normative order: intellectual critique of the social order of knowledge and commonsense features of bodies of knowledge, in Young (1971).

Blyth, W. A. L. (1974) One development project's awkward thinking about objectives, *Journal of Curriculum Studies*, Vol. 6, pp. 99–111.

Blyth, W. A. L. (1984) *Development, Experience, and Curriculum in Primary Education*, Croom Helm, London.

Blyth, W. A. L. (ed.) (1988) *Informal Primary Education Today: Essays and Studies*, Falmer, London.

Bobbitt, F. (1918) *The Curriculum*, Houghton Mifflin, Boston.

Brennan, W. K. (1979) *Shaping the Education of Slow Learners*, Routledge & Kegan Paul, London.

Bristol, University of (1983) *Guidelines for Review and Institutional Development in Schools (GRIDS): Handbook for Primary Schools* (mimeo), Bristol University School of Education.

Broadfoot, P. (ed.) (1983) *Selection, Certification and Control*, Falmer, London.

Brown, R. (1980) A visit to the APU, *Journal of Curriculum Studies*, Vol. 12, pp. 78–81.

Charters, W. W. (1924) *Curriculum Construction*, Macmillan, New York.

Connolly, K. and Bruner, J. (eds.) (1974) *The Growth of Competence*, Academic Press, London.

Cooksey, G. (1972) Stantonbury Campus – Milton Keynes, *Ideas*, Vol. 23, pp. 28–33.

Cooksey, G. (1976a) The scope of education and its opportunities in the 80s, in Kelly (1976).

Cooksey, G. (1976b) Stantonbury Campus: the idea develops – December 1975, *Ideas*, Vol. 32, pp. 58–63.

Cox, C. B. and Dyson, A.E. (eds.) (1969a) *Fight for Education: A Black Paper*, Critical Quarterly Society, Manchester.

Cox, C. B. and Dyson, A. E. (eds.) (1969b) *Black Paper Two: The Crisis in Education*, Critical Quarterly Society, Manchester.

Curtis, S. J. (1948) *History of Education in Great Britain*, University Tutorial Press, London.

Davies, I. K. (1976) *Objectives in Curriculum Design*, McGraw-Hill, Maidenhead.

Davies, W. (1980) Administrative and historical aspects, in Kelly (1980b).

Dawson, J. (1984) The work of the Assessment of Performance Unit, in Skilbeck (1984).

Dearden, R. F. (1968) *The Philosophy of Primary Education*, Routledge & Kegan Paul, London.

Dearden, R. F. (1976) *Problems in Primary Education*, Routledge & Kegan Paul, London.

Dearden, R. F., Hirst, P. H. and Peters, R. S. (1972) *Education and the Development of Reason*, Routledge & Kegan Paul, London.

Dewey, J. (1916) *Democracy and Education*, Macmillan, New York (page references are to 1961 edn).

Dewey, J. (1938) *Experience and Education*, Collier-Macmillan, New York.

Donaldson, M. (1978) *Children's Minds*, Fontana/Collins, Glasgow.

Donaldson, M., Grieve, R. and Pratt, C. (eds.) (1983) *Early Childhood Development and Education*, Blackwell, Oxford.

Downey, M. E. and Kelly, A. V. (1979) *Theory and Practice of Education: An Introduction*, 2nd edn (revised 3rd edn 1986), Harper & Row, London.

Ebbutt, D. (1983) *Educational Action Research: Some General Concerns and Specific Quibbles* (mimeo), Cambridge Institute of Education.

Eisner, E. W. (1969) Instructional and expressive educational objectives: their formulation and use in curriculum, in Popham *et al.* (1969).

Eisner, E. W. (1982) *Cognition and Curriculum*, Longman, New York and London.

Eisner, E. W. (1985) *The Art of Educational Evaluation: A Personal View*, Falmer, London and Philadelphia.

Eliot, T. S. (1948) *Notes Towards a Definition of Culture*, Faber, London.

Elliott, G. (1981) *School Self-Evaluation – The Way Forward* (mimeo), University of Hull.

Elliott, J. (1976) Preparing teachers for classroom accountability, *Education for Teaching*, Vol. 100, pp. 49–71.

Elliott, J. (1981) *Action Research: A Framework for Self-Evaluation in Schools*, Cambridge Institute of Education.

Elliott, J. and Adelman, C. (1973) Reflecting where the action is, *Education for Teaching*, Vol. 92, pp. 8–20.

Elliott, J. and Adelman, C. (1974) *Innovation in Teaching and Action-Research*, Centre for Applied Research in Education, Norwich.

Finn, D. (1987) *Training Without Jobs. New Deals and Broken Promises*, Macmillan, London.

Freire, P. (1972) *Pedagogy of the Oppressed*, Penguin, Harmondsworth.

Galton, M., Simon, B. and Croll, P. (1980) *Inside the Primary Classroom*, Routledge & Kegan Paul, London.

Gipps, C. (1987) The APU: from Trojan horse to angel of light, *Curriculum*, Vol. 8, no. 1, pp. 13–18.

Goddard, A. (1983) Processes in special education, in Blenkin and Kelly (1983).

Goddard, D. (1985) Assessing teachers: a critical response to the government's proposals, *Journal of Evaluation in Education*, Vol. 8, pp. 35–8.

Goodson, I. F. (1981) Becoming an academic subject: patterns of explanation and evolution, *British Journal of Sociology of Education*, Vol. 2, no. 2, pp. 163–80.

Goodson, I. F. (1983) *School Subjects and Curriculum Change*, Croom Helm, Beckenham.

Goodson, I. F. (1985a) Subjects for study, in Goodson (1985b).

Goodson, I. F. (ed.) (1985b) *Social Histories of the Secondary Curriculum: Subjects for Study*, Falmer, London and Philadelphia.

Goodson, I. F. and Ball, S. J. (eds.) (1984) *Defining the Curriculum: Histories and Ethnographies*, Falmer, London and Philadelphia.

Gribble, J. H. (1970) Pandora's box: the affective domain of educational objectives, *Journal of Curriculum Studies*, Vol. 2, pp. 11–24.

Gross, N., Giacquinta, J. B. and Bernstein, M. (1971) *Implementing Organizational Innovations: A Sociological Analysis of Planned Change*, Harper & Row, New York.

Halpin, A. W. (1966) *Theory and Research in Educational Administration*, Macmillan, New York.

Halpin, A. W. (1967) Change and organizational climate, *Journal of Educational Administration*, Vol. 5.

Hamilton, D. (1976) *Curriculum Evaluation*, Open Books, London.

Hamingson, D. (ed.) (1973) *Towards Judgement: The Publications of the Evaluation Unit of the Humanities Curriculum Project 1970–1972*, Occasional Publications No. 1, Centre for Applied Research in Education, Norwich.

Hamlyn, D. W. (1972) Objectivity, in Part 2 of Dearden *et al.* (1972).

Harlen, W. (1971) Some practical points in favour of curriculum evaluation, *Journal of Curriculum Studies*, Vol. 3, pp. 128–34.

Harlen, W. (1973) Science 5–13 Project, in Schools Council (1973).

Havelock, R. G. (1971) *Planning for Innovation through the Dissemination and Utilization of Knowledge*, Centre for Research and Utilization of Knowledge, Ann Arbor, Michigan.

Hextall, I. (1983) Rendering accounts: a critical analysis of the APU, in Broadfoot (1983).

Hirst, P. H. (1965) Liberal education and the nature of knowledge, in Archambault (1965), also in Peters (1973b).

Hirst, P. H. (1969) The logic of the curriculum, *Journal of Curriculum Studies*, Vol. 1, pp. 142–58, also in Hooper (1971).

Hirst, P. H. (1975) The curriculum and its objectives – a defence of piecemeal rational planning, in *Studies in Education 2. The Curriculum. The Doris Lee Lectures*, University of London Institute of Education.

Hirst, P. H. and Peters, R. S. (1970) *The Logic of Education*, Routledge & Kegan Paul, London.

Hogben, D. (1972) The behavioural objectives approach: some problems and some dangers, *Journal of Curriculum Studies*, Vol. 4, pp. 42–50.

Hollins, T. H. B. (ed.) (1964) *Aims in Education: The Philosophic Approach*, Manchester University Press.

Holly, D. (1973) *Beyond Curriculum*, Hart-Davis, MacGibbon, St Albans.

Holt, M. (1981) *Evaluating the Evaluators*, Hodder, London.

Holt, M. (1987a) *Judgement, Planning and Educational Change*, Harper & Row, London.

Holt, M. (ed.) (1987b) *Skills and Vocationalism: The Easy Answer*, Open University Press, Milton Keynes.

Hooper, R. (ed.) (1971) *The Curriculum: Context, Design and Development*, Oliver and Boyd in association with the Open University Press, Edinburgh.

House, E. R. (ed.) (1973) *School Evaluation: the Politics and Process*, McCutchan, Berkeley.

House, E. R. (1974) *The Politics of Educational Innovation*, McCutchan, Berkeley.

Hoyle, E. (1969a) How does the curriculum change? 1. A proposal for inquiries, *Journal of Curriculum Studies*, Vol. 1, pp. 132–41, also in Hooper (1971).

Hoyle, E. (1969b) How does the curriculum change? 2. Systems and strategies, *Journal of Curriculum Studies*, Vol. 1, pp. 230–9, also in Hooper (1971).

Illich, I. D. (1971) *Deschooling Society*, Calder, London.

James, C. M. (1968) *Young Lives at Stake*, Collins, London.

Jeffcoate, R. (1984) *Ethnic Minorities and Education*, Harper & Row, London.

Jenkins, D. (1973) Integrated Studies Project, in Schools Council (1973).

Jenkins, D. and Shipman, M. D. (1976) *Curriculum: An Introduction*, Open Books, London.

Keddie, N. (1971) Classroom knowledge, in Young (1971).

Keddie, N. (ed.) (1973) *Tinker, Tailor: The Myth of Cultural Deprivation*, Penguin, Harmondsworth.

Kelly, A. V. (1973) Professional tutors, *Education for Teaching*, Vol. 92, pp. 2–7.

Kelly, A. V. (ed.) (1975) *Case Studies in Mixed Ability Teaching*, Harper & Row, London.

Kelly, A. V. (ed.) (1976) *The Scope of Education: Opportunities for the Teacher*, Report of a Conference, Goldsmiths' College, London.

Kelly, A. V. (1980a) Ideological constraints on curriculum planning, in Kelly (1980b).

Kelly, A. V. (ed.) (1980b) *Curriculum Context*, Harper & Row, London.

Kelly, A. V. (1981) Research and the primary curriculum, *Journal of Curriculum Studies*, Vol. 13, pp. 215–25.

Kelly, A. V. (1986) *Knowledge and Curriculum Planning*, Harper & Row, London.

Kelly, A. V. (1987) The Assessment of Performance Unit and the school curriculum, *Curriculum*, Vol. 8, no. 1, pp. 19–28.

Kelly, A. V. (1988) Schools, teachers and curriculum planning at a time of economic recession, *Compass*, Vol. 17, no. 2, pp. 7–30.

Kelly, A. V., Kimbell, R. A., Patterson, V. J., Saxton, J. and Stables, K. (1987) *Design and Technological Activity: A Framework for Assessment*, HMSO, London.

Kelly, P. J. (1973) Nuffield 'A' level biological science project, in Schools Council (1973).

Kerr, J. F. (ed.) (1968) *Changing the Curriculum*, University of London Press.

Kogan, M. (1978) *The Politics of Educational Change*, Fontana, London.

Kohlberg, L. (1963) Moral development and identification, in *National Society for the Study of Education 62nd Yearbook*, University of Chicago Press.

Kohlberg, L. and Mayer, R. (1972) Development as the aim of education, *Harvard Educational Review*, Vol. 4, pp. 449–96.

Kratwohl, D. R. (1965) Stating objectives appropriately for program, for curriculum, and for instructional materials development, *Journal of Teacher Education*, Vol. 16, pp. 83–92.

Kratwohl, D. R. *et al.* (1964) *Taxonomy of Educational Objectives. II. Affective Domain*, Longman, London.

Lawton, D. (1969) The idea of an integrated curriculum, *University of London Institute of Education Bulletin*, Vol. 19, pp. 5–11.

Lawton, D. (1973) *Social Change, Educational Theory and Curriculum Planning*, University of London Press.

Lawton, D. (1975) *Class, Culture and the Curriculum*, Routledge & Kegan Paul, London.

Lawton, D. (1980) *The Politics of the School Curriculum*, Routledge & Kegan Paul, London.

Lee, S. G. (1977) *The Role of the Change Agent in the Cooperative Model of Curriculum Innovation*, unpublished MA thesis, University of London.

Leeming, K., Swann, W., Coupe, J. and Mittler, P. (1979) *Teaching Language and Communication to the Mentally Handicapped*, Evans/Methuen Educational for the Schools Council, London.

MacDonald, B. (1971) Briefing decision makers, internal paper, Evaluation Unit of the Humanities Curriculum Project, later reprinted in Hamingson (1973), House (1973) and Schools Council (1974b).

MacDonald, B. (1973) Humanities Curriculum Project, in Schools Council (1973).

MacDonald, B. (1975) Evaluation and the control of education, in Tawney (1975).

MacDonald, B. and Rudduck, J. (1971) Curriculum research and development projects: barriers to success, *British Journal of Educational Psychology*, Vol. 41, pp. 148–54.

MacDonald, B. and Walker, R. (1976) *Changing the Curriculum*, Open Books, London.

MacIntyre, A. C. (1964) Against utilitarianism, in Hollins (1964).

Maclure, J. S. (1970) The control of education, *History of Education Society Studies in the Government and Control of Education since 1860*, Methuen, London.

Mack, J. (1976) Assessing schools, *New Society*, 25 Nov.

Mager, R. F. (1962) *Preparing Instructional Objectives*, Fearon, Palo Alto, California.

Metz, M. (1988) The development of mathematical understanding, in Blenkin and Kelly (1988b).

Money, T. (1988) Early literacy, in Blenkin and Kelly (1988b).

Parlett, M. and Hamilton, D. (1975) Evaluation as illumination, in Tawney (1975).

Peters, R. S. (1965) Education as initiation, in Archambault (1965).

Peters, R. S. (1966) *Ethics and Education*, Allen & Unwin, London.

Peters, R. S. (1967a) In defence of Bingo: a rejoinder, *British Journal of Educational Studies*, Vol. 15, pp. 188–94.

Peters, R. S. (1967b) What is an educational process?, in Peters (1967c).

Peters, R. S. (ed.) (1967c) *The Concept of Education*, Routledge & Kegan Paul, London.

Peters, R. S. (ed.) (1969) *Perspectives on Plowden*, Routledge & Kegan Paul, London.

Peters, R. S. (1973a) Aims of education: a conceptual inquiry, in Peters (1973b).

Peters, R. S. (1973b) *The Philosophy of Education*, Oxford University Press.

Petter, G. S. V. (1970) Coherent secondary education, *Trends in Education*, Vol. 19, pp. 38–43.

Phenix, P. H. (1964) *Realms of Meaning*, McGraw-Hill, New York.

Piaget, J. (1969) *Science of Education and the Psychology of the Child* (1971 edn), Longman, London.

Pirsig, R. (1974) *Zen and the Art of Motorcycle Maintenance*, Bodley Head, London.

Popham, W. J. (1969) Objectives and instruction, in Popham *et al.* (1969).

Popham, W. J., Eisner, E. W., Sullivan, H. J. and Tyler, L. L. (1969) *Instructional*

Objectives, American Educational Research Association Monograph Series on Curriculum Evaluation No. 3, Rand McNally, Chicago.

Postman, N. (1970) The politics of reading, *Harvard Educational Review*, Vol. 40, pp. 244–52, also in Keddie (1973).

Pring, R. (1971) Bloom's Taxonomy: a philosophical critique (2), *Cambridge Journal of Education*, Vol. 2, pp. 83–91.

Pring, R. (1973) Objectives and innovation: the irrelevance of theory, *London Educational Review*, Vol. 2, pp. 46–54.

Pudwell, C. (1980) Examinations and the school curriculum, in Kelly (1980b).

Purcell, F. A. (1981) *The Role of the Change Agent in Curriculum Development*, unpublished MA thesis, University of London.

Raymond, J. (1985) *Implementing Pastoral Care in Schools*, Croom Helm, London.

Reid, W. A. (1978) *Thinking about the Curriculum*, Routledge & Kegan Paul, London.

Richards, R. (1979) Learning through science. *Schools Council Newsletter*, Vol. 30, pp. 5–7.

Rodger, I. A. and Richardson, J. A. S. (1985) *Self-Evaluation for Primary Schools*, Hodder, London.

Rudduck, J. (1976) *Dissemination of Innovation: The Humanities Curriculum Project*, Schools Council Working Paper 56, Evans/Methuen Educational for the Schools Council, London.

Russell, B. (1950) *Unpopular Essays*, Allen & Unwin, London.

Scheffler, I. (1960) *The Language of Education*, Thomas, Springfield, Illinois.

Schon, D. A. (1971) *Beyond the Stable State*, Temple-Smith, London.

Schools Council (1967) *Society and the Young School Leaver*, Working Paper 11, HMSO, London.

Schools Council (1969) *Education through the Use of Materials*, Working Paper 26, Evans/Methuen Educational for the Schools Council, London.

Schools Council (1970) *The Humanities Project: An Introduction*, Heinemann, London.

Schools Council (1971a) *A Common System of Examining at 16+*, Examinations Bulletin 23, Evans/Methuen Educational for the Schools Council, London.

Schools Council (1971b) *Choosing a Curriculum for the Young School Leaver*, Working Paper 33, Evans/Methuen Educational for the Schools Council, London.

Schools Council (1972) *With Objectives in Mind: Guide to Science 5–13*, Macdonald Educational for the Schools Council, London.

Schools Council (1973) *Evaluation in Curriculum Development: Twelve Case Studies*, Schools Council Research Studies, Macmillan Education for the Schools Council, London.

Schools Council (1974a) *Social Education: An Experiment in Four Secondary Schools*, Working Paper 51, Evans/Methuen Educational for the Schools Council, London.

Schools Council (1974b) *Dissemination and In-service Training: Report of the Schools Council Working Party on Dissemination (1972–1973)*, Schools Council Pamphlet 14, Schools Council, London.

Schools Council (1975a) *The Whole Curriculum 13–16*, Working Paper 53, Evans/Methuen Educational for the Schools Council, London.

Schools Council (1975b) *Examinations at 16+: Proposals for the Future,* Examination Bulletin 23, Evans/Methuen Educational for the Schools Council, London.

Schools Council (1975c) *The Curriculum in the Middle Years*, Working Paper 55, Evans/Methuen Educational for the Schools Council, London.

Schools Council (1978a) *Examinations at 18+: the N and F Studies*, Working Paper 60, Evans/Methuen Educational for the Schools Council, London.

Schools Council (1978b) *Impact and Take-up Project. A First Interim Report*, Schools Council, London.

Schools Council (1979) *Examinations at 18+: Report on the N and F Debate*, Working Paper 66, Methuen Educational for the Schools Council, London.

Schools Council (1980) *Impact and Take-up Project. A Condensed Interim Report on Secondary Schools*, Schools Council, London.

Schools Council (1981) *The Practical Curriculum*, Working Paper 70, Methuen Educational for the Schools Council, London.

Scriven, M. (1967) The methodology of evaluation, in Stake (1967).

Shipman, M. D. (1971) Curriculum for inequality?, in Hooper (1971).

Shipman, M. D. (1972) Contrasting views of a curriculum project, *Journal of Curriculum Studies*, Vol. 4, pp. 145–53.

Shipman, M. D. (1973) The impact of a curriculum project, *Journal of Curriculum Studies*, Vol. 5, pp. 47–57.

Simon, B. (1985) *Does Education Matter?*, Lawrence & Wishart, London.

Simons, H. (1980) The evaluative school, *Forum*, Spring.

Skilbeck, M. (1973) Openness and structure in the curriculum, in Taylor and Walton (1973).

Skilbeck, M. (1976) School-based curriculum development, in Open University Course 203, Unit 26, Open University Press, Milton Keynes.

Skilbeck, M. (ed.) (1984) *Evaluating the Curriculum in the Eighties*, Hodder, London.

Sockett, H. (1976a) *Designing the Curriculum*, Open Books, London.

Sockett, H. (1976b) Teacher accountability, *Proceedings of the Philosophy of Education Society*, July, pp. 34–57.

Stake, R. E. (ed.) (1967) *Perspectives of Curriculum Evaluation*, American Educational Research Association, Monograph Series on Curriculum Evaluation No. 1, Rand McNally, Chicago.

Stake, R. (1972) Analysis and portrayal, paper originally written for AERA Annual Meeting presentation 1972, republished as Responsive Education in *New Trends in Education*, no. 35 (1975) Institute of Education, University of Göteborg.

Stenhouse, L. (1969) The humanities curriculum project, *Journal of Curriculum Studies*, Vol. 1, pp. 26–33, also in Hooper (1971).

Stenhouse, L. (1970) Some limitations of the use of objectives in curriculum research and planning, *Paedagogica Europaea*, Vol. 6, pp. 73–83.

Stenhouse, L. (1975) *An Introduction to Curriculum Research and Development*, Heinemann, London.

Stenhouse, L. (ed.) (1979) *Educational Analysis*, Vol. 1, no. 1, Falmer, Lewes.

Stenhouse, L. (1980a) Reflections, in Stenhouse (1980b).

Stenhouse, L. (ed.) (1980b) *Curriculum Research and Development in Action*, Heinemann, London.

Swann, W. (1981) *The Practice of Special Education*, Blackwell in association with Open University Press, London.

Taba, H. (1962) *Curriculum Development: Theory and Practice*, Harcourt, Brace and World, New York.

Tawney, D. (1973) Evaluation and curriculum development, in Schools Council (1973).

Tawney, D. (ed.) (1975) *Curriculum Evaluation Today: Trends and Implications*, Schools Council Research Studies, Macmillan Education, London.

Taylor, P. H. (1970) *How Teachers Plan their Courses*, National Foundation for Educational Research, Slough.

Taylor, P. H., Reid, W. A., Holley, B. J. and Exon, G. (1974) *Purpose, Power and Constraint in the Primary School Curriculum*, Macmillan, London.

Taylor, P. H. and Walton, J. (eds.) (1973), *The Curriculum: Research, Innovation and Change*, Ward Lock Educational, London.

Thompson, K. and White, J. (1975) *Curriculum Development: A Dialogue*, Pitman, London.

Tizard, B. and Hughes, M. (1984) *Young Children Learning: Talking and Thinking at Home and at School*, Fontana, London.

Tyler, R. W. (1932) *The Construction of Examinations in Botany and Zoology. Service Studies in Higher Education*, Ohio State University, Bureau of Educational Research Monographs, no. 15, pp. 49–50.

Tyler, R.W. (1949) *Basic Principles of Curriculum and Instruction*, University of Chicago Press.

Warnock, M. (1977) *Schools of Thought*, Faber, London.

Weingartner, C. and Postman, N. (1969) *Teaching as a Subversive Activity*, Penguin, Harmondsworth.

Weiss, R. S. and Rein, M. (1969) The evaluation of broad aim programmes: a cautionary tale and a moral, *Annals of the American Academy of Political and Social Science*, Vol. 385, pp. 133–42.

Wells, G. (1981a) Becoming a communicator, in Wells (1981b).

Wells, G. (ed.) (1981b) *Learning through Interaction: The Study of Language Development*, Cambridge University Press.

Wheeler, D. K. (1967) *Curriculum Process*, University of London Press.

White, J. P. (1971) The concept of curriculum evaluation, *Journal of Curriculum Studies*, Vol. 3, pp. 101–12.

White, J. P. (1973) *Towards a Compulsory Curriculum*, Routledge & Kegan Paul, London.

Whitehead, A. N. (1932) *The Aims of Education*, Williams and Norgate, London.

Whitty, G. and Young, M. F. D. (eds.) (1976) *Explorations in the Politics of School Knowledge*, Nafferton Books, Nafferton.

Williams, R. (1961) *The Long Revolution*, Chatto, London (also Penguin 1961 and 1963).

Wilson, P. S. (1967) In defence of Bingo, *British Journal of Educational Studies*, Vol. 15, pp. 5–27.

Wilson, P. S. (1971) *Interest and Discipline in Education*, Routledge & Kegan Paul, London.

Young, M. F. D. (ed.) (1971) *Knowledge and Control*, Collier-Macmillan, London.

Young, M. F. D. (1973) On the politics of educational knowledge: some preliminary considerations with particular reference to the Schools Council, in Bell *et al.* (1973).

Young, M. F. D. (1976) The rhetoric of curriculum development, in Whitty and Young (1976).

GOVERNMENT REPORTS AND OTHER OFFICIAL PUB-
LICATIONS REFERRED TO IN THE TEXT

Assessment of Performance Unit (1982) *Language Performance in Schools: Primary Survey Report No. 2*, HMSO, London.

Board of Education (1926) *The Education of the Adolescent* (the Hadow Report on Secondary Education), HMSO, London.

Board of Education (1931) *Primary Education* (the Hadow Report on Primary Education), HMSO, London.

Board of Education (1933), *Infant and Nursery Schools* (the Hadow Report on Infant and Nursery Schools), HMSO, London.

Central Advisory Council For Education (1959) *15 to 18* (the Crowther Report), HMSO, London.

Central Advisory Council for Education (1963) *Half Our Future* (the Newsom Report), HMSO, London.

Central Advisory Council for Education (1967) *Children and Their Primary Schools* (the Plowden Report), HMSO, London.

Department of Education and Science (1975) *A Language for Life* (the Bullock Report), HMSO, London.

Department of Education and Science (1977a) *A New Partnership for our Schools* (the Taylor Report), HMSO, London.

Department of Education and Science and the Welsh Office (1977b) *Education in Schools: A Consultative Document* (Green Paper), cmnd. 6869, HMSO, London.

Department of Education and Science (1977c) *Curriculum 11–16*, HMSO, London.

Department of Education and Science (1978) *Primary Education in England: A Survey by HM Inspectors of Schools*, HMSO, London.

Department of Education and Science (1979) *Aspects of Secondary Education in England: A Survey by HM Inspectors of Schools*, HMSO, London.

Department of Education and Science (1980a) *A View of the Curriculum*, HMI Series, *Matters for Discussion*, no. 11, HMSO, London.

Department of Education and Science and the Welsh Office (1980b) *A Framework for the School Curriculum*, HMSO, London.

Department of Education and Science (1980c) *Special Needs in Education* (the Warnock Report), HMSO, London.

Department of Education and Science and the Welsh Office (1981) *The School Curriculum*, HMSO, London.

Department of Education and Science (1983) *Teaching Quality*, a White Paper, cmnd. 8836, HMSO, London.

Department of Education and Science (1984a) *English from 5 to 16. Curriculum Matters 1*, HMSO, London.

Department of Education and Science (1984b) *Curriculum 11–16: towards a statement of entitlement*, HMSO, London.

Department of Education and Science (1985a) *The Curriculum from 5 to 16. Curriculum Matters 2*, HMSO, London.

Department of Education and Science (1985b) *Mathematics from 5 to 16. Curriculum Matters 3*, HMSO, London.

Department of Education and Science (1985c) *Music from 5 to 16. Curriculum Matters 4*, HMSO, London.

Department of Education and Science (1985d) *Home Economics from 5 to 16. Curriculum Matters 5*, HMSO, London.

Department of Education and Science (1986a) *Health Education from 5 to 16. Curriculum Matters 6*, HMSO, London.

Department of Education and Science (1986b) *Geography from 5 to 16. Curriculum Matters 7*, HMSO, London.

Department of Education and Science (1987a) *The National Curriculum 5–16: a consultative document*, HMSO, London.

Department of Education and Science (1987b) *Modern Foreign Languages to 16. Curriculum Matters 8*, HMSO, London.

Department of Education and Science (1987c) *Craft, design and technology from 5 to 16. Curriculum Matters 9*, HMSO, London.

Further Education Unit (1981) *Vocational Preparation*, HMSO, London.

House of Commons Expenditure Committee (1976) *Policy-Making in the DES*, HMSO, London.

Inner London Education Committee (1976) *Report of the Public Enquiry into Teaching, Organisation and Management of William Tyndale Junior and Infant Schools* (the Auld Report), ILEA, London.

Report of the Schools Inquiry Commission (the Taunton Report) (1868).

Secondary Schools Examinations Council (1960) *Secondary School Examinations other than the GCE* (the Beloe Report), HMSO, London.

AUTHOR INDEX

SUBJECT INDEX